ADDING UP TO PEACE

The Cumulative Impacts of Peace Initiatives

Diana Chigas and Peter Woodrow

CDA Collaborative Learning Projects

April 2018

CDA improves the effectiveness of peacebuilding, development, and humanitarian organizations and corporations working in fragile and conflict-affected contexts. Through its unique collaborative learning approach, CDA combines rigorous analysis and evidence-based methodologies to produce useful tools and guidance for practitioners and policymakers alike. In strengthening the work of its partners, CDA contributes to positive, systematic, and lasting change for people and communities, while also influencing policy and practice across the sectors in which it works.

ISBN-13: 978-0-9882544-0-4

CDA Collaborative Learning Projects Inc.
186 Hampshire Street
Cambridge MA 02139
USA
www.cdacollaborative.org

CDA is keen to hear how you are using our materials. Your feedback informs our ongoing learning and impact assessment processes. Email your feedback to feedback@cdacollaborative.org

The finalization of this book was generously funded by Humanity United. The opinions expressed are those of the authors and do not necessarily reflect the views of Humanity United or of CDA Collaborative Learning Projects.

Suggested Citation: Chigas, Diana and Peter Woodrow. *Adding Up to Peace: The Cumulative Impacts of Peace Programming*. Cambridge, MA: CDA Collaborative Learning Projects, 2018.

TABLE OF CONTENTS

Acknowledgements

This book represents a massive amount of work by many people over many years. Mary B. Anderson, Executive Director of CDA Collaborative Learning Projects when this effort started, helped to conceptualize the "cumulative" case studies and engaged in all of the early consultations and several staff analysis sessions. A number of other colleagues at CDA participated in various aspects of the project: organizing case studies, facilitating case writers' travel and local contacts, editing draft cases, analyzing and coding case material, and helping to organize and run consultations and feedback workshops. Colleagues who provided crucial support in those ways included: Chloe Jaleel, Carrie O'Neal, Andrew Wei-Chih Yang, and Ethan Schechter. Some staff worked more intensively: Isabella Jean not only helped in the ways cited above, but also developed two of the case studies and did crucial work on case coding and analysis. Most of these staff members were also pressed into service writing Issue Papers containing preliminary findings that were then used in consultations and feedback workshops.

We also owe a considerable debt to the case writers themselves (see list of cases and writers in Annex A), who took on a challenging assignment and performed well in and good spirits, in spite of the difficulty of assessing cumulative impacts in an entire country or conflict area in a limited amount of time. Most of the case writers also participated in consultations—and listened to feedback and questions to finalize the case studies.

We would like to thank the "core group" of colleagues, who, for the first several years of the cumulative case effort, helped shape the inquiry. In some cases, they took on case research and writing, and often stayed extra days after consultations to take deeper dives on key topics: Sue Williams, Niall Fitzduff, Frederic Kama-Kama Tutu, Emma Leslie, Jos De La Haye, Graeme Simpson, Cordula Reimann, Rob Ricigliano, Andy Carl, and Koenraad van Brabant. Almost 300 peace practitioners participated in the fifteen feedback workshops, which significantly expanded the breadth and depth of the information available and helped to refine and validate the findings. We also appreciate the numerous partner organizations who hosted those events all over the world. (See Annex C for a list of the feedback workshops.)

In the final stages of manuscript development, Anita Ernstorfer and Andy Carl provided valuable feedback, leading to vital improvements. Our profound thanks, also, to our colleagues Sweta Velpillay, who kept us on track through the final steps of text editing, and Jasmine Walovitch, who organized the copyediting, indexing, formatting and online production of the book.

Of course, none of this would have been possible without the generous support of several donors. These include AusAID (now the Australian Department of Foreign Affairs and Trade); the Office of Conflict Management and Mitigation at USAID; the UK Department for International Development; the Swedish International Development Cooperation Agency; and the Norwegian Ministry of Foreign Affairs. And, last but certainly not least, our colleagues at Humanity United, Elise Ford and Carrie DuLaney, not only provided funding to enable finalization of the book but also insisted that this book be made available to the peacebuilding field and the public. Thank you for making that final push!

Diana Chigas
Peter Woodrow
Cambridge, MA
December 2017

INTRODUCTION

The Reflecting on Peace Practice Project (RPP) was launched in 1999 to answer the question: *What works—and what doesn't work—in peacebuilding?* The first phase of RPP lasted from 1999 through 2002 and resulted in the publication of *Confronting War* (2003),[1] based on twenty-six case studies and multiple consultations and feedback workshops focused mainly on single-program efforts in a range of conflict zones.

The second phase of RPP concentrated on disseminating lessons from the first phase, mainly through developing training materials and delivery of workshops, especially in East/Central Africa, West Africa, and the Balkans. The authors of this book were engaged for that second phase effort and were asked to address a small number of outstanding questions raised but not answered during the first phase. These included the question that was the primary inquiry for the "cumulative impact" case studies conducted for this book:

> **How do numerous peace efforts add up to produce progress towards peace over time?**

Other questions included a conundrum regarding conflict analysis, discussed at length in later chapters. We were also asked to expand on the notion of "linkages," which were identified during the first phase as making important positive contributions to peace efforts., but with little substantive detail. The question about linkages was also incorporated into the cumulative impact case studies.

Why the Cumulative Impact Case Studies?

Towards the end of the first phase of RPP, participants in a final consultation identified a need to better understand how multiple peacebuilding initiatives in the same conflict zone[2] interacted and added up—looking beyond the effectiveness of individual projects or programs, which was the focus of the twenty-six original cases. This became one of several questions for further exploration during the RPP phase that started in 2003.

---

1   Mary B. Anderson and Lara Olsen, *Confronting War: Critical Lessons for Peace Practitioners*, Collaborative for Development Action, 2003. Available at www.cdacollaborative.org. Referred to hereafter as simply *Confronting War*.

2   A "conflict zone" can be an entire country or a smaller geographic area within a country—or a cross-border area. For instance, several of the cases involve particular provinces, such as Aceh in Indonesia and Mindanao in the Philippines.

Peace Writ Large is a term introduced in *Confronting War* to describe changes at the macro level of society, comprising two basic goals which RPP found the wide array of programs examined in the first phase aimed to achieve:

- **Stopping violence and destructive conflict by working to end war and violence**

- **Building just and sustainable peace by addressing the political economic and social grievances driving conflict and forming the foundations for sustainable peace.**

Confronting War, p. 12

As a result, RPP staff began to explore systematically how multiple peace efforts in the same conflict zone have cumulative impacts, and how they "add up"—or don't add up—to producing significant progress towards Peace Writ Large (the larger societal-level peace, a term introduced in *Confronting War*). This effort aimed to identify how cumulative impacts in peace practice operate at all levels, in order to provide practical lessons that would assist policymakers, donors, and practitioners to develop more effective strategies for greater progress towards peace.

Confronting War identified factors that inhibited programs from adding up to an impact on the overall conflict situation. For instance, RPP found that the effectiveness of peace initiatives depends in large part on their ability to address the driving factors of conflict and to translate or link individual/personal change (such as, attitudes, skills, or relationships) to socio-political change (institutional or structural change, or changes in group behavior, norms and attitudes). In addition, effectiveness was associated with efforts to link "key" people (those with power and influence over the conflict) with wider constituencies in the population. This often involved connecting efforts at different levels, sectors and groups of actors. However, there was little practical evidence at that stage about what constitutes an effective linkage. It was clear that we needed to learn more about what contributes to adding up processes, what effective linkages look like and, consequently, how practitioners can work to improve the cumulative impacts of all peace efforts in a conflict zone.

In order to address the interrelated questions of cumulative impacts and linkages, starting in 2007, and continuing through 2012, RPP undertook a new series of case studies, variously called our "cumulative impact" or "adding up" cases. Each case was focused on a conflict context in which there had been some progress towards peace at the time the case was undertaken, although in some cases this progress was sustained and in others not. The cases gathered the perceptions of both local and international stakeholders regarding what accounted for these periods of progress towards peace, asking each interviewee, "*What kinds of progress took place, and what, in your view made that progress possible or helped propel it?"* This was deliberately an open-ended question inviting the interviewees to determine how and why progress occurred. We did not start with a list of peace initiatives and ask whether they had been effective or contributed to Peace Write Large. Rather, we asked interviewees to identify moments of momentum and progress toward peace and let them decide whether any particular efforts should be named.[3]

The case studies were conducted over a five-year period—now several years ago. It is important to note that the cases explored perceptions of how and why progress was made **during a particular period of time**. The purpose was not to provide a current analysis of those contexts, but rather to explore how progress was accomplished during specific periods of progress—even if that progress was not sustained. Interviewees were asked to identify particular key turning points towards peace in the situation, and then to explain why those took place. Some of the cases were conducted some time ago—and some examined the course of progress going back as much as twenty years. While we have attempted to keep abreast of later developments in these conflict zones, we have not re-opened the cases to consider later relapses into violence or further progress towards durable peace.

As noted, the purpose of the case study exercise was not to develop a definitive model of what will add up to peace, but rather to understand how and why efforts "add up" to generate progress. Thus, we sought to understand whether and how multiple peace efforts added up to progress that had been achieved at a specific time, not to determine whether those gains were sustained, nor to provide guidance about approaches to those specific situations in the current context. However, as the reader will see, important concerns emerged regarding what was addressed and unaddressed in formal peace agreements and whether or not drivers of conflict were dealt with—which does suggest an ongoing agenda for peacebuilding. The cases also examined whether activities at the community or local level were linked to higher levels to provide sustainable changes and momentum toward peace.

CDA's Collaborative Learning Process

For more than twenty years, CDA has used a case-based methodology in all of its work. The process draws on qualitative field experience in an inductive manner to analyze what the experience tells us. In other words, CDA does not start with a hypothesis and then attempt to prove or disprove it. Rather, we let the evidence in the case studies speak for itself and draw lessons from that evidence. Preliminary findings from the case studies are further refined through a series of interactions (consultations and feedback workshops) with policymakers, practitioners and researchers in a collaborative process of analysis and generation of practical and generalizable lessons.

---

3   While the case studies did not identify all the interventions in the context, the case writers did develop a broad map of peacebuilding initiatives and programs by a variety of actors – international organizations, international NGOs, local NGOs and CSOs and individuals. They then assessed the density and relevance of initiatives to the areas identified by interviewees as significant for progress. They did not, however, examine or assess the impact of each individual effort.

This is a *collaborative* learning process because we engage a wide range of people to research and write cases, and to participate in their roles as staff in the field offices or headquarters of local and international implementing agencies, as well as staff members and policymakers from intergovernmental and international organizations, donors and academic institutions. This wide-ranging group of individuals works with us as co-analysts of the case data and refiners of preliminary findings through a series of consultations and, later, feedback workshops. Typically, by the time we have come to the end of a collaborative learning process, several hundred people have participated in one way or another in generating the evidence, analyzing it and developing the lessons.

Figure 1 below depicts the general pattern of a CDA collaborative learning process—and the RPP cumulative impact process followed this pathway, from identification of the question, through the development of an initial set of cases, a first consultation, development of additional cases, further consultations on those cases and preliminary issue papers, case analysis (involving, among other things, identifying common themes and coding the cases with the help of qualitative data analysis software), writing of issue papers, conduct of about fifteen feedback workshops and, finally, writing of this volume.[4]

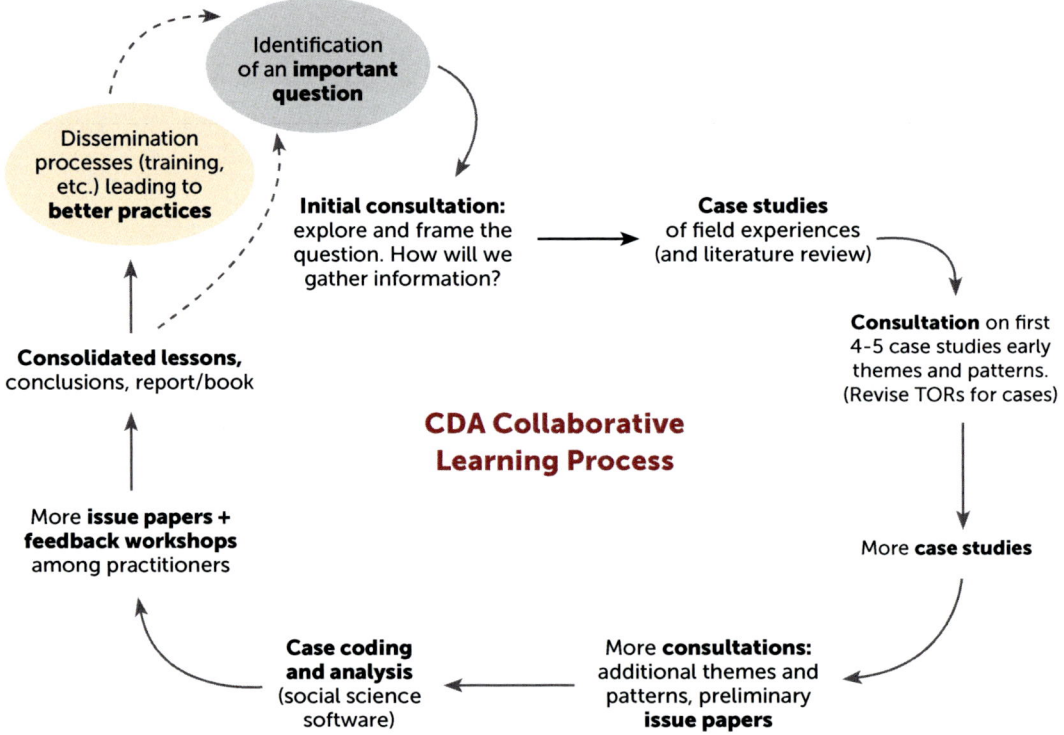

Figure 1: CDA Collaborative Learning Process

---

4   Further explication of the CDA collaborative learning methodology can be found on the CDA website: http://www.cdacollaborative.org.

Throughout the collaborative learning process, the case studies are considered raw material and the primary source of evidence for any conclusions drawn. The methodology does emphasize the validation and refinement of findings through the repeated consultations and feedback workshops, in which participants also add their own considerable experiences to support or contradict the case evidence.

Specific Process & Methodology for the Cumulative Impact Case Studies

For almost all of the case studies in this series, RPP engaged two case writers to research and write each case study, most often including one "external" researcher and one "internal" researcher. Where we engaged two local authors, we ensured that they represented the important differences inherent in the situation—which sometimes made for interesting team dynamics. In one or two cases, a single well-informed external author worked with local research assistants to produce the case study.

The case writers were asked to perform a short literature review to collect relevant documents and conflict analyses developed by others. Several weeks in the field were devoted primarily to conducting semi-structured interviews and focus groups with a wide range of people representing different perspectives, including peacebuilding practitioners, civil servants and political representatives at various levels, civil society, the business community, media, international community (UN, INGOs, donors, humanitarian, and development actors), and relevant local academics. Typically, case writers interviewed thirty to forty people, sometimes more. The case writers were recruited based on their knowledge of the situation—and were encouraged to draw on their own experience as well, being careful to indicate clearly when they were doing so.

The authors worked with common Terms of Reference[5] which asked them to:

1. Develop an understanding of the **causes of conflict** and obstacles to settlement: brief historical overview, analysis of the conflict.

2. Identify the main positive **turning points** in the conflict: What key events, initiatives, processes led to change? Why; what laid the groundwork for change?

3. **Map peacebuilding efforts:** What was done, by whom, with whom, about what? What were the areas of concentration or gaps? How were women engaged or not?

4. **Analyze cumulative impacts:** Where, when and how did they occur? How/why did peacebuilding efforts contribute to positive change? What patterns/themes emerged? What kinds of linkages occurred across levels, sectors, and constituencies? What was the role of leadership? What was neglected or left unfinished?

5. Analyze **reversals of progress:** In certain cases, why was positive change followed by reversals, blockages or outright failure of peace efforts? Were there missed opportunities?

---

5   The Terms of Reference for case authors is presented in Annex B.

The case writers were not asked to develop a full, comprehensive map of the peace-building efforts undertaken by the myriad actors working in the context, including efforts by diplomats, UN, government, as well as international and local civil society. (That said, a few of the researchers did try, but found this quite challenging, except in quite contained contexts.) Case writers also limited their inquiry to efforts that self-described or were characterized by interviewees as peacebuilding efforts. The cases were not intended to provide an evaluation of the "success" or "impact" of any individual peacebuilding effort, type of effort or methodology. Rather, they sought to develop an understanding of the factors contributing to progress and to deepen inquiry into the types of efforts identified as relevant to generating such progress. Further research would be needed to identify with more specificity which specific initiatives were more or less successful in contributing to the elements of progress.

Most cases showed interesting interactions among questions 2, 3 and 4 above. Turning points in a conflict (positive or negative) might be attributed to military engagements, action by a key ally or regional power, a changed government policy, provision or denial of humanitarian and/or development assistance, or expansion of the civil society and media—none of which would necessarily be seen as explicitly "peacebuilding." It also turned out to be impossible to gain a comprehensive catalog of all peace efforts (Question #3)—which is why case writers let interviewees identify any initiatives they considered as particularly influential, while also obtaining a broad overview of peace-building processes and their scale. Cumulative impacts could be attributed, therefore, to a combination of both explicit peacebuilding efforts and other initiatives that would not fit most definitions of peacebuilding.

As noted, the case studies were developed over a five-year period (2007-2012). Due to the lag time from the completion of some of the cases until the current writing, we commissioned a brief update for three cases (Burundi, Haiti, and Liberia) in which developments were still quite fluid at the time of the writing of the original case. The updates were based on literature review and a few key interviews. Of course, events unfold rapidly in all of these situations, and a rigorous process of constant updating would take enormous resources. Questions do remain regarding sustainability and, as we shall see, what we call "persistent issues." Nevertheless, the case studies capture an analysis of progress made prior to the case writing process. For purposes of this effort, because the primary focus of the case studies was retrospective—why progress towards peace was made during key points in the past—it was sufficient to understand *whether* the progress made had been sustained, and whether there were unanticipated areas of progress, in order to check the reliability of our analysis.

Throughout the cumulative impact collaborative learning process, we also benefitted from engagement with other groups undertaking similar efforts that provided helpful resources and insights. At early stages of the process, we collaborated with Jason Calder, who was then at Future Generations, which was conducting a multi-year global study of the role of citizens and communities in building peace.[6] Their case studies in Nepal and Guyana incorporated CDA's lines of inquiry related to cumulative impacts and were also examined in one of the consultations for this process. We also conferred with Thania Paffenholz at the Graduate Institute of International and Development Studies, University of Geneva, who developed a series of case studies regarding the role of civil society in peacebuilding, some of which were in the same countries where we are doing cumulative cases.[7] The cases in that study focused on the civil society role, which enabled us to look more closely at other issues, rather than repeat her work.

The Cumulative Impact Case Studies

Ultimately, RPP produced sixteen case studies,[8] and also referenced studies done by other organizations as noted above. The sixteen cumulative impact cases include:

Aceh (Indonesia)	Guatemala	Liberia	Solomon Islands
Burundi	Haiti	Mozambique	South Africa
Cambodia	Israel/Palestine	Mindanao (Philippines)	Sri Lanka
Cyprus	Kosovo[9]	Northern Ireland	Tajikistan

These cases can be characterized in several ways:

- Four cases were in Africa, two in the Middle East, two in Europe, six in Asia/Pacific, and two in Latin America/Caribbean.

- Eleven of these conflicts achieved some form of settlement/peace agreement: South Africa, Burundi, Northern Ireland, Tajikistan, Aceh, Cambodia, Liberia, Solomon Islands, Mozambique, Mindanao, Guatemala.

- In the cases of Liberia, Mindanao, Aceh, Solomon Islands and Burundi, the settlements were relatively recent, and the situation was quite fluid.

- Three of the cases represented significant progress towards peace followed by reversals: (Cyprus, Israel/Palestine, Sri Lanka), or no significant improvement (Kosovo).

The Haiti case represents a different form of conflict and a more elusive path towards peace, as there has not been a protracted war there, but rather periodic cycles of extreme violence followed by periods of relative peace.

---

6   The case studies and summary of findings from their project (2009-2012), *Understanding How Communities Create Peace*, can be found at https://www.future.edu/research/peacebuilding-research.html (accessed December 4, 2017).

7   Paffenholz, Thania. *Civil Society & Peacebuilding: A Critical Assessment*. Boulder, CO: Lynne Rienner Publishers, 2010.

8   The full list of case studies and their authors are provided in Annex A. All of the case studies are also available online at www.cdacollaborative.org.

9   The Kosovo case was not developed specifically as a cumulative impact case study for this project. Rather, we drew on two previous studies related to cumulative impacts of initiatives. One was conducted as part of RPP on the cumulative impacts of peacebuilding in 2006, and a second was a field visit of the Listening Project in 2007. The latter mobilized teams of "listeners" composed of Kosovar and international staff from different aid agencies and CDA to listen to the perspectives and experiences of people in communities regarding international assistance. See Listening Project, "Field Visit Report: Kosovo." Cambridge, MA: CDA Collaborative Learning Projects, July 2007 and Chigas, D. *et al. Has Peacebuilding Made a Difference in Kosovo? A Study of the Effectiveness of Peacebuilding in Preventing Violence: Lessons Learned from the March 2004 Riots in Kosovo*." Cambridge, MA: CDA Collaborative Learning Projects and CARE International, 2006. Both reports are available at www.cdacollaborative.org

The case studies were written by well-informed teams representing diverse perspectives, usually permitting a balanced viewpoint. Although the case studies were not specifically peer-reviewed, they were all discussed thoroughly during consultations, in which the case authors also participated. Comments and critiques offered during those consultations (and later feedback workshops) led to revisions before the final posting of the cases to the CDA website. None of the conclusions presented in this book is based on a single case; they represent important cross-case analysis and examination of the full range of experiences.

The case studies are repeatedly referenced, especially in Part I of this book, which focuses on the findings of the collaborative learning project (cases, consultations, and feedback workshops), to provide examples and clarification of the results discussed. Most of those references are in text boxes using the format shown immediately below, stating the case location in bold and, where applicable, a page number. Where there is no page number, the text box presents a general inference drawn from the overall analysis of the case.

> **Example text box.** Case study evidence from **Cambodia** shows that, in 2009, text text text text text text text text text text text text text text text text text text text text text text text text text text text text text text text text text text text text text text text text text text text text text text text text text text text text text text text text text. [p.17]

Case Analysis Process

The CDA case analysis process is intensive and iterative. This mainly involves reading and rereading the cases and noting key issues and themes across the full set of cases. We also used qualitative data analysis software to code the cases, based on themes that had been identified in consultations with colleagues as well as internal discussions among staff and close collaborators. The software-based coding enabled us to pull text from all of the cases pertaining to a particular theme or issue, and then further analyze it comparatively. We were also able to conduct simple inquiries regarding the use of specific terms or to find text related to a specific topic.

In the past, CDA case studies had mainly focused on projects or programs as the unit of analysis. For the cumulative impact cases, though, the unit was an entire conflict zone (whether country or province) and the work of multiple agencies (governments, international organizations, local and international NGOs, etc.) in promoting peace. This complicated the process of cross-case analysis considerably. We also struggled to find analytical frameworks and tools that would help in this process. We experimented with tools and concepts from systems thinking, at first for conflict analysis, and later for understanding the core questions regarding cumulative impacts. These efforts are explained fully in subsequent chapters.

Consultations

The cumulative impact case process included a series of consultations involving case authors and a wide range of colleagues from headquarters and field operations of UN agencies, donors, and local and international organizations. Participants in each consultation analyzed several cases (usually 4-5) comparatively and identified cross-cutting themes and outstanding questions to pursue further. From January 2008 through February 2011, we held six consultations, four of them in Cambridge, Massachusetts and one each in Washington, DC and Kathmandu. The discussions in these consultations, along with the case study analysis, formed the basis for the development of issue papers exploring the emerging themes and findings. The consultations focused on sets of case studies, as they were completed, as well as early drafts of Issue Papers, which summarize staff analyses of themes and patterns identified in earlier consultations. Ultimately, nine Issue Papers were produced (see list in Annex B), which were used as the basis for discussion in a series of Feedback Workshops.

Feedback Workshops

The CDA collaborative learning process recognizes that it is difficult to produce generalizable lessons based on a limited number of cases. Therefore, the collaborative learning process always includes important steps for expansion, refinement, and verification of preliminary findings among active policymakers and practitioners with relevant experiences, through what we call "feedback workshops." Each feedback workshop represents an opportunity to test preliminary conclusions with a well-informed audience. In the course of discussions, participants are also encouraged to add their experiences from work in other places. For instance, a consultation in Nairobi in October 2011 brought together peace practitioners from Uganda, South Sudan, Somalia, and Kenya—none of them the focus for any of the cumulative impact case studies. This produced an insightful conversation about the applicability to the situations in their countries of the preliminary findings captured in the Issue Papers.

Ultimately, RPP conducted sixteen feedback workshops in diverse locations, each involving as few as ten and as many as forty participants. While most of these were one-day events, they were as short as three hours and as long as two days. The results have been incorporated into this publication. (See list of Feedback Workshops in Annex C.) In addition, a consultation on a preliminary draft of this book was held in 2015—which resulted in many helpful comments and a significant rewriting process to produce the current text.

Overview of the Book

Part I of this book presents the most significant findings from the case study process. Chapter 1 reviews what we found—and did not find—from the overall study. Chapter 2 presents, in detail, a key finding in the form of a Peace Progress Factor Tree, a systems thinking tool that we found was useful in identifying patterns regarding cumulative impacts across the cases, and can be used to assess progress towards peace (or the lack thereof). Chapter 3 explores the key concept of Linkages: the different types and how they work in the context of peacebuilding. Chapter 4 examines how "insiders" and "outsiders" can best collaborate in promoting peace. Chapter 5 delves into the role of Leadership in the adding up process.

Part II is explicitly prescriptive. It builds on the case study findings presented in Part I, but also draws on our own experience working with peace practitioners since 2003 and before to apply the findings of the first phase of RPP. We incorporate insights from other fields, particularly systems thinking and the emerging knowledge about how to achieve collective impacts that we have found to be useful in that work. Chapter 6 lays out the current state of the peacebuilding field, including a systems analysis of the current challenges and dysfunctions. Chapter 7 explores the concept of collective impact—and adapts some of the models from other sectors to propose a framework for collective impact in peacebuilding. Chapter 8 summarizes the accumulated experience of RPP staff and partners in performing conflict analysis using systems thinking tools, as an aid in achieving a shared understanding of a conflict context as the basis for more effective program design. Chapter 9 offers a series of suggested forward actions, building on the findings from the cumulative impact cases and the other activities of the Reflecting on Peace Practice program over the years.

PART I

THE ELEMENTS OF "ADDING UP"

WHAT WE FOUND— AND DID NOT FIND

This chapter provides an overview of our findings from the cumulative case study process, many of which are then elaborated further in subsequent chapters. We were also intrigued by things we *did not find*, some of which are as significant as those we did. During this collaborative learning process, the analytical challenge was to identify, across sixteen diverse cases, patterns of progress (and lack of progress) towards peace, as well as cogent explanations of how the actions of multiple individuals and organizations contributed to that improvement.

As noted in the Introduction, the sixteen case studies each focused on a specific conflict area or zone—in many cases a whole country, but sometimes a subregion (e.g., Mindanao, Aceh, Northern Ireland) or a more complex situation (Cyprus, Israel/Palestine). Eleven of these conflicts had achieved some form of settlement/peace agreement (South Africa, Burundi, Northern Ireland, Tajikistan, Aceh, Cambodia, Liberia, Solomon Islands, Mozambique, Mindanao, Guatemala). In three cases, there had been significant progress towards peace followed by reversals (Cyprus, Israel/Palestine, Sri Lanka), or no significant improvement (Kosovo). The Haiti case represents a different form of conflict, as there has not been a protracted war, but rather periodic cycles of extreme violence followed by periods of relative peace.

Understanding "Progress"

In choosing the case studies, we deliberately emphasized conflict contexts in which some discernable progress had been made—although, in some cases, progress was followed by backsliding (Israel/Palestine, Sri Lanka, Cyprus) or no significant progress (Kosovo). "Progress" does not mean that the conflict factors[10] are fully resolved, or

---

10 "Conflict factors" refer to dynamics or activities, social/economic political structures, or a social norms or attitudes that contribute to disputes, grievances, and disagreements that lead, over time to violence.

even that forward movement was substantial at any point in time. There will almost always be unresolved, unfinished, or persistent issues that are not addressed, as discussed further below. Rather, in this study, we were interested in shifts or developments in the situation that people inside the context (those interviewed from a wide range of perspectives) acknowledge as representing an improvement in the situation or in the conditions for achieving peace.

Progress almost never happens in a linear fashion, and advances at a different pace in different domains. The presence of unresolved issues or lack of progress on less prominent sub-factors does not mean overall progress in the larger domain will not continue.[11] Many dimensions of change in each of the major domains need to work together to advance towards peace. How can one recognize progress then? The following observations emerged as significant from the cases and practitioner experience.

What does "progress" entail? A major finding from the cumulative impact cases is the need to make progress in six significant "domains" that represent essential concerns. The six domains are:

1. Physical security and sense of security;

2. Acknowledgment of key conflict drivers and commitment to address them;

3. A durable political arrangement for handling power;

4. Resilient relationship between government and society;

5. Economic fairness and opportunity; and

6. Social cohesion.

Each of these domains is discussed in detail in Chapter 2, including the factors that contribute to them.

These domains do not constitute the elements necessary for a just and sustainable peace. Therefore, they do not represent an alternative to the multiple articulations of frameworks and goals for just and sustainable peace that have been developed over the last decade. Examples include the Peacebuilding and Statebuilding Goals (PSGs),[12] Goal 16 of the Sustainable Development Goals (SDGs)[13] and the Institute for Economics and Peace's Eight Pillars of Positive Peace.[14] Rather, they represent significant areas of concern affecting the *transition from war* that the cases suggested need to be addressed to make progress towards a just and sustainable peace. They are necessarily

---

11 The next chapter will identify a set of "high level" factors or domains that contribute to durable peace—and subsidiary factors that contribute to those larger issues. See also: Bell, C., & Pospisil, J. (2017). Navigating Inclusion in Transitions from Conflict: The Formalised Political Unsettlement. *Journal of International Development* 29: 576–593.

12 The PSGs identify legitimate politics, security, justice, employment and livelihoods, and revenues and accountable service delivery as key goals and the basis for working in fragile contexts (https://www.newdeal4peace.org/about-the-new-deal/).

13 SDG 16's targets relating to rule of law and equal access to justice, reduction of corruption, effective and accountable institutions, participation and inclusive decision making, violence prevention and non-discrimination

14 See Institute for Economics and Peace, Positive Peace Report 2016 (http://visionofhumanity.org/app/uploads/2017/02/Positive-Peace-Report-2016.pdf); *Positive Peace: The lens to achieve the Sustaining Peace Agenda* (IEP Brief, 2017).

narrower than the full range of factors that "support an environment where human potential flourishes," which the Institute for Economics and Peace proposes as factors for positive peace.[15]

How does one assess "progress" in a complex situation—where there are areas in which progress is detectable, but also areas where there is none? Progress in a major domain such as social cohesion or governance must necessarily be based on an aggregate assessment—that is, there will be both significant improvements and areas that are stuck or even experience backsliding. The importance or weight of any contributing factors matters—as determined in context. For instance, factors that contribute to social cohesion, such as various forms of reconciliation or increased commercial and social interactions, may remain static, while other factors, such as government policies that encourage exchanges and fairness, may improve. In situations involving such mixed reviews, it is necessary to determine how the various factors result in progress, or the lack thereof, in a major domain.

In this regard, it is not necessary that all contributing causes or factors to progress in an area (such as social cohesion) experience progress. In a particular situation, it was important to ask people, both about overall perceptions of how the situation has evolved in each area, such as security, economics or social cohesion, as well as about the different factors influencing progress in that area. In other words, it helps to understand the relative importance of the contributing factors, as well as how momentum toward progress can develop in the larger domains.

In **Aceh**[16], people considered that significant progress had been made in the governance arena in 2008, despite the fact that issues of corruption and rule of law remained severe, and neither the Human Rights Court nor the Commission for Truth and Reconciliation had been established, even though the peace accords had mandated them. (The TRC was finally appointed in 2016.)

In **Northern Ireland,** advances due to the Fair Employment Acts of 1976 and 1989, and the establishment of the Fair Employment Tribunal in 1989 were seen as key initiatives for sustainable peace. Although discrimination in housing, education, and political gerrymandering, as well as the presence and actions of security forces, were also significant issues, these initiatives represented for people an acknowledgment of a long-standing grievance and provided channels for redressing it. They contributed to progress in governance, not only because they addressed a specific issue of concern for the Catholic population, but they also held out a credible promise that (eventually) the same would occur for other grievances.[17]

How do people living in the area see changes in the context? How people characterize changes in the context—as positive or negative, progress or not—is critical, as the very

---

15 Ibid., p. 8.

16 As noted in the Introduction, examples placed in text boxes are all citations from the RPP cumulative cases, with the case location highlighted in bold. Where applicable, a page number is provided [in brackets]. In this reference to the Aceh case, and the Northern Ireland case below, these are general observations drawn from the cases, without citing a specific page.

17 Note that citations of RPP cases without page numbers refer to the sense of the whole case.

framing of the changes affects the evolution of the peace process itself and can help to create momentum toward peace. Understanding how people view changes in the context, and how they perceive peace initiatives, is thus very important. The perceptions of progress and the vital evidence of progress can only be determined *in context*, and by people immersed in the situation because the factors contributing to sustainable peace cannot be separated from the people that influence them and that they influence. Understanding these dynamics requires investment in processes and skills to listen to a wide range of people's views. Of course, while perceptions are important, they not the only possible measures of progress; objective and quantifiable measures can and should be identified that can complement more qualitative and perceptual information. We will return to this issue in Chapter 7 to delve more deeply into how we can develop shared measures across multiple organizations trying to achieve collective impact.

How does progress evolve over time? Progress, including negotiated agreements and both formal and informal settlements, can be reversed quite quickly, especially in vulnerable situations. Progress is often delayed, slow, and evolves in a nonlinear way—which becomes apparent over time and presents a complex set of interactions among developments in security, social, economic, structural, political and perceptual (attitudinal) domains. Progress may proceed quickly or lag behind in different domains. If peacebuilding work neglects important factors or is ineffective, new strategies for promoting progress may need to be developed, taking account of the systemic complexity of conflict.[18] Thus, to understand a conflict context, it is essential to look at the evolution of progress over time (rather than just immediate achievements) and to identify patterns across different domains.

RECOGNIZING AND TRACKING VULNERABILITY

In Burundi, in 2007-8, people we interviewed judged that significant progress had been made, even if vulnerabilities to recurring violence persisted. The process that led to the Arusha Accords (2000) and the accords themselves were widely seen as a "training ground" for learning the values of tolerance and compromise. However, the government elected in 2005 arose from a rebel group that had not participated in the Arusha negotiations—which was seen to have deprived it of the experience of developing a "culture of tolerance" as the other parties had, and undermine its ownership of the negotiated agreements. Thus, progress had been achieved in security, development of political processes for handling power and the relationship between government and citizens, but by 2008, these had deteriorated under the new government, ultimately finding expression in election-related violence in 2015. Certain dynamics foreshadowed a worsening of the situation: key parties, including the government, regressed in open acknowledgment of conflict drivers and in their commitment to address them, retreated from political accommodations, and slowed progress on mechanisms to address grievances (e.g., justice reform, police).

---

18 Chapter 8 will present methods for conducting conflict mapping using systems thinking tools.

What Promotes Progress?

The cases and practitioner experience suggest that identifying and focusing on areas of progress or "traction" (and identifying points of resistance) are important for generating cumulative impacts.

Shocks to the system sometimes promote progress. Some initiatives or events produce shocks to the existing conflict system, resulting in a realignment of relationships, or key actors change their thinking, which opens possibilities for progress in other areas. Of course, such shocks can (and often do) also produce adverse reactions and worsening of conflict, depending partly on how governments and citizens respond to the events.

SHOCKS CAN LEAD TO STRUCTURAL CHANGES OR POSITIVE ACTIONS THAT OPEN POSSIBILITIES FOR PROGRESS

In 1985, the British and Irish governments concluded the Anglo-Irish Agreement, giving the Irish government a consultative role in **Northern Ireland**'s affairs in exchange for Ireland's recognizing the 'principle of consent' that Northern Ireland should remain part of the United Kingdom, while the majority of people there wished it. The agreement was developed without consulting the people or politicians in Northern Ireland and provoked fury and opposition. However, it constituted a critical structural change in the situation, laying the groundwork for joint responsibility of the governments of Britain and Ireland for the situation. This was a first step toward allaying the fears of both sides that their identity was under threat—while at the same time removing a source of polarization between the sides. The Anglo-Irish Agreement is seen as a key turning point in the extended process toward peace. [p. 23]

Negative "shocks" can catalyze positive actions and progress. In **Mindanao,** the Supreme Court's invalidation of critical points of the Memorandum of Understanding reached between the Government of the Philippines and the MILF "shocked many in Track 2" to recognize the gap in harmonization in their efforts that was undermining their influence on peace. This led to a "new spirit of sharing information," respect and development of common agendas. [p.36]

In **Cyprus,** positive international developments, such as Greek-Turkish rapprochement and a change of government in Turkey, along with the pressure of a rapidly approaching date for Cyprus' accession to the EU. These were significant factors in mobilizing the Turkish Cypriot population against their leadership, leading to a change in government and in positions toward the Cyprus problem.

Progress in an area opens space for engagement of more people in peacebuilding. Traction exists when progress in one area provides signals of hope and encourages and opens space for new actors to take initiative to promote and consolidate peace.

The 2005 elections **Liberia** were a key turning point in the peace process because they were not only the most open (and peaceful) democratic political contest the country had ever had, but they also signaled a break with the power-sharing that had paralyzed

> the transitional government. These competitive yet peaceful elections were seen as a major milestone in the peace process. Moreover, progress on elections also provided a big boost to broader civic life and activism in Liberia; many civil society groups were able to expand their programming and get involved in civic voter campaigns or election monitoring, without becoming politicized. [p.26]

Existing system change provides opportunities to reinforce and accelerate progress. Because "systems change best when they change themselves, the best peacebuilders can do (both from within and outside a particular social context) is to nurture change from within the system...."[19] When an important factor is already in flux, this supports other changes in the system. Change that is already happening in the system decreases "friction" and the amount of effort needed to affect the direction of change, as there will be less resistance.[20] The fair employment legislation example in Northern Ireland above illustrates this point.

Understanding Lack of Progress: "Persistent Issues"

While the main focus of the case studies was on the cumulative impacts of multiple peace efforts, it was impossible to ask questions about what was accomplished without eliciting information about what had *not* been done—or how progress was incomplete or stalled. Each case study, therefore, recounted not only the advances towards peace but also what came to be identified as "unfinished business" or "persistent issues." It was clear that these are important dynamics that must be included in findings regarding the adding up process. Several observations emerged about how these persistent issues influence the sustainability of progress.

What are the persistent issues – or unresolved business? We found twenty types of persistent conflict issues in the cases and consultations that were seen to remain blockages to consolidation of peace. Table 1.1 below lists these issues, grouped in categories, along with the frequency with which they are found.

These are familiar themes in post-war peacebuilding. They represent key conflict drivers that are often not addressed or addressed inadequately. A common trajectory post-agreement is that significant gains are made in the security situation, in the conclusion of a peace agreement and establishment of new rules of the game that limit *violent* handling of political struggles, and minimum legitimacy of government. However, old patterns of political culture, inequity, corruption, and social, economic and political exclusion persist, even with new formal rules—resulting in what Christine Bell and Jan Pospisil have called a "formalized political unsettlement."[21] These factors hinder further progress toward a more positive and durable peace.

---

19 Ricigliano, *Making Peace Last*, 63.

20 Ibid, 146-148.

21 Bell, C. and J. Pospisil, "Navigating Inclusion in Transitions from Conflict: The Formalised Political Unsettlement." *Journal of International Development* 29: 576–593. The formalized political unsettlement manages and contains the conflict, pursuing it in new political and legal institutions, rather than resolving it.

Table 1.1: Persistent Conflict Issues

	# cases*
A. SECURITY DOMAIN	
Incomplete/unfair DDR, SSR, small arms	8
Stability prioritized over peace/justice	4
Dependence on external forces/roles	4
B. POLITICAL DEAL	
Structural inequalities, power struggles [global variable]	11
Threat to indigenous/minority rights, identity, land, traditions	8
Peace agreements/laws vs. implementation	5
Inclusion/exclusion from peace processes, spoilers [global variable]	2
C. RESILIENT RELATIONSHIP BETWEEN GOVERNMENT AND CITIZENS	
Poor governance, democracy, rule of law	11
Corruption/impunity	8
Exclusionary policies/practices [global variable]	8
Institutional dysfunction	6
Human rights abuses	4
Incomplete transitional justice/impunity	6
Need for judicial reform/strengthening	6
D. ECONOMIC DOMAIN	
Inequitable development, distribution of benefits, resource management, unemployment [global variable]	12
Specific disputes over land, returns...	8
E. SOCIAL FABRIC DOMAIN	
Need for improved inter-group relations	10
Lack of a sense of national identity, unity, vision	5
Inadequate dealing with the past, reconciliation	9
Need for deeper dialogue (local or national)	8

* Based on a total of 12 cases in which peace agreements had been concluded and held, even if not fully implemented.

The most prevalent persistent issues, as the table suggests, are issues related to power struggles and structural inequalities, governance and rule of law, inequitable economic development and access to resources and inter-group relations. These trends in post-war settings are of particular concern when these factors constitute, in whole or in part, the original reasons for the war and violence. In other words, the historic causes of the conflict persist, despite years, sometimes decades, of fighting and concerted efforts to establish peace, often supported by enormous amounts of international assistance.

In many settings, war and a subsequent political settlement (and/or a series of agreements) become the context for a renewed cycle of violence. At times, this is due to a flawed peace process or incomplete or contested agreements, as key issues are not addressed, particularly when negotiators represent political elites that may or may not serve the interests of large segments of the population. In other cases, post-war regimes have no intention of abiding by agreements, especially when to do so would hurt their interests. As we have noted, leaders must acknowledge key conflict issues and make commitments to address them—but few do.

PERSISTENT ISSUES AND INCOMPLETE "SETTLEMENTS"

In **Mindanao,** interviewees noted the need for changes in the autocratic—even feudal—systems of local dynasties that dominate politics, often in collaboration with central government powers in Manila. [p.14]

Similar language is used in **Mozambique** to describe a zero-sum mindset in which political parties vie for total control over the state, in order to perpetuate the entrenched patron-client system, resulting in an increasingly politicized state and trends toward one-party control. [p.12]

Similarly, democratic developments in other cases, such as **Cambodia** and **Tajikistan,** have been stalled by the persistence of historical patterns of political decision-making, leading to one-party capture of the state.

In **Liberia,** the underlying patron-client (or "Big Man") model of governance was seen as problematic. The persistent marginalization of rural areas over Monrovia and the relative neglect of some tribes remain points of contention and has led many to conclude that nothing fundamental has changed. To quote the RPP case study:

"Many interviewees, apart from those subjective assessments of the current situation, stressed that they found the conditions in post-war Liberia to resemble pre-war Liberia and that the root causes of the war had not been properly addressed. One observer noted that the fact that many people were "disgruntled and marginalized" had not changed. Widespread poverty, underdevelopment, exclusion of parts of the country and the marginalization of parts of the population were all cited as root causes of the conflict that have largely remained unchanged. According to those interviewed, most development remains focused on Monrovia at the expense of the countryside, and "resources are not being distributed as they should be." The government is seen to take action mainly for its own benefit or for the benefit of the rich. One informant summed it up as follows: "Those who were wealthy sent their kids abroad and they are coming back now and get all the good jobs. Corruption and lack of opportunities [continue], just like in the history of our country." [p.41]

When do persistent issues make a difference? Not all persistent issues, or lack of progress, stall or reverse progress towards sustainable peace. These persistent issues exist both in cases of sustained progress toward a more just and sustainable peace and in more fragile situations. What makes the difference? How can one assess whether the persistent issues or unfinished business, will block progress toward sustainable peace or result, eventually, in relapses into violence?

Some cases show a higher number of issues (see Table 1.2 at the end of this chapter, indicating which issues were found in which cases). Liberia, for example, showed eighteen out of the twenty issues in 2008, and Burundi seventeen in the same time frame. In Northern Ireland, our sources identify eleven and in South Africa only seven. Tajikistan exhibits sixteen issues, Haiti thirteen,[22] and Aceh ten.

The cases and experiences gathered suggest that while the number of unresolved issues is not unimportant, their "density," severity or depth, and their relation to the conflict context are most important. By "density" we mean the degree to which they are concentrated in a particular domain (rather than spread over many domains). Although this should not be taken as yet another index of fragility,[23] the "density" of issues in a single conflict zone likely represents an indicator of vulnerability to renewed violence over time. In situations such as Tajikistan, Burundi or Liberia, where international attention and assistance have been declining as time has elapsed since the peace agreement and violence has remained minimal, this may suggest both an urgency and an agenda for conflict prevention—and indeed, unrest and violence has reemerged in two of these countries. If the issues are severe or profound, important in the conflict context (e.g., related to drivers of conflict), and concentrated in particular domains (rather than spread out), they are more likely to be destabilizing in the long run.

Vertical and Horizontal Linkages Contribute to Adding Up

As noted in the Introduction, one of the areas of inquiry for the cumulative case studies centered on the role of "linkages" in promoting peace. Linkages refer to how initiatives support and complement each other, increasing their combined impacts. Therefore, each case study examined how a range of peace efforts was linked, both horizontally (across sectors, constituencies, and geography) and vertically (from local communities to national and international levels), to discover more precisely what types of linkage contributed to progress towards peace. We note a few key findings here—and then discuss these issues more fully in Chapter 3.

The issue of "linkages": Progress in one area affects progress in others. Momentum or traction can be gained when efforts and progress in one area (e.g., social cohesion) also have effects in other areas, either because the issues cut across several different

---

22 The absence of a "peace agreement" and issues related to implementation of peace agreements in Haiti makes some of the factors less applicable in that case and may explain the relatively low number.

23 See, for example, the Global Peace Index (http://visionofhumanity.org/indexes/global-peace-index/), developed by the Institute for Economics and Peace, as well as the Positive Peace Report (http://visionofhumanity.org/app/uploads/2017/10/Positive-Peace-Report-2017.pdf), which provide an index and a score that can be used to assess overall fragility.

domains, or because change in one area has "ripple" effects in others.[24] The issue of vertical linkages from local communities to sub-national, national and regional levels was identified as an important factor for peace in earlier phases of RPP—and we continued to explore those issues in these case studies.[25] Horizontal linkages across programming approaches, sectors and constituencies are also important—as explored further in Chapter 3.

> The 1991 National Peace Accord in **South Africa** helped to contain political violence in many areas that could have been worse, though in many places it was unable to break cycles of violence. The NPA catalyzed progress, not only in the security arena, where the results were mediocre but also because it got the political parties involved, constituting the first step in real negotiations. It also promoted a 'peace culture' and established procedures for crisis management. The negotiation of the NPA was, as chief negotiator for the National Party noted, "our first introduction in negotiating the details of a document," and could be seen as progress toward a negotiated settlement. It also contributed to democratization by bringing together "political opponents and representatives from a wide range of groups to promote peace, political tolerance, mutual understanding and the building of trust." It allowed South Africans to imagine a future without violence, contributed to the possibility of a negotiation process, and provided a voice for civil society. [p.20]

Progress on some issues can be seen as symbolic—representing political will and possibilities for addressing grievances. When an issue is tightly connected to a fundamental grievance (e.g., Fair Employment in Northern Ireland), progress on that issue can represent the possibility of progress on grievances more generally. Progress in areas that are conceptually linked with each other communicates a willingness to change and address grievances. Not all issues in a similar area (e.g., related to exclusion, or related to national identity) are linked in this way; in some cases, progress on one issue can raise fears among groups that "their" issues will not be addressed. Whether problems or issues are conceptually linked, and whether one problem can be representative of the possibility of solving other related or similar issues, can only be identified by listening to people in the context itself.

> The "7 Million Fund," was a **Mozambican** government initiative, created as part of the decentralization program in the early to mid-2000s, to provide loans to small business and individuals for projects to improve food security, create jobs, and fight poverty. Despite problems of corruption, party favoritism, inefficiency and lack of strategy, the 7 Million Fund was one of the most prized government programs, because it offered hope and opportunity to people to change their condition. In this sense, it communicated both an acknowledgment of and commitment to address a key conflict driver, and the possibility of economic opportunity. [p.20]

---

24 This is supported by systems thinking principles: see Ricigliano, *Making Peace Last.*

25 See Chapter 3 and Ernstorfer, Anita, Diana Chigas, and Hannah Vaughan-Lee. 2015. "From Little to Large: When does Peacebuilding Add up." *Journal for Peacebuilding and Development* 10 (1): 72-77.

The role of "insiders" and "outsiders" in peace processes

It was clear from the case material that external assistance to peace efforts is not the driving force for change, unless it reinforces internal initiatives. External forces (international agencies and actors) seldom have a decisive influence in promoting peace, with some exceptions. Therefore, those of us who "meddle" in other people's conflict need a degree of humility regarding our own importance to peace processes; local people have the greatest influence over progress towards peace—or the lack of it.

The case studies reveal support for locally-led peace initiatives is crucial—if also sometimes difficult in a highly politicized environment. The cases also point to examples where outsiders—often regional powers and the primary supporters of internal groups—can take decisive action that pushes the conflicting parties to negotiate peace. On the other hand, external organizations, including donors, often create dependency on external technical support and funding, which can weaken local efforts and undermine local legitimacy. The cases also provide numerous examples in which external actions failed to align or link with local initiatives, decreasing the effectiveness of both. We explore these "insider-outsider" dynamics further in Chapter 4.

Leadership matters

In examining the case material, we were cautious about issues of leadership, not wishing to reinforce the idea that attributes progress towards peace to unique and heroic individuals, like Nelson Mandela. Nevertheless, as in other domains, it became clear that there are specific ways that leaders can promote or impede movement towards peace. While leaders or "champions" can act decisively in any of the domains, they play a particularly important role in a critical factor: *the degree to which there is progress in the acknowledgment of key conflict drivers and commitment to address them.* This is one of the six key domains noted above, discussed further in Chapter 2 as an essential element of sustainable peace and in Chapter 5 as a dimension of leadership.

The failure to acknowledge key drivers of conflict or denial of their importance is perhaps more important to increasing vulnerability to relapse than other individual factors. In some cases, progress, accompanied by open recognition or identification of ongoing (unresolved) issues and commitment to a process for addressing them has supported further momentum—as people are willing to be more patient when there is a credible hope that some of the knottier problems will be tackled. Where, for example, a new government has not been connected with the old system and has articulated a clear commitment to pursue change, peace processes can continue to "add up," despite the incomplete nature of the peace process.

> The post-apartheid government in **South Africa** has been intent on dismantling all of the institutions, policies, and practices that entrenched white privilege in the country. Progress on the political front and in new policies and institutions has occurred, and while economic progress for large numbers of people has been slow, and economic inequality and unequal access to resources and opportunity continues. While accu

sations of corruption and abuse of power have plagued the government, this did not undermine overall progress—although failure to make progress over a prolonged time on these issues can, and has, created dissatisfaction and contributed to unrest.

In **Northern Ireland,** as of 2007, people described the process as "irreversible," even though progress in social cohesion had been minimal, and concerns over government policies (especially the police) and about political participation remained, following the Good Friday Agreement. However, acknowledgment of the problems and the development of processes to deal with them helped ensure they did not undermine overall progress, despite serious challenges and setbacks.

In **Liberia,** a majority of interviewees in 2010 felt that the deep inequality from which the country suffers has not been tackled in the Poverty Reduction Strategy (PRS), which is the guide for peacebuilding. And the way the PRS had been implemented was following the same patterns of power and wealth distribution that existed in the country previously. As one person put it, the "poverty reduction strategy has turned into a poverty reproduction strategy." According to this critical perspective, the PRS neither represented a true vision, nor did its implementation help to construct peace in the country. Nonetheless, the PRS did acknowledge that peacebuilding in Liberia required efforts to tackle the "structural conditions and processes and attitudes that sustain social and political division and encourage the use of violence." Some, therefore considered the PRS to be an essential first step, but in need of an additional explicit national vision and peacebuilding strategy to contribute to peace and reconciliation, rather than reconstituting and reinforcing previous inequalities and patterns of power that have been causes of conflict. [p. 20-22]

What we did *NOT* find

There is no dominant pattern in the "adding up" process

When we launched the cumulative case study process, we knew that many organizations and individuals prefer a particular approach to peacebuilding or rely on a set of assumptions (theories of change) that inform their work. We had hoped to discover through the cumulative cases whether some approaches and their associated theories of change contributed more effectively to the cumulative effects of multiple efforts than others, or whether the different approaches complement each other in effective ways to produce cumulative effects.

While each case study presented a coherent "story" about how progress towards peace was achieved in that context, we did not find convincing evidence of patterns that were repeated across contexts. *There was no dominant pattern in the adding up process.* In other words, we did not find that any one approach facilitated cumulative impacts consistently, and we found no patterns regarding sequencing—i.e., there was no consistent pattern that any one domain must always be addressed before any other; moreover, progress in one area does not automatically lead to progress in another.

It is worth noting that in none of the cases was there a deliberate joint peace effort across multiple organizations, with some minor exceptions. The cases examined how different initiatives resulted in progress—even though they were not intentionally linked. Although the six high-level domains emerged as of importance overall, no one of those domains was found to be more important than any other across all of the cases. Instead, whether specific domains and sub-factors were seen as significant areas of progress or high priorities for action depended entirely on the context. In addition, we discovered that the *interactions* among the domains are as important as achieving progress in the individual domains—a concept supported by systems thinking principles.

Because a factor is important in one setting will not predict its importance in another. There is no substitute or shortcut for listening carefully, generating a shared analysis of the situation, and developing a multifaceted strategy for promoting progress in key locally-defined priority areas. Over time, it will be necessary to generate advances in each of the six domains of progress.

There is no one sequence for "adding up"

Our failure to find any dominant patterns or pathways to cumulative impacts means that we also found no formula for sequencing peacebuilding activities or initiatives to ensure that they all "add up." Much attention has been dedicated in the peacebuilding community over the years to the question of what the right sequencing and phasing for initiatives and activities ought to be.[26] People feel that some sequencing and phasing is necessary, because they do not have the resources to do everything at once. Sequencing also recognizes that things do not change at the same rate, and advances in some areas will open up possibilities for progress in others, while focusing on some issues first may undermine or block further progress on others. At the same time, practitioners and policymakers increasingly recognize that sequencing and timing depend on context. Thus, any plan or sequence will likely be disrupted by the unpredictability of events and activities on the ground. "Forget linearity," the Army Peacekeeping and Stability Operations Unit and USIP warned.[27]

We performed a careful exercise to identify, case by case, which initiatives came first, second, etc. While there was some evidence that progress in security preceded advances in other domains, this was not always the case; in some instances, negotiation of key issues permitted movement in security arrangements—and vice versa. While the peacebuilding community puts a lot of time and energy into efforts to increase "social cohesion," such efforts rarely showed immediate results—this was usually a "lagging indicator" for change. In many cases, concerted work to build better inter-group relations paid off at the point when efforts in other domains began to move, especially when people key to change in other domains participated and were influenced by

---

26 See, e.g., Langam, A. & G. Brown, *Building Sustainable Peace: Timing and Sequencing of Post-Conflict Reconstruction and Peacebuilding. Oxford Scholarship Online, 2016.*

27 See United States Institute of Peace and US Army Peacekeeping and Stability Operations Institute. 2009. *Guiding Principles for Stabilization and Reconstruction.* Washington, DC: USIP, p. 5-32.

social cohesion-focused work. The classic example is the fact that many of the Israeli and Palestinian negotiators in the Oslo process knew each other from many years of inter-group dialogue work and problem-solving workshops.

Other things we did NOT find

We were surprised by findings that did *not* emerge from the case studies, despite our best efforts to discern additional "adding up" elements. In addition to those issues discussed above, a few other "non-findings" were as follows.

Economic Factors. *We found no substantial linkage to economic factors in particular.* Our methods elicited the views of a wide range of local people and close observers regarding what, in their views, contributed to progress towards peace in their situation. Surprisingly, given the attention and resources devoted to economic issues and programming in post-conflict peacebuilding, we did not find a strong correlation to economic issues. This does not mean that economic issues are unimportant and do not influence conflict dynamics. As explained further in the next chapter, what we found is that in the dynamics of progress toward peace, economic factors contributed to progress either as a factor shaping motivations for supporting peace processes (e.g., the prospect of economic gains with an agreement, and the concomitant prospect of loss in the absence of a peace agreement), or in relation to issues of equity and fairness. Progress on common economic measures (growth in GDP, employment rates, etc.) were not identified as major contributing forces.

The Role of Women. *We found very little evidence regarding the contributions of women to the adding up process, with a few exceptions.* This was a surprise, as the terms of reference for the case writers included an explicit question regarding the role of women. It should also be noted that among the sixteen cases, five were developed by women-only teams, nine by mixed teams of a man and a woman, and two by men only. While being female does not automatically guarantee more sensitivity to gender issues, it usually helps—so we doubt that gender bias on the part of the case writers provides an explanation.

Currently, there is considerable emphasis on expanding the role of women in peace processes, through the application of UN Resolution 1325 and other initiatives. However, in these *retrospective* cases, we did not find that women played important roles in most settings. Three *important* exceptions were Liberia, Northern Ireland, and Solomon Islands, in which women were fully engaged and quite influential. Womens' groups had an important influence in promoting peace in Liberia at the national level; in the Solomons women took strong leadership at the community and sub-national levels.

This lack of evidence in the case studies about the role of women can be interpreted in various ways. First, it supports the observation that women have often been left out of peace *processes*, especially at official levels, and therefore reinforces the need for improvement in this area, as called for by Resolution 1325. Second, because the case study inquiry focused on the question of whether and how a range of peace efforts added up, it may be that the roles women were playing in many settings were effective in their own right, but simply less visible or not involved in those initiative deemed by diverse observers as critical to forward motion towards peace.

The next chapter will further explore the six domains of progress and introduce a systems thinking tool, factor trees, which enable us to identify the elements that contribute to progress in the key domains. Subsequent chapters in Part I will address the how linkages function, the potential roles for outsiders in peace efforts, and the contributions of leadership.

Table 1.2: Persistent Issues in RPP Cumulative Case Studies (Cases with peace agreements only)

	Aceh	Brundi	Cambodia	Guatemala	Haiti	Liberia	Mindanao	Mozambique	No. Ireland	Solomon Islands	South Africa	Tajikistan	# cases
A. SECURITY DOMAIN													
Incomplete/unfair DDR, SSR, small arms	X	X	X		X	X	X	X				X	8
Stability prioritized over peace/justice			X		X	X						X	4
Dependence on external forces/roles	X				X	X				X			4
B. POLITICAL DEAL													
Structural inequalities, power struggles		X	X	X	X	X	X	X	X	X	X	X	11
Threat to indigenous/minority rights, identity, land, traditions	X	X	X	X		X	X				X	X	8
Peace agreements/laws vs. implementation	X	X	X	X								X	5
Inclusion/exclusion from peace processes, spoilers		X							X				2
C. RESILIENT RELATIONSHIP BETWEEN GOVERNMENT AND CITIZENS													
Poor governance, democracy, rule of law	X	X	X	X	X	X	X	X	X	X		X	11
Corruption/impunity		X	X	X	X	X	X	X				X	8
Exclusionary policies/practices	X	X		X	X	X		X	X			X	8
Institutional dysfunction		X		X	X	X			X	X			6
Human rights abuses	X	X					X					X	4
Incomplete transitional justice/impunity		X	X	X		X			X			X	6
Need for judicial reform/strengthening		X		X	X	X		X	X				6

	Aceh	Brundi	Cambodia	Guatemala	Haiti	Liberia	Mindanao	Mozambique	No. Ireland	Solomon Islands	South Africa	Tajikistan	# cases
D. ECONOMIC DOMAIN													
Inequitable development, distribution of benefits, resource management, unemployment	X	X	X	X	X	X	X	X	X	X	X	X	12
Specific disputes over land, returns...		X	X			X	X	X		X	X	X	8
E. SOCIAL FABRIC DOMAIN													
Need for improved inter-group relations	X	X		X	X	X		X	X	X	X	X	10
Lack of a sense of national identity, unity, vision					X	X			X	X		X	5
Inadequate dealing with the past, reconciliation	X	X	X	X		X			X	X	X	X	9
Need for deeper dialogue (local or national)	X	X		X	X	X		X			X	X	8
Number of issues per case	11	17	11	13	13	17	8	10	11	9	7	16	

2

MAJOR DOMAINS OF PROGRESS & FACTOR TREES

The first phase of the Reflecting on Peace Practice project (1999–2003) explored the question of what peacebuilders understood to be the "peace" they were aiming to contribute to. We found that the goals and visions for peace programs varied widely.[28] The meaning of "peace" ranged from an end to overt violence, to transformation of social, political and economic arrangements that fuel conflict, to redress injustices, as well as transformation of culture and attitudes about violence and domination. Through the consultative process, practitioners asserted that "peace" must be defined in context, with the participation of stakeholders in the conflict, and that there would inevitably be different (though not always inconsistent) views on priorities for action or what might be feasible. There was, however, consensus that peace programs must strive to accomplish two broad goals that reach beyond just achieving a negative peace.[29] These goals comprise "Peace Writ Large," or the broader peace involving changes in the overall conflict dynamics beyond program or sectoral-level accomplishments. These two goals are:

- Stopping violence and destructive conflict, that is, ending war and cycles of physical violence; and

- Supporting social change to address political, economic and social grievances that drive conflict and to achieve sustainable and just structures.[30]

How do we know if we have made progress toward these broad goals? In *Confronting War* and through subsequent RPP work with practitioners, we identified five benchmarks[31] for assessing whether programs contribute meaningfully to Peace Writ Large:

---

28 *Confronting War,* p 10.

29 The concepts of 'positive peace' and 'negative peace' were first introduced by Johan Galtung in an editorial in the *Journal of Peace Research* (published by PRIO) in 1964, and expounded upon in multiple subsequent publications into the 1990s.

30 *Confronting War,* 10-11

31 The five elements were terms "Criteria of Effectiveness" in Confronting War, and have been referred to as "Building Blocks for Peace" in later RPP materials.

1. **The effort results in the creation or reform of political institutions to handle griev-ances in situations where such grievances do, genuinely, drive the conflict.** In other words, the effort develops or supports institutions or mechanisms (formal and in-formal) that address the specific inequalities, injustices and other grievances that are drivers of the conflict.

2. **The effort contributes to a momentum for peace by causing participants and com-munities to develop their own peace initiatives in relation to critical elements of context analysis.** This benchmark stresses the importance of local "ownership" and sustainability of action and efforts to bring about peace, as well as creating momen-tum for peace, involving increasing numbers of people.

3. **The effort prompts people increasingly to resist violence and provocations to vio-lence.** In most circumstances, one important aspect of Peace Writ Large is a signifi-cant and sustained reduction in violence. This building block is a stepping stone to that long-term goal. Where people have been drawn into violence in the past, they seek other means of change and become more wary of political manipulation.

4. **The effort results in an increase in people's security and in their sense of security.** Security and people's perceptions of it contain many different aspects, which must be identified and attained based on the local context.

5. **The effort results in meaningful improvement in inter-group relations,** as reflected in, for example, changes in group attitudes, public opinion, social norms, or public behaviors. Improved relationships between conflicting groups constitute an import-ant building block for peace—often a preliminary step towards other initiatives.[32]

Evidence in the first phase of RPP showed that when peacebuilding programs meet these criteria, they contribute to the larger peace, and that such contributions can be even more significant when they are timely (rather than delayed), sustained, and "big enough," that is, proportional to the scale and level of the conflict, making linkages between levels and across sectors and constituencies. The five criteria are also addi-tive—that is, the more elements are addressed, the more likely that programs will make a significant contribution to peace.[33]

These benchmarks remain useful for individual programs as they define goals and assess whether and how those individual initiatives might contribute to the larger goal of Peace Writ Large. However, they do not help us understand what progress toward Peace Writ Large looks like. For this, in analyzing the rich material of the RPP cumula-tive cases, we turned to systems mapping as a possible tool for seeing the larger picture and how various initiatives address different conflict factors.

---

32 "Criteria of Effectiveness in *Confronting War* 15-19; RPP Training Manual 29-30 (and sometimes called "Building Blocks for Peace").
33 *Confronting War,* p 19; RPP Training Manual 2013, p. 30

Peacebuilding practitioners and policymakers have found systems dynamics maps (or causal loop diagrams) helpful in conflict analysis and strategy development.[34] The systems maps depict the *interrelations* of causes and consequences relating to conflict and peace, help to identify what possible systemic effects a strategy might have, and provide a way to test theories of change. They are also useful for placing different kinds of work by different peace actors in relation to the factors that they affect and affect them, and for identifying gaps, overlaps and synergies among efforts—all of this important for understanding cumulative impacts.

We found these systems maps less helpful in analyzing cumulative impacts—in understanding what *progress* looks like from a collective perspective. While they can and have been used to assess cumulative impacts in a single conflict area, they are not helpful for *comparative* analysis of what progress towards sustainable peace looks like across different cases, and do not depict benchmarks of progress.

Factor Trees that Show What Progress Looks Like from a Collective Perspective

As we analyzed progress towards peace in the cumulative cases within and across these common factors, we found it helpful to use a complementary tool for seeing trends and patterns in the system. This helps us understand how the more visible markers of progress were changing over time as a result of changes in conflict dynamics. This systems-based tool is called a "factor tree," as elaborated by Paul K. Davis and his colleagues at the Rand Corporation. Davis developed factor trees to synthesize fragmented and heterogeneous knowledge from different disciplines and strands of work into a more comprehensive understanding of the dynamics of violent extremism and the factors that motivate an individual to undertake acts of terrorism. Later, he used factor trees to integrate social science knowledge from different disciplines about stabilization and reconstruction.[35] Factor trees convey a snapshot of causal factors at work in a system with a "modest indication" of how they interact or influence each other.[36] They depict factors contributing to a phenomenon (such as sustainable peace) at a particular point in time in an approximate hierarchical tree, showing how a host of subordinate factors cascade upwards to achieve a higher order goal or change.

Figure 2.1 shows this basic concept. Lower-level nodes lead to the top-most node (larger goal/outcome), meaning that they are factors contributing to that effect. These contributing factors may themselves be effects of still other factors (e.g., A1 and A2 contributing to Key Factor A). The curved dotted lines and the notation "~ands" and "~ors" suggest how the factors tend to combine. In Figure 2.1, the "~and" notation indicates that Key Factors A, B and C must all be present to achieve the higher goal. The "~ors" between B1 and B2, indicates that either factor could by itself lead to the higher-level factor B.

---

34 We will return to consideration of systems thinking tools for conflict analysis in Chapter 8.

35 Davis, Paul K., "Primer for Building Factor Trees to Represent Social-Science Knowledge." *Proceedings of the 2011 Winter Simulation Conference*, S. Jain, R.R. Creasey, J. Himmelspach, K.P. White, and M. Fu, eds. and Davis, Paul K. (ed.), *Dilemmas of Intervention: Social Science for Stabilization and Reconstruction*, Santa Monica, Calif.: RAND Corporation, 2011.

36 Davis, *Dilemmas of Intervention*, p 11.

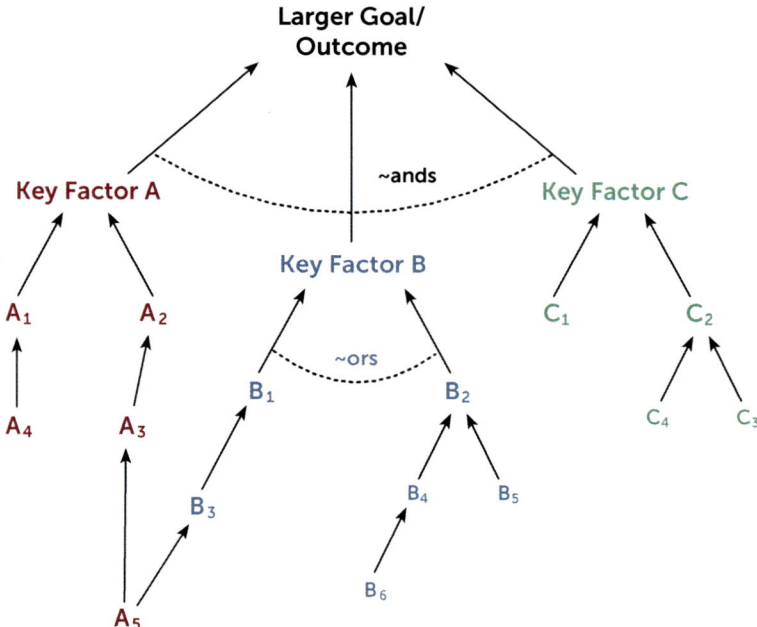

Figure 2.1: Factor Tree Concept

The factor trees are deliberately simplified pictures. Unlike the causal loop diagrams (or systems maps), they do not depict dynamics of interrelationships, feedback processes, time delays, or relationships across different branches of the trees.[37] Although the factor trees appear fairly linear, they do facilitate a larger view of the whole, while providing some detail at the same time.[38] We found them useful for visualizing patterns of "progress" across a number of normally fragmented domains, and analyzing case-based and experience-based observations of what progress towards peace has occurred over time and how.

The Peace Progress Factor Tree as a Tool for Assessing Progress Towards Peace

Initial participatory analysis of the case studies and testing against further experience through consultations and feedback workshops revealed common general clusters of factors or domains of progress toward sustainable peace. There was remarkable consistency in people's judgments of what factors of "progress" looked like, even if they differed regarding the details. They also often identified areas where more work was needed—what we have called "persistent issues" or "unfinished business," as introduced in the previous chapter.

---

37 These aspects of causal loop diagrams or systems maps are discussed in Chapter 8.
38 Davis, *Primer for Building Factor Trees to Represent Social-Science Knowledge,* 3124

Building on these initial analyses, we developed an initial rough draft factor tree for "sustainable progress toward peace," by looking at the factors leading towards peace across all sixteen RPP cumulative case studies (see Figure 2.2).[39] This "generic" Peace Progress Factor Tree was refined through multiple rounds of analysis of the peacebuilding work undertaken and the resulting progress towards sustainable peace in all of the case studies. We analyzed each case based on the draft factor tree, highlighted the factors that appeared important to progress in that specific case, and showed, through color coding, where significant progress had been made, where some progress had been made, and where there were serious outstanding issues that had not been addressed. We also noted and compared factors that were important to the specific case, but missing in the generic tree—which prompted us, in some instances, to change or add factors to the generic tree. However. factors that appeared unique to a particular case (or only a few cases) were not added to the generic tree, as we assumed that important factors could be added when working with practitioners in a specific context.

The generic factor tree is depicted in Figure 2.2. The ultimate goal, indicated at the top, is "degree and sustainability of progress towards durable peace." This highest-level factor (and effect) has two implied measures: the "degree of progress" and the "sustainability of progress;" progress itself is not sufficient without being sustained. The first row of the factor tree shows six high-level factors or domains that emerged as essential for the adding up process (already introduced, briefly, in Chapter 1):

1. Physical security and sense of security;

2. Acknowledgment of key conflict drivers and commitment to address them;

3. A durable political arrangement for handling power;

4. Resilient relationship between government and society;

5. Economic fairness and opportunity; and

6. Social cohesion.

The higher-level categories (the six major domains) are common to all of the cases, to a certain extent, but none of them is sufficient, in itself, to bring about sustainable progress, even if the degree and rate of progress across the domains may be different. In the convention of factor trees, the first level of factors (tied together by the notation "~ands") are considered necessary *collectively* for the achievement of the higher-level goal.

It should be noted that the factor tree includes a set of "Global Variables" (in the box at the bottom of the diagram) that influence everything—that is, they are so pervasive in the system that they cannot be treated separately and attached to any specific branch of the tree. These include: horizontal inequalities, sense of grievance, patterns of inclusion/exclusion, and mental models and political culture regarding power. These and each of the major domains are further explained below.

---

39 We are grateful to Paul Davis for his kind feedback on our early attempts at these factor trees.

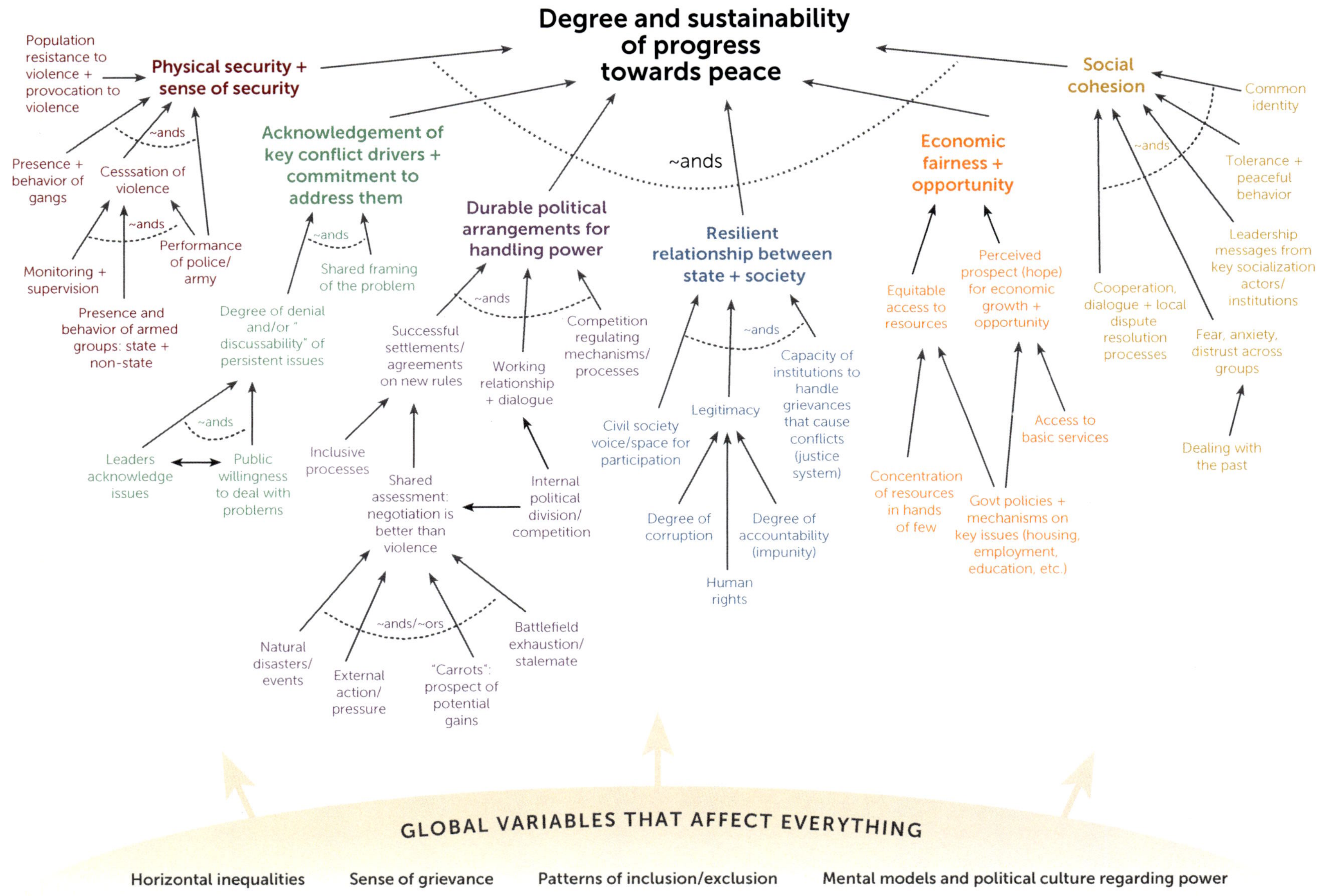

Degree and sustainability of progress towards peace

Physical security + sense of security

- Population resistance to violence + provocation to violence
- Presence + behavior of gangs
- Presence and behavior of armed groups: state + non-state
- Monitoring + supervision
- Performance of police/army
- Cessation of violence
- ~ands

Acknowledgement of key conflict drivers + commitment to address them

- Degree of denial and/or "discussability" of persistent issues
- Shared framing of the problem
- ~ands
- Public willingness to deal with problems
- Leaders acknowledge issues
- ~ands

Durable political arrangements for handling power

- Successful settlements/ agreements on new rules
- Inclusive processes
- Working relationship + dialogue
- Competition regulating mechanisms/ processes
- ~ands
- Internal political division/ competition
- Shared assessment: negotiation is better than violence
- ~ands/~ors
- Battlefield exhaustion/ stalemate
- "Carrots": prospect of potential gains
- External action/ pressure
- Natural disasters/ events

Resilient relationship between state + society

- Capacity of institutions to handle grievances that cause conflicts (justice system)
- ~ands
- Legitimacy
- Degree of accountability (impunity)
- Human rights
- Degree of corruption
- Civil society voice/space for participation

Economic fairness + opportunity

- Perceived prospect (hope) for economic growth + opportunity
- Access to basic services
- Equitable access to resources
- Concentration of resources in hands of few
- Govt policies + mechanisms on key issues (housing, employment, education, etc.)

Social cohesion

- Common identity
- Tolerance + peaceful behavior
- Leadership messages from key socialization actors/ institutions
- ~ands
- Cooperation, dialogue + local dispute resolution processes
- Fear, anxiety, distrust across groups
- Dealing with the past

- ~ands

GLOBAL VARIABLES THAT AFFECT EVERYTHING

Horizontal inequalities   Sense of grievance   Patterns of inclusion/exclusion   Mental models and political culture regarding power

Figure 2.2: "Generic" Peace Progress Factor Tree

CAUTIONARY NOTES ABOUT THE PEACE PROGRESS FACTOR TREE

The basic high-level factors should be familiar to most peacebuilding practitioners. They are similar to the International Dialogue on Peacebuilding and Statebuilding (IDPS)'s Peacebuilding and Statebuilding Goals.[40] And, they overlap in part with other models of the components of peace.[41] However, the high-level factors should not be confused with the PSGs, or with the various sectors (silos) of the liberal peace, such as security, governance, etc. Several notes are important.

First, the domains do not represent sectors. They reflect aspects of these broad areas that practitioners, policymakers, and other observers thought were important for progress towards peace. In identifying these factors from the case material, we kept asking, "What is it about 'governance' that is important for peace," and "What elements of the economic realm appear to support peace?" In the governance realm, the relationship of government to the population, and especially its ability to deal with grievances, was found to be the important issue. In the economic sphere, the factors have to do less with economic progress than with equity, fairness, and opportunity. The factor of "acknowledgment and commitment to addressing conflict drivers" appears fairly simple on the chart—but turns out to be fundamental to sustained progress, even if it is rarely addressed (or addressable) directly.

Second, the generic factor trees are decontextualized. No single case will exactly match this "generic" model; each situation has its own distinctive dynamics. What may be a crucial factor for progress in one setting may be relatively insignificant in another. What looks like progress on a factor in one context may look like stagnation or regression in another. The generic factor tree shows broad patterns across the different cases; it can be used as a starting point for a context-specific application, an indication of what might be important in a specific situation. But distinct factors will be important in each context, and specific factors (such as the mechanisms that regulate competition) will look different in different contexts—and the ways to achieve progress will differ. It is important to listen to stakeholders in the context to determine what factors look like in any specific context.

Third, the Peace Progress Factor Tree is not a substitute for conflict analysis. Factor trees should be considered in conjunction with other forms of (repeated) analysis. How, for example, will we know that mechanisms to handle grievances are working, without understanding what the grievances are in a particular context? Or, how will we know if fear and anxiety are reduced unless we understand what fears and

---

40 The goals of the New Deal for Engagement in Fragile States include: 1) Legitimate Politics - foster inclusive political settlements and conflict resolution; 2) Security - establish and strengthen people's security; 3) Justice - address injustices and increase people's access to justice; 4) Economic Foundations – generate employment and improve livelihoods; and 5) Revenues & Services – manage revenue and build capacity for accountable and fair service delivery.

41 For instance, Conciliation Resources, International Alert and the Institute for Economics and Peace each have models for peacebuilding components.

anxieties exist? The factor trees provide an indication of where progress has been made and what areas may still need to be addressed; how progress has been made, why progress has been made, and what and how conflict and peace drivers should be addressed require a deeper conflict analysis.

Finally, application of the Peace Progress Factor Tree does not provide a blueprint for peacebuilding work. The cases and practitioner experience show us that we cannot assume that efforts to produce change in any particular domain will necessarily result in progress. That is, we cannot measure progress by assessing the amount of effort. The factor trees can be used to produce a broad snapshot of progress at a particular time, but they do not tell us whether and how our work might affect these factors.

Domains and Sub-Factors

Each of the major domains is explained further below, including the contributing sub-factors.

Increase in physical security and sense of security[42]

This domain (shown in the Figure 2.3 below) is widely recognized as a fundamental element of sustainable peace. In the first phase of RPP, it emerged as a key criterion of effectiveness—a sign that a particular effort, however small, has contributed to the larger peace.[43] It includes both an objective dimension (reduction in observable conditions of insecurity) *and* a subjective one (decrease in perceptions of threat and fear of violence). The perceptual element is included because, in many places, perceptions of threat can lead to acts of preemptive violence. People often experience things that do not rise to the level of a physical violence (such as graffiti, verbal insults, offensive gestures, or other forms of intimidation) as forms of psychological harm that contribute to their sense of insecurity.[44] Moreover, indicators of progress—such as increased freedom of movement— may not reflect real improvements in security, especially when the threat (and sometimes perpetration) of physical violence is wielded effectively to control people's behavior.[45]

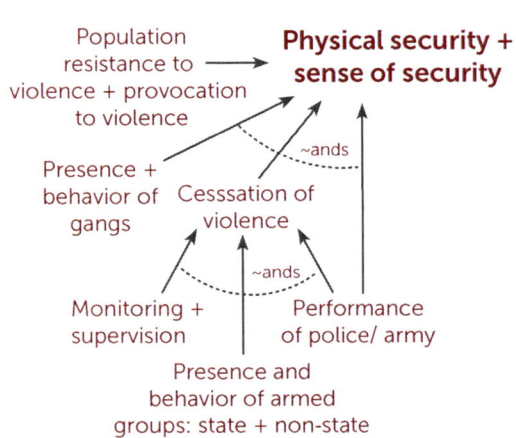

Figure 2.3: Physical Security and Sense of Security

---

42 Note that this factor echoes one of the "Criteria of Effectiveness" presented in Confronting War and summarized at the beginning of this chapter. Several other elements in the factor tree do so as well.

43 *Confronting War,* p. 18

44 Chigas, Diana, et al, "Has Peacebuilding Made a Difference in Kosovo?" CDA Collaborative Learning Projects, 2006, p. 14

45 Ibid.

The figure above is a summary depiction of what helps to bring about security. Security depends on whether conflict-related violence has ended, how the police and military carry out their duties, as well as how gangs and other forms of criminal violence have emerged in some settings (e.g., South Africa and Guatemala), after peace agreements have been concluded. Peace agreements often include provisions for cessation of violence, and other forms of provisional ceasefire may be agreed as a precursor to negotiations, followed by a permanent peace agreement that may also include broader security arrangements and conditions that assure the end of destructive violence.

The three factors leading to "cessation of violence" are often the focus of ceasefire or peace agreements and are shown here as lower level factors because they affect whether an end to violence related to the conflict can be sustained. These factors include effective monitoring and supervision (international or local), the presence and behavior of armed groups (state and non-state), and the willingness and capacity of the police and army to perform their duties. Performance of the police and army is crucial, as it contributes both to the immediate cessation of violence, and, longer term, to the degree to which people feel protected or threatened by security forces—a factor key to their sense of security. Peacebuilding work often targets these factors, and may be effective in influencing them, along with contextual developments, such as the calculus each group makes regarding the costs and benefits of continued fighting. In many cases, regional and international dynamics play a role, as armed factions are often supported in terms of morale and/or funding and supplies by outside groups, diasporas, and governments.

Finally, where state institutions, politicians or non-state actors attempt to perpetrate or attempt to provoke violence, people in local communities and civil society may resist violence or provocations to violence by state groups, politicians, or non-state armed groups.[46] Such enhanced resistance to violence can have a significant influence on security and violence.

> In **Mindanao,** peace covenants were revived in communities that were plagued by violence. While they did not necessarily fully address the underlying causes of violence that result in cattle rustling, car theft, rido (revenge), and the like, they did provide a structure that can quickly mobilize resources to address the surface violence and give time and space to come to agreements, thus preventing further violence. [p.19]

Acknowledgment of key conflict drivers and commitment to address them

Turning points in the peace processes described in the case studies were frequently associated with changes in how the conflict was "framed" by stakeholders, usually involving a shared analysis or shared (even if not common) characterization of the problem, along with a commitment to address it.[47] This increase in understanding and commitment functions both as an effect of the peace process and as a factor influenc-

---

46 See the third Criterion of Effectiveness above, p. 29
47 Note: a turning point could lead to a change in framing, or a change in framing could support a turning point.

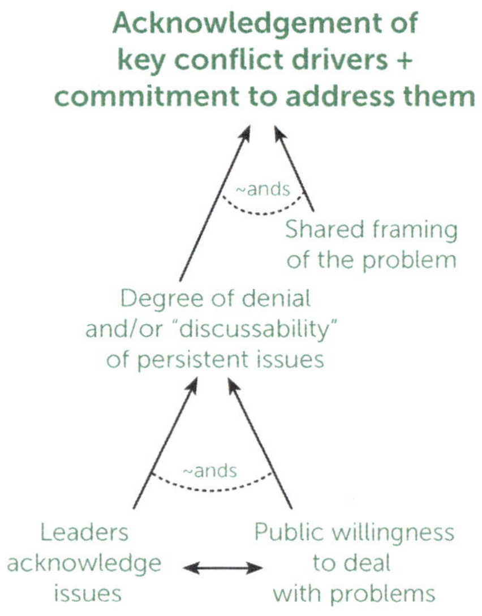

ing further momentum toward peace. It is not required that the parties *agree* on the causes of conflict, nor on what solutions should be pursued. Indeed, in most situations, stakeholders have differing views on the nature of the problem and what is needed to resolve it. However, people in the context—especially key people and decision makers, engaging as well as the public at large—must at least acknowledge the fundamental conflict issues, incorporating different viewpoints, and make a commitment to address them.

Acknowledgement of key conflict drivers + commitment to address them

~ands

Shared framing of the problem

Degree of denial and/or "discussability" of persistent issues

~ands

Leaders acknowledge issues ⟷ Public willingness to deal with problems

Figure 2.4: Acknowledgment of Key Conflict Drivers + Commitment to Address Them

In **Northern Ireland,** interviewees characterized what changed: "It's better than where we were, but still needs a lot of work to get right." Changes included dramatic decline in sectarian violence, structural changes in housing, employment, and education, economic improvement, changes in what is considered to be acceptable behavior, less fear and anxiety among other changes in conflict drivers. Interviewees from a wide spectrum in Northern Ireland noted that people's understanding of the situation had changed, and a widespread acceptance that real grievances had led to nationalist agitation—a shared analysis. This attitude was both made possible by the progress in (other areas) of the peace process, and made the peace process possible. [p.9]

In **Tajikistan,** a significant factor that brought opposing Tajik sides together was a recognition that continuing civil would could jeopardize further existence of Tajikistan as a sovereign state. The emergence of a shared understanding of the problem as a threat to Tajikistan's sovereignty and territorial integrity, along with a shared commitment to Tajikistan as an independent state, contributed to the emergence of common ground. [p.28]

Such recognition of conflict drivers by a wide range of stakeholders can be seen in "iconic events" that provide a public symbol that significant change is underway and communicate to the wider public that the key actors acknowledge the conflict drivers and are willing (and able) to promote change.

In **Northern Ireland,** certain iconic events were seen as signs of change underway. A handshake in 2007 between the prime minister of Ireland and the leader of the Democratic Unionist Party, the party most committed to union with Great Britain and most opposed to closer integration with Ireland, was an indicator of huge shifts in politics, and an acceptance by the key Northern Irish parties of their commitment to govern together. Similarly, in the context of the 1998 Good Friday Agreement, Ireland's offer of a referendum to change its constitutional provisions laying claim to Northern Ireland, along with public willingness to support it, indicated a commitment to address a significant grievance among Protestants and a conflict driver in Northern Ireland. [p.33]

In **Burundi,** Pierre Buyoya's relinquishing power in 2003 to a Hutu successor, in accordance with the provisions of the Arusha peace accords, had significant psychological and symbolic importance; it was seen as a demonstration of respect for commitments and the binding nature of the law itself—and a commitment to address conflict drivers related to rule of law and enforcement of the law, as well as exclusionary governance. [p.14]

In some cases, a shared framing of the conflict exists and facilitates acknowledgment of conflict drivers, and, in particular, the development of an agenda for negotiation or reform. This does not imply necessarily a commitment to implement reforms, but is an important step toward a shared analysis and commitment to change. In other cases, the shared analysis and framing emerged during the peace process. In Northern Ireland, for example, at least three of the four key initiatives characterized as having had a significant impact on the situation involved a degree of shared analysis among people who disagreed.

In both **Mozambique and South Africa,** the resolution of the conflict was facilitated by the fact that the parties shared an understanding of the problem and of what would be needed to establish peace, even if they disagreed on specific provisions. In South Africa, there was agreement that, at its core, the conflict was a struggle over the form of the state and how power would be held. In Mozambique, the conflict was understood widely to have begun as a result of disagreements over the kinds of economic and social development policies the government should adopt after independence, and the parties agreed that to end the conflict, the issue of what form of government should rule the country needed to be addressed. After the signing of a 1994 peace agreement, it came to be understood in terms of economic development. These common framings facilitated convergence of a wide variety of efforts and initiatives.

In cases where there was no shared analysis or framing, progress was more difficult.

In **Guatemala,** as of 2011, there were different views about the war and Peace Accords. One perspective, shared by members of the "cosmopolitan network," [p.11] was that the war was fought between the army and state (in collaboration with the elite) and the four guerrilla organizations. At the local level, however, people's experience of the war differed from the ideological or class-based framework that dominated among national level actors. The Peace Accords were scarcely mentioned by local people, and have not had the compelling reality or urgency of other issues.[48] This disagreement on how to define the problem (and its solution) had implications for the failure of the 1998 referendum in which key elements of the Accord were voted down by Guatemalan citizens and the implementation of the provisions of the Accords that dealt with structural reorganization of the state. Similarly, reconciliation and dealing with the past is a conflict in itself. Along with the government's refusal to acknowledge its role in the war, domination of peacebuilding by those who sought to repair the damage caused by the state, and do not see those who did not suffer "innocently" at the hands of the state as "victims," has undermined the possibilities for national reconciliation. The peacebuilding work enjoys little legitimacy among those who don't share those views, and the deep divisions have made it difficult to pass a coherent

---

48 Adams, Tani M. 2010. Reconstructing Community amid Chronic Social Violence in Post War Guatemala.

national reconciliation policy and practice. "The notion of building a new state and new society in which the violations and damages of the past are repaired, and opponents reconciled, remains an elusive goal." [p.42-45]

The cases, especially those in which progress was halting or reversed, denial or "un-discussability" of key drivers or persistent issues had an important effect on progress toward peace. In other words, conflict-related issues and drivers had not yet been resolved, but need to be addressed in order to move beyond a "negative peace."[49] Therefore, we have included this concept as a significant element of the factor tree. When significant unaddressed issues are put on the table and made discussable, through public acknowledgment and debate or in dialogue forums, confidence in the peace process increases, as well as parties' willingness and ability to tackle issues. When parties communicate a willingness to deal with difficult issues, it increases trust that all issues will eventually be addressed, even if not resolved immediately. Failure to acknowledge the conflict drivers as significant issues can undermine a peace process, or, in post-agreement phases, hinder implementation or freeze progress beyond a mere absence of violence, toward a "just and sustainable" peace. It will also inhibit the possibility of establishing shared priorities towards specific peace goals, thus making cumulative impacts less likely.

In **Haiti,** as of 2009 (shortly before the January 2010 earthquake), there was a wide variety of explanations for the persistence of conflict—from development, poverty and unemployment to governance and political leadership to the effects of historical injustices and deep social divisions. However, differences in how to make sense of these, and of terms of "peacebuilding" and "stability," were rarely acknowledged or mentioned. As one development worker noted, the real issues of conflict and violence have yet to be addressed, and, as long as conflict is not defined and addressed as a national issue, through a process that forges common understandings, everyone's efforts will be compromised. [p.22]

In **Mindanao,** the Philippines government and the MILF signed a Memorandum of Agreement in 2008, covering, among other things, the controversial issue of Moro geographical claims of ancestral domain (MOA-AD). The failure of the MOA-AD, due to a legal challenge by local government officials in the Supreme Court and subsequent violence and displacement, forced stakeholders to look at the "elephants in the room"— unacknowledged, undiscussed and difficult issues, such as the different understandings of "ancestral domain," corruption, and those with interests in derailing talks that were contentious and potentially polarizing. These issues had been neglected in peace initiatives by governmental and non-governmental stakeholders alike, for fear of upsetting negotiations. [p.38]

An important element of this dynamic is the interaction between actions and statements by leaders and the dominant views of the general public. This observation mirrors an earlier RPP lesson regarding the need for communication and common purpose across

---

49 Term first introduced by Johan Galtung. See Galtung, J. "Violence, Peace and Peace Research." *Journal of Peace Research* (1969).

"more people" (the wider public) and "key people" (those who have the power to affect the course of conflict or peace).[50] If leaders get too far in front of other stakeholders and the public, they may not survive. Likewise, the public often needs to push leaders to take the necessary steps to secure peace and to address the underlying problems.[51]

> John Hume, leader of the Social Democratic and Labour Party (SDLP), the social-dem-ocratic and main "constitutional" Irish nationalist party in **Northern Ireland,** from 1979-2001, exerted leadership by articulating concepts and visions that initially seemed far-fetched but encapsulated the dominant discourse about the situation. He is widely credited with changing the understanding of the conflict by defining it as having three strands: within Northern Ireland, within the entire island of Ireland, and between Ireland and Great Britain. [p. 20 and 26]

The most common pattern—as exhibited by many of the other RPP cases—is for post-war leaders to seek a return to "normalcy" and to suppress any implications that problems persist. The incentive systems favor this approach, as national leaders wish for infusions of development assistance and, more importantly, foreign investment. Under these circum-stances, it is vital to maintain the appearance of a stable society that is safe for investment. As a result, the fundamental drivers of conflict and violence are usually ignored or sup-pressed—and the seeds of a new round of violence are sown. In some cases, it is not in the interest of elites or leadership to acknowledge the key conflict drivers—as they see their continued power, privilege and access to (often illicit) economic benefits tied to continua-tion of the prevailing status quo systems.

> In **Haiti,** the need for a fundamental change in power structures continues to be contest-ed. In the post-Duvalier period (after 1986), a struggle ensued over who would control Haiti's future. Competing visions played out in slogans between those demanding elec-tions and democratic governance, on one side—Chak Kat Ans (Every Four Years)—and recidivist forces who countered Viva l'Armee, on the other. Between those extremes was a more moderate group of Haitian elites who acknowledged a need for reforms, but whose strategy for change aimed to preserve the traditional structure of Haitian society. [p.13] As one observer put it, at the root of Haiti's conflict is deep denial, on the part of the rich, of the realities of the poor—a denial that is masked, and perhaps reinforced, by "emergency" programs, such as the United Nations' stabilization program, that do not reach these drivers. [p.20]
>
> The Peace Accord of 1997 in **Tajikistan** is significant, as it allowed an end to violence, en-sured that Tajikistan survived as a sovereign state, and created conditions for the strength-ening and centralization of state power. But, as one former participant in the peace talks noted, "We celebrated the relatively quick resolution, but unfortunately it meant that many issues were left unresolved." [p.31] At a fundamental level, as another negotiator noted, the characterization of the conflict as ideological (Islamist vs. communist/secular, communist vs. democratic) has allowed a key driver of conflict—the struggle between regional elites for control of political power—to continue to operate unabated. [p.14]

---

50 *Confronting War,* p.47-50 and RPP training materials available on www.cdacollaborative.org.

51 For an interesting discussion of the role of elites and how international assistance can influence settlement processes. Yanguas, Pablo. (2017) "The Role and Responsibility of Foreign Aid in Recipient Political Settlements." Journal of International Develop-ment, 29: 211–228.

Durable political arrangements for handling power

Much attention has been paid to the role of inclusive or "inclusive enough"[52] "political settlements," and "elite pacts" as a key factor promoting sustainable peacebuilding and statebuilding.[53] While there are myriad definitions of what "political settlements" are,[54] broadly they refer to agreed (explicitly or implicitly) rules for how power is held and exercised—primarily among key political and economic elites, but also in relation to wider society, whose conformity to elite wishes cannot be taken for granted. We use the language, "durable political arrangement for handling power" to reflect that it involves both the formal and informal interactions and dynamics among political actors over time. These may be shaped by more formal negotiations of political arrangements—through peace accords (or a series of agreements) and their subsequent implementation arrangements, constitutional conferences, electoral rules, etc. Peace agreements almost always include provisions determining who has access to power, how power is gained, held and transferred, and who is included in subsequent governing entities—for example, through elections, power-sharing and other arrangements—presumably permitting more equitable, or "inclusive," access to political power and resources.

Durable political arrangements for handling power

~ands

Successful settlements/ agreements on new rules

Competition regulating mechanisms/processes

Working relationship + dialogue

Willingness to negotiate

Inclusive processes

Shared assessment: negotiation is better than violence

Internal political division/ competition

~ands/~ors

Natural disasters/ events

External action/ pressure

"Carrots": prospect of potential gains

Battlefield exhaustion/ stalemate

Figure 2.5: Durable Political Arrangements for Handling Power

The case studies and practitioner and policymaker experience suggest that formal agreements and rules (such as peace agreements) are essential but not sufficient for progress toward *sustainable peace*.[55] It is necessary to transform the political rules of the game that generate behavior that leads to conflict. Therefore, this factor goes beyond formal negotiated settlements to include informal dynamics, political culture and accepted modes of handling power. It is directly concerned with how key political

---

52 "World Development Report 2011: Conflict, Security and Development," World Bank 2011.

53 See, for instance, DFID Peacebuilding and Statebuilding Framework; OECD 2011, From Power Struggles to Political Settlements; World Development Report 2011; Dudouet, V. & S. Lundstrom, "Post-War Political Settlements: From Participatory Transition Processes to Inclusive State-building and Governance." Berghof Foundation Research Report, 2016; Di John & Putzel 2009; Lindemann 2008; Asia Foundation.

54 Examples include: Menocal, A. "Inclusive Political Settlements: evidence, gaps and challenges of institutional transformation." Birmingham, UK: International Development Department, University of Birmingham, 2015; Laws, E. "Political Settlements, Elite Pacts and Governments of National Unity: A conceptual study," DLP Background Paper 10, 2012; Jones, B., Elgin-Cossart, M. and Esberg, J. 'Pathways Out of Fragility: The Case for a Research Agenda on Inclusive Political Settlements in Fragile States'. New York: Centre for International Cooperation, 2012; Evans, W. "A review of the evidence informing DFID's 'Building Peaceful States and Societies' Practice Paper." Paper 1: Political Settlements, Peace Settlements, and Inclusion. London: DFID, 2012.

55 See UN Security Council Resolution 2282 under the notion of "Peacebuilding and Sustaining Peace," 27 April 2016.

and economic actors regulate or channel power struggles, which are influenced by deeper constructs of political power—a less tangible dimension concerning *mental constructs about power and how to gain and exercise it*—which is found among the Global Variables that influence the entire array of factors. For instance, the "big man" or patron-client political systems that operate in many places are more powerful than the formal institutions and rules of electoral democracy that are put in place, often as a result of peace agreements and as an aspect of gaining independence from colonial rule. "Big man"/patron-client systems rely on a mental model (or way of thinking) that assumes that, in order to advance in society, any particular individual must seek out a powerful patron who will secure a job, protect a family (etc.) in return for loyalty and willingness to respond to the needs and demands of the patron. This mental model can be contrasted with other ways of thinking, such as an individualistic mode (I can do it on my own—an entrepreneurial spirit) or collective interdependence (we all contribute to advancing our community).

In **Mozambique,** a new constitution was adopted in 1990, two years before the peace agreement was concluded. It called for a multiparty state and is seen to be an important cornerstone for peace. It was evidence that the regime was willing to change, and provided an incentive for the rebels (RENAMO) to come to the table. The General Peace Agreement of 1992 further institutionalized multiparty democracy—effectively addressing one of the key causes of conflict, the government's adoption of economic centralization and a one-party political system. Although most Mozambicans recognize that the multiparty rules do not guarantee inclusion of opposition forces, and indeed many have noted increased trends towards authoritarianism and politicization of the state, a multiparty system with regular elections is a form of tolerance that offers opportunity for opposing political forces to compete peacefully.[56] [p. 19]

In **Burundi,** the Arusha Accords (2000), despite being signed without putting a ceasefire in place, are considered to be a decisive turning point. The Accords addressed a key driver—political exclusion—by providing for the possibility of alternation of government (between Tutsi and Hutu) through a transition government and electoral rules, as well as integration of Hutu into the army, police and other government institutions. Further, the negotiation process leading to the accords is seen by many to have initiated dialogue between the warring factions that has attenuated ethnic tension, reduced the salience of ethnicity, and promoted respect for commitments—evidenced initially when the Tutsi President surrendered power to his Hutu Vice President during the transition and later electoral victory by a Hutu-dominated party, CNDD-FDD, in 2005. Some believe that the CNDD-FDD's increased authoritarianism and moves to appropriate political space for itself, to the exclusion of other political parties, is due to the fact that they did not participate in the Arusha negotiations and, as a consequence, see electoral success as a "military victory" and a license to exclude others and pursue corrupt practices. [p. 21]

Political arrangements for handling power are not always democratic. **Cambodia's** experience illustrates the complexity of this process. While the country formally gained democratic institutions (elections, assembly, independent judiciary, etc.) as a result of the peace accords, in reality, decision-making is characterized as taking place among

---

56 Indeed, tensions and fighting have resumed in recent years, as RENAMO has experienced exclusion from power.

a handful of political leaders and the business elite. Cambodia experienced significant changes in institutional structures but few changes in implementation or in relationships. Government structures operate still according to authoritarian and patron-client principles. At the same time, there is a high level of popular satisfaction with the political system. [p.16] The Cambodian People's Party (CPP) has followed a strategy of consolidating dominance since 1992 through a "carrot and stick" policy, offering positions and patronage to some, while encouraging divisions in and taking coercive action against the opposition. [p.24] At the same time, the CPP shifted from a strategy of exclusion of the Khmer Rouge to political negotiation and reintegration, as well as integration of some leaders from the opposition into the CPP itself. [p.22] People have noted that security has improved, even if land conflicts have intensified, and the government has taken some steps to address the public's grievances (such as corruption). The CPP's decisions to share power were decisive. Initially they agreed to organize fresh elections to legitimize their power, rather than resort to overt violence. They also chose to continue policies, after it gained dominance, that had been developed jointly with the opposition, and to make partners of their former adversaries. [p.45]

Durable arrangements for handling power thus depend on three things, which must be present together:

1. Peace agreements (and subsequent negotiations on specific issues), which in all the cases that achieved them have led to an end of violence and pursuit of competition through political means—a significant achievement.

2. Working relationships and dialogue among key actors. While some assert that peace processes provide windows of opportunity to reshape existing political settlements, experience suggests that this is very difficult; peace agreements have limited power to transform political interactions and dynamics. The intensity of competition among political forces in the country drives the ability of key parties to develop reasonable relationships and to enter into dialogue about important policy issues, including how power is held—a capacity that helps both to negotiate formal agreements and to deal with power struggles peacefully.

3. Establishment of effective mechanisms (formal or informal) for regulating competition or power struggles among different parties.

The **Guatemalan** peace process was one of few that comprised a comprehensive redefinition of the State and of Guatemalan society itself. The Peace Accords contemplated broad transformation, reform, and modernization of the State as well as measures to combat racism and promote greater equity and inclusion in society. Yet while the war-related accords (ceasefire, DDR, refugee return) have been relatively effective, assessments of the Accords that deal with structural reorganization of the State and society, have been less so. The ambivalence of the Government toward the UN mission, along with incapacity to establish rule of law, are significant factors slowing progress in many of the agreed reforms—many of which were rejected by referendum or by the Government, while others have proven difficult to implement.

Whether warring factions or governments are even willing to negotiate is affected by their calculus (both rational and emotional) regarding the potential benefits from continued fighting. In many of the RPP cases, there was a precipitating event that caused a shift in this calculus, whether a natural disaster (such as the tsunami in Aceh), exhaustion or stalemate on the battlefield (in Burundi, Mindanao, and Cambodia), or shifting regional or international dynamics leading to increased external pressure to negotiate, as in regional powers forcing negotiations in Tajikistan, Solomon Islands, Northern Ireland and Guatemala, and the end of the Cold War. Such regional efforts were sometimes accompanied by promised gains, or, in some cases like South Africa, the prospect of devastating losses. Peace scholars note that a precondition for negotiation is that the parties consider negotiation better than their alternatives to negotiation (i.e. continued fighting or stalemate)—either because there is a mutually hurting stalemate and/or a mutually enticing opportunity.[57] The lack of progress in situations such as Cyprus and Israel/Palestine can be explained in part by the perception by one or both parties that continuation of the status quo or escalation will yield better results than negotiation.[58] These precipitating factors are depicted at the bottom of Figure 2.5, leading to a shared assessment that negotiation is better than violence.

While a shared assessment that negotiation is better than violence is a key factor driving a willingness to negotiate, the success of settlement processes depends on several additional factors, including internal politics, or divisions, within parties, and the inclusiveness of the negotiation process(es). In the case of Burundi, leaders had made the decision to negotiate, but factions organized roadblocks to prevent the negotiation team from reaching the airport.[59] Internal dynamics may be influenced by the depth of grievances and, at times, the depth of hostility generated by conduct of the war itself (massacres, ethnic cleansing, assassinations, treatment of women and children, etc.).

Here the "global variables" noted at the bottom of the full factor tree chart come into play, especially horizontal inequalities (which groups are favored/disfavored politically, economically and socially) and patterns of exclusion and inclusion from political and economic power and privileges—often leading to long-term grievances. There is some evidence suggesting that more inclusive processes lead to stronger and more durable agreements,[60] although, as the Guatemala case demonstrates, it is no *guarantee* of implementation or even of sustainability.

---

57 See, e.g., Zartman, I. William. "Timing and Ripeness." In The Negotiator's Fieldbook, by Andrea Kupfer Schneider and Christopher Honeyman. Washington, DC: American Bar Association, Section of Dispute Resolution, 2006; Haass, R. *Conflicts Unending: The United States and Regional Disputes.* New Haven: Yale University Press, 199; Stein, J. *"Getting to the Table: The Triggers, Stages, Functions and Consequences of Prenegotiation."* In Stein, J. Ed. Getting to the Table: The Processes of International Prenegotiation. Baltimore: Johns Hopkins University Press, 1989.

58 These findings from the cases and experience echo various theories of "ripeness" and other considerations in international negotiations. See Chigas, D. "The Harvard Study Group on Cyprus: Contributions to an Unfulfilled Peace Process." In Lund, M. (Ed.) *Across the Lines of Conflict: Facilitating Cooperation to Build Peace. New York: Woodrow Wilson Center International Center for Scholars and Columbia University Press (2015);* Fen Osler Hampson, Chester Crocker and Pamela Aall, "Negotiating International Conflict," in Handbook of Peace and Conflict Studies, Routledge, 2007.

59 RPP Burundi case, p. 12.

60 Kew, D. and A. Wanis-St. John. "Civil Society and Peace Negotiations: Confronting Exclusion," with Anthony Wanis St. John, *International Negotiation* 13 (2008): 11-36; Nilsson, D. "Civil Society in Peace Accords and the Durability of Peace." *Accord,* Issue 25. London: Conciliation Resources, 2014; Paffenholz, T. 2015. http://i.unu.edu/media/cpr.unu.edu/attachment/1005/Inclusivity-in-peace-processes.pdf.

Resilient governance relationships between the state and society

The dimension of state-society relations, or governance, was mentioned in nearly all the cases as a driver of conflict and an area of needed progress. Among all of the major factors, this one was among the most difficult to sort out, because there is so much emphasis among donor governments and implementing agencies on development of governance institutions—and so many embedded assumptions about the relationship between "good governance" (poorly defined) and "peace" (also poorly defined). The idea of a negotiated agreement between "state" and "society" (whether explicit or implicit) is embedded in the notion of governance and a social contract. But this concept is too abstract and too broad to be actionable, taking into account the diversity of interests, and divisions within and across the "state" and "society."

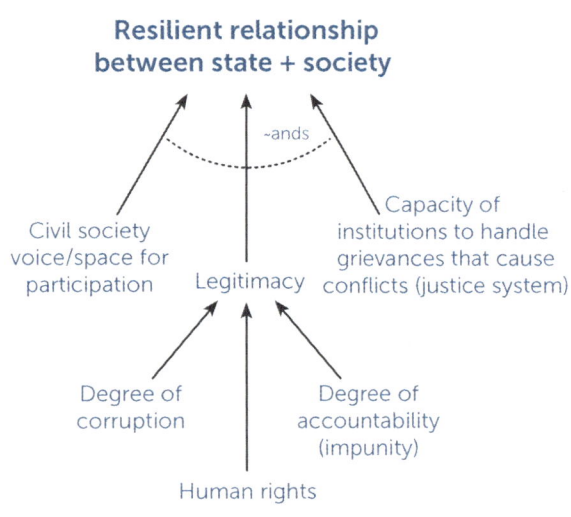

Figure 2.6: Good Enough Governance

Yet the effectiveness of political settlements—processes for handling power—also depend on their capacity to accommodate and manage fundamental cleavages in society, as well as the degree to which the elites are seen as legitimate representatives of the social groups to which they belong and are able to meet their interests.[61] We found that the framing of "the relationship between government and society" was the important dimension of this expansive arena. If the essential relationship is sound, people are willing to wait for progress in institutional development. The relationship is influenced by how people are treated and allowed a "voice," whether fundamental grievances are taken seriously and addressed, and whether government representatives from top to bottom are seen as working towards common progress as opposed to simply lining their own pockets.

Progress in this area is often visible when the government takes action to address the source of grievances—through policies, laws, rules or institutions that determine how it manages societal relations and how government behaves towards its citizens.

The elements of legitimacy and the capacity of institutions to handle grievances are both important in this arena. Legitimacy involves not only how a government comes to power, how it organizes political power, and whether it is perceived as rightful, but also how it exercises that power.[62] While legitimacy is influenced by many things, we found that the degree of corruption and whether/how officials are held accountable for potentially illegal actions are critical in the context of sustainable peace, as they affect whether citizens viewed the state as primarily concerned with the narrow interests of

---

61 See Lindemann, S. "Do Inclusive Elite Bargains Matter? A Research Framework for Understanding the Causes of Civil War in Sub-Saharan Africa." London: LSE Development Studies Institute, 2008.

62 For more on state legitimacy, see Claire McLoughlin, "State Legitimacy." Development Leadership Program, University of Birmingham, Concept Brief 02, December 2014; and OECD, "The State's Legitimacy in Fragile Situations unpacking complexity." Conflict and Fragility Series, Paris, 2010.

elite powerbrokers or, alternatively, also concerned with and willing to address the welfare of everyday citizens. Both corruption and accountability, therefore, need to be considered in context, in relation to how they are connected to grievances that drive conflict and to peoples' attitudes toward the state. In this sense, legitimacy needs to be "grounded"—connected to and consistent with people's values and beliefs on the ground—rather than based solely on instrumental performance.[63]

> In **Liberia,** fears that corruption put reconstruction and peace in danger, and an understanding that corruption and elite capture of the state was a driver of conflict, led international donors in 2006 to make future funding conditional on adoption of an ambitious anti-corruption plan, in which the heads of Liberian Government agencies involved with revenue collection, procurement and disbursement were shadowed by international experts, who also had co-signing power. The Governance and Economic Management Assistance Program (GEMAP), which ran from 2006-2009, is considered to have been successful. Corruption effectively declined and revenues went up. However, its legitimacy was undermined by Liberian objections to the erosion of their sovereignty. The sustainability of the effects on corruption were also questionable, as the program did not deal with practices rooted in deeper social and political structures and shifted responsibility for accountability toward the international community rather than the government. [p.36]

The capacity to handle grievances (an important global variable) relates to a wide range of institutions, from local dispute resolution mechanisms, to more formal judicial systems, but also to the extent to which institutions can deliver a sense of equity by addressing past abuses, marginalization and neglect. This latter element requires political structures that can deliver policies that embody fairness—and following through with their implementation. On the negative side, unaddressed grievances fester over time and, if they continue to be neglected, can lead to more and more vociferous demands that ultimately escalate to violence.

A final dimension of the relationship between government and society concerns whether or not there is space for civil society participation in governance, both in terms of people's ability to speak up on important issues and whether such political speech actually has influence on policy decisions.

> In **Mozambique,** people distinguish between "conquered spaces" and "offered or invited space." They describe conquered spaces as those created by civil society itself of their own accord in response to the need for a common approach to a problem. "Offered spaces," such as the Development Observatory, are created by the government (or international community) with little input from civil society. These "offered spaces" are perceived to be imposed and have been unable to gain civil society confidence. The

---

63 Clements, 2014. "What is legitimacy and why does it matter for peace?" In Wennmann, A. and Ramsbotham, A., Eds. *Legitimacy and peace processes: from coercion to consent.* Accord Series No. 25. London: Conciliation Resources. http://www.c-r.org/sites/default/files/Accord25_WhatIsLegitimacy%3F.pdf. The Institute for Economics and Peace also identifies a strong statistical link between corruption and peace—both negative peace (as measured by the Global Peace Index) or positive peace. Institute for Economics and Peace. "Peace and Corruption: Lowering Corruption—a transformative factor for peace." London: IEP, 2015.

> government is also seen as not recognizing or respecting the opinions of civil society in those spaces. But in "conquered spaces" like the Election Observatory, the state is compelled to pay attention because the groups have become a force with which to be reckoned. [p.59]

Economic fairness and opportunity

Poverty and economic deprivation are mentioned by people in nearly all the cases as a cause of conflict and a threat to peace. We found little evidence in the case material that actual progress on economic indicators (growth in GDP, reductions in poverty rates or other key economic factors) were correlated with progress towards peace.[64] This is consistent with research findings that low economic growth is weakly correlated with civil war or between income and civil war onset.[65] This is also consistent with findings in the World Development Report (2011) and in more recent research by Mercy Corps on youth and violence that the principal drivers of violence are not rooted in poverty or unemployment, but in experiences of injustice.[66] When speaking about conflict and progress toward peace, people interviewed for case studies nearly always discussed poverty and economic development in association with inequality, injustice, lack of access to resources/exclusion and thwarted (or hopeful) expectations. The Global Variable of *horizontal inequalities* is clearly involved here as well, as the issue is not necessarily whether you are poor yourself, but how you and your group are faring in comparison with others.

Two key factors stand out in relation to economic dimensions of progress toward peace: the degree to which people feel that access to resources is equitable (that is, not unjust), and the degree to which they feel they have prospects for improving their lives. It appears important that individuals gain a sense that they, their families or group (clan, ethnic group, religious group, geographic area…) are playing on a relatively even economic playing field. They do not necessarily expect immediate and tangible gains (or even the much-touted "peace dividends"). Rather, they require a sense that, over time, their group has the possibility of making progress towards improved wellbeing. If they feel excluded from economic opportunity, due to delib-

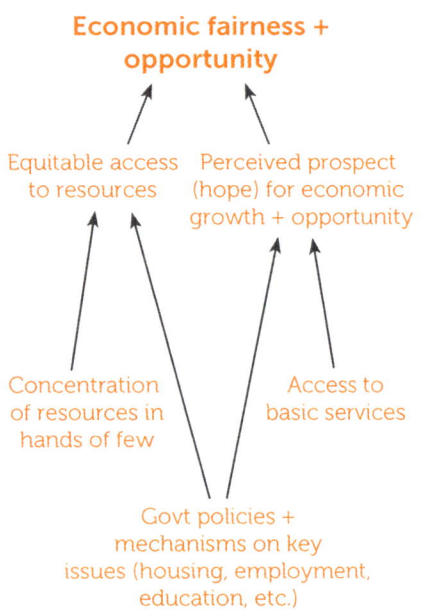

Figure 2.7: Economic Fairness and Opportunity

---

64 Interestingly, the Institute for Economics and Peace's (IEP) Positive Peace Framework also does not identify economic progress as a significant factor in positive peace, even though several of the domains they identify (such as sound business environment, well-functioning government, high levels of human capital and low levels of corruption) would naturally provide a foundation for economic progress. IEP also identifies equitable distribution of resources (including income, but also access to health and education) as a significant domain for positive peace. See "Positive Peace Report 2017: Tracking Peace Transitions Through a Systems Thinking Approach." Report # 54. Sydney: IEP.

65 Collier, Paul; Sambanis, Nicholas. 2005. *Understanding Civil War: Evidence and Analysis," Volume 1. Africa.* Washington, DC: World Bank. "Ethnicity, Insurgency, and Civil War," James D. Fearon and David D. Laitin. American Political Science Review, Vol. 97, February 2003, p. 75-90; Stewart, F. Horizontal Inequalities and Conflict: Understanding Group Violence in Multi-ethnic Societies. New York: Palgrave-Macmillan, 2008.

66 See World Bank. *World Development Report 2011.* Washington, DC: World Bank. Mercy Corps. "Youth & Consequences: Unemployment, Injustice and Violence."

erate policies of exclusion or more subtle practices of discrimination, their sense of grievance will obstruct progress towards sustainable peace. Here, access to resources, (jobs, land, natural resources, funding...) becomes crucial, and often reflected in or determined by key governmental policies. Note that the global variables of inclusion/exclusion, horizontal inequalities and grievance are powerful forces here.

The necessary action required to generate progress in the key contributing factors will depend on the context. That is, each situation will exhibit its own dynamics in terms of whether the main concerns are about land tenure and resource policies, employment policies and programs, housing, education or other basic services. However, the effects of these economic programs on peace will be determined by how they promote economic equity and hope for progress.

Social cohesion

The domain of social cohesion concerns the degree of unity or disunity among groups that have been in conflict. In nearly all of case studies, inter-group relations were identified as problematic and in need of additional efforts. The issue was often coupled with calls for more effective efforts to heal past trauma and violence and to promote reconciliation, or for more general dialogue as a means of improving communication, increasing mutual understanding and developing a better *modus vivendi*. In most cases, concerns regarding social cohesion were not sufficient, by themselves, to undermine the peacebuilding process or produce great gains. These issues—relating to mutual understanding, trust, common identity and dealing with the past—are long term. In this sense, the various aspects of social cohesion are "lagging indicators"—that is, the re-

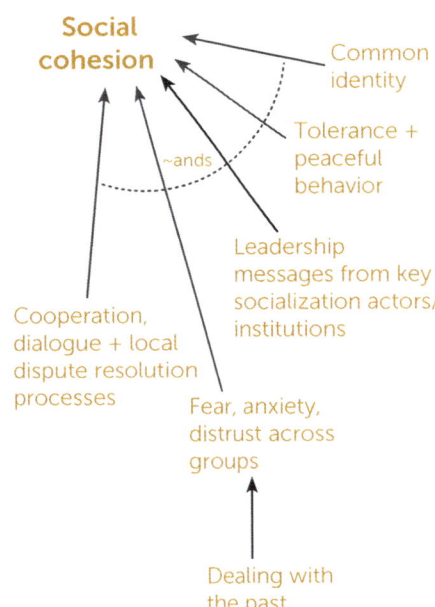

Figure 2.8: Social Cohesion

sults are not immediately apparent. While a significant amount of peace work focuses on social cohesion, visible progress occurs more quickly in other areas. At the same time, incremental gains in social cohesion, especially among key groups and at the local level, provide a basis for making headway in other domains.

In **Solomon Islands,** as of 2009, the integration of traditional community dispute reconciliation processes with longer-term development outcomes and community-led approaches to restoring peace, demobilizing combatants, and enhancing community resilience were used to help people reengage with each other within communities. The conflict had destabilized village life, reigniting old grievances and making people afraid

> to leave their houses. The community reconciliation processes became a mechanism by which the different sectors of communities could experiment with working together again. Healing and reconciliation ceremonies and processes likewise increased people's sense of security. Yet, it was acknowledged that building peace across the islands will very much depend upon the idea of nationhood taking root in Solomon Islander consciousness—a long-term endeavor. [p.25]

Contributing factors to social cohesion included various aspects that work together in mutually supportive ways (represented as "ands" in the factor tree):

- Reducing fears, anxiety, and suspicion of the "other" (one aspect of a sense of security).

- Changes in behavior toward more tolerant and peaceful interactions with other groups. This is often supported by changes in attitudes/stereotypes.

- Cooperation, dialogue, and local dispute resolution processes. Cooperation and dialogue support the development of mutual understanding, relationships, and mutual interests at all levels. While these processes at the local level do not necessarily "add up" to national level social cohesion, "top down" or national level efforts also do not necessarily produce cohesion at the local level. Local level processes can support "bottom-up" social cohesion, and prevent difficult national level dynamics from provoking local-level violence.

- Messages and efforts by leaders and key socialization actors—a recognition of the fact that it is difficult to promote social cohesion when these key people do not support it.

> In **Mindanao,** as of 2009, years of grassroots efforts to promote understanding of the context, conduct analysis, and develop a culture of peace has fostered communal tolerance. Instead of reacting with violence, people in communities are more likely now to engage first in dialogue about significant events. [p.37]

> In **Cyprus,** as of 2008, both Turkish Cypriots and Greek Cypriots reported powerful changes and learning. For the Turkish Cypriots, a feeling of solidarity and of "being Cypriots" was important, and engagement in conflict resolution workshops helped create trust, relationships, capacities to see the other side's perspective, and changed views about peace and the Cyprus conflict. Similarly, Greek Cypriots reported understanding the "other" better and realizing that they have common goals, reducing stereotypes and developing relationships and recognizing that the Turkish Cypriots did want a solution. Realizing the common humanity and bond between the communities, despite the conflict, fostered understanding and hope for the future. [p.23]

The need to deal with past trauma, abuses, and violations of human rights through some process was mentioned universally as necessary to alleviate fears, anxiety, and hostility (as well as promote justice). In many cases, Truth and Reconciliation Commissions were used, but as they often encountered significant obstacles and resistance and took years to implement, their ultimate contribution is uncertain.

Global variables

The box at the bottom of the factor tree diagram is labeled "global variables." Global variables are crucially important and cross-cutting factors that are not associated with any one area, but affect all of them. For instance, patterns of inclusion/exclusion are fundamental to conflict issues in social cohesion, economic life, governance, the nature of political arrangements, security and the degree to which there is commitment to dealing with key conflict drivers, and so forth. Because exclusion and marginalization are quite often key conflict drivers, explicit commitment to addressing them is important for making progress towards peace. Similarly, pronounced horizontal inequalities (in income, power, resources, etc.) can be underlying factors in any of the areas.

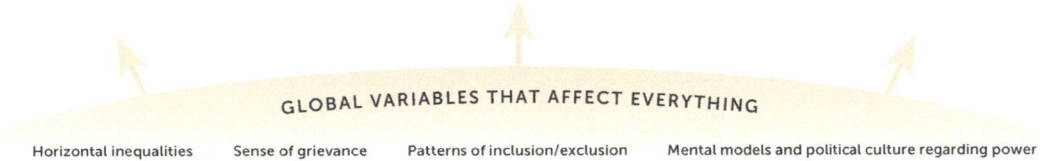

GLOBAL VARIABLES THAT AFFECT EVERYTHING

Horizontal inequalities   Sense of grievance   Patterns of inclusion/exclusion   Mental models and political culture regarding power

A sense of grievance might arise due to patterns of exclusion and/or horizontal inequalities, but may also result from a myriad of other issues, some of them from ancient or more recent history. For instance, in Liberia, various military and political factions had engaged in mutual cycles of massacres based on ethnicity, leading to residual grievances. In addition, the dominance of one particular ethnic group over many decades generated deep resentment (and grievance) in all of the other tribes, and attempts by each to attain power as a way to gain "their turn" in the dominant role. This is seen as a fundamental driver of conflict in Liberia. Therefore, in order to achieve sustained progress towards peace, these grievances need to be addressed.

A "mental model" is a systems thinking concept that refers to "deeply ingrained assumptions, generalizations, or even pictures or images that influence how we understand the world and how we take action."[67]—often providing important "fuel" to the ways the system functions. Thus, a fundamental belief about fairness may drive a sense of grievance about how people are treated. Among the global variables, we identified the prevailing mental model regarding how power is held and the associated political culture as important cross-cutting issues. Returning to the Liberia example, the entire system is influenced by the pervasive patron-client system, in which political factions are lined up behind powerful political players, who are associated with ethnic identities and extended family and clan structures—without the counterbalancing influence of functioning state laws and institutions (regarding land tenure, for example). The political culture is defined by those relationships, supported by a mental model that says, "In order to get ahead, I have to hook my star to the wagon of that Big Man,

---

67 Senge, P. The Fifth Discipline: The Art and Practice of the Learning Organization. New York: Doubleday, 1990. Another prominent systems thinker, Donella Meadows, refers to them as "an abstraction of all [a person's] perceptions and experiences in the world, which he uses to guide his decisions." Meadows, D. et al. Dynamics of Growth in a Finite World. Cambridge, MA: Wright-Allen Press, 1975.

who will get me a job and help my family survive." The political culture and mental models about power may be quite different in other settings, of course—but they will always represent important and pervasive global variables affecting the entire system.

The Peace Progress Factor Tree & Cumulative Impacts

We have described the factors of progress toward sustainable peace and the patterns of relationships among them that emerged from the cases and practitioner experience. This allows us to see a cumulative picture of the whole, to understand trends, and to identify which of the major domains (and the array of sub-factors) is making progress towards peace—and which ones are lagging behind. What have we learned about cumulative impacts by mapping progress in the factor trees?

All high-level factors are critical components

> *The RPP cases suggest that some degree of progress is necessary in all of the six high-level factors or domains, in order to attain a significant "degree and sustainability of progress towards peace." If any major domain is missing from the equation or lags behind to a considerable degree, progress towards peace will be impeded, only partial, or unsustained.*

In looking across the case studies, it was apparent that a significant delay or blockage in any of the major domains could hold back overall progress towards sustainable peace. Therefore, attention is needed regarding each of the key domains: the degree and quality of security and sense of security; acknowledgment of conflict drivers and commitment to address them; durable political arrangements; a resilient relationship between government and society; economic fairness and opportunity; and social cohesion. If any domain fails, or if one area falls significantly behind the others for an extended period of time, progress is likely to be stymied or regress. Tripling efforts in one area in order to "compensate" for lack of progress in another might work in the short term. It may keep some momentum going and provide a pathway to tackling difficult issues, but, over time, it will not overcome failure or "stuckness" in others.[68] If a significant imbalance in progress persists, it is difficult to move from negative peace to sustainable peace, and in some cases, the risk of future unrest or violence continues or is heightened.

Why? First, the various factors, although depicted in hierarchical form in the factor trees, do interact with each other; progress in one area may require progress in another to contribute to sustainable peace.

---

68 Our findings are consistent with Davis' hypotheses in his 2011 synthesis of literature on stabilization and reconstruction. See Davis, Paul. (Ed.) 2011. *Dilemmas of Intervention: Social Science for Stabilization and Reconstruction.* Washington, DC: Rand Corporation.

More than ten years after the signing of the **Guatemalan** Peace Accords in 1996, democratization processes and the recommendations of the Historical Clarification Commission (CEH) had led to a substantial expansion of the state and greater citizen participation in a wide range of social, economic and political processes. Modernization of the political system (voting, Electoral Tribunal, for example) and development of a more transparent government executive had proceeded well. However, success in one sector can induce failure in another, and the lack of progress in several areas had undermined progress toward sustainable peace. For example, the success of the Forensic Anthropological Foundation in exhuming and identifying the remains of over 21,000 people over 17 years represented an enormous burden on the judicial system, which had no capacity to process these legal dossiers. Overall, modernization of the justice sector lagged, and the incapacity of state institutions to respond to social demands frustrated or truncated citizen participation in many cases, which stimulated social conflict and violence. The consistent relative lack of progress in dealing with socio-economic inequality was a "fatal flaw" in the post-war development of Guatemalan society. Successive governments have been unable to construct a long-term plan to implement either the Peace Accords or the recommendations of the CEH, the link in the Accords between peace and development had been severed. This failure, along with the chronic inability of the state to provide basic human services, obliged people to "fend for themselves," finding solutions in illicit or illegal activities or other means to meet their economic needs. It also directly contributed to social violence, social disintegration, and opened the door for increased social involvement in criminal activities and de-legitimization of the state. [p.54-57]

Second, different constituencies, or key stakeholders, are concerned with different issues in different domains; lack of progress in one area while others make headway can leave a constituency behind and provoke resistance. For instance, in Cyprus, Greek Cypriots engaged in peacebuilding are more concerned with social cohesion and security-related progress, while Turkish Cypriots are more concerned with political arrangements and governance issues.

Israelis and Palestinians have experienced different motivations and concerns, and the failure to make progress on one set of issues while also making progress on the other has been one reason for what has been characterized by some as the "failure" of people-to-people initiatives. An activist Israeli commented, "The people-to-people initiatives failed for various reasons. One is that Israelis came thinking that all the political problems were solved, and so they came to 'make a friend.' Palestinians, knowing their own current realities, came to convince Israelis to make concessions. The gap between expectations and reality was huge and disappointing to many." A Palestinian involved in joint efforts also queried: "People to people efforts are important for the larger peace process but only when the two are linked." [p.30]

Table 2.1 below summarizes the broad degree of progress for the high-level factors in each of the cases, in order of year of agreement (the oldest first and those in which there has been no settlement last). It is based on more detailed analysis of the factor trees of each case and coding of all of the factors (including lower-level factors) by color: areas where significant progress has been made (green), where some progress has been made (blue), **and where there are serious outstanding issues that have not been addressed or that have worsened** (red). An illustrative coded factor tree base on the Guatemala case can be found at the end of this chapter. In each case, the characterization of the quality of "progress" is based on assessments by a wide range of stakeholders in the case itself; where there is no indication in the chart, there was no characterization, so we have left it blank.

As the high-level comparison suggests, *at least at the time that the cases were written*, the processes in which peace has been sustained to a greater degree have fewer "red" (no progress or urgent) areas (Mozambique, South Africa, Northern Ireland, Cambodia), while those that are vulnerable have more uneven progress, with significant "red" areas and, in some cases (such as Burundi), deterioration in some areas.

Table 2.1: Progress in Cumulative Cases

Case	Security	Framing/ Commitment	Political Deal	Resilient Relationship	Economic Equity	Social Cohesion
Aceh	X		X	X	X	X
Burundi[I]	X		X	X	X	X
Cambodia	X	X	X	X	X	X
Cyprus	X	X	X	X		X
Guatemala	X	X	X	X/X	X	X
Haiti	X	X	X	X	X	X
Israel-Palestine	X	X	X	X	X	X
Liberia	X	X	X	X/X	X	X
Mindanao[II]	X	X	X	X	X	X/X
Mozambique[III]	X	X/X	X	X	X	X
Northern Ireland	X	X	X	X	X	X/X
Solomon Islands[IV]	X	X	X	X	X	X
South Africa	X	X	X	X	X	X
Sri Lanka[V]	X	X	X		X/X	X
Tajikistan	X	X/X	X	X	X	X

I   In Burundi, events since 2008 have reversed many of the security gains that had been made, and cast doubt on the political deal.

II   The Comprehensive Agreement on Bangsamoro was concluded between the Government of the Philippines and the MILF in 2014. This has significantly affected security conditions, as well as political and governance conditions since the case was written in 2008.

III   Progress has been tempered over time by concerns about increasing politicization of the state and questions whether the initial hopes about opportunities for economic development are being brought about.

IV   Progress on social cohesion has occurred within communities, but little progress has been made on inter-group relations at a national level.

V   Subsequent developments in the war from the time the case was written and electoral developments in Sri Lanka in 2015 have changed the assessment of progress in Sri Lanka. Security has improved, and the political deal could be considered to have improved somewhat.

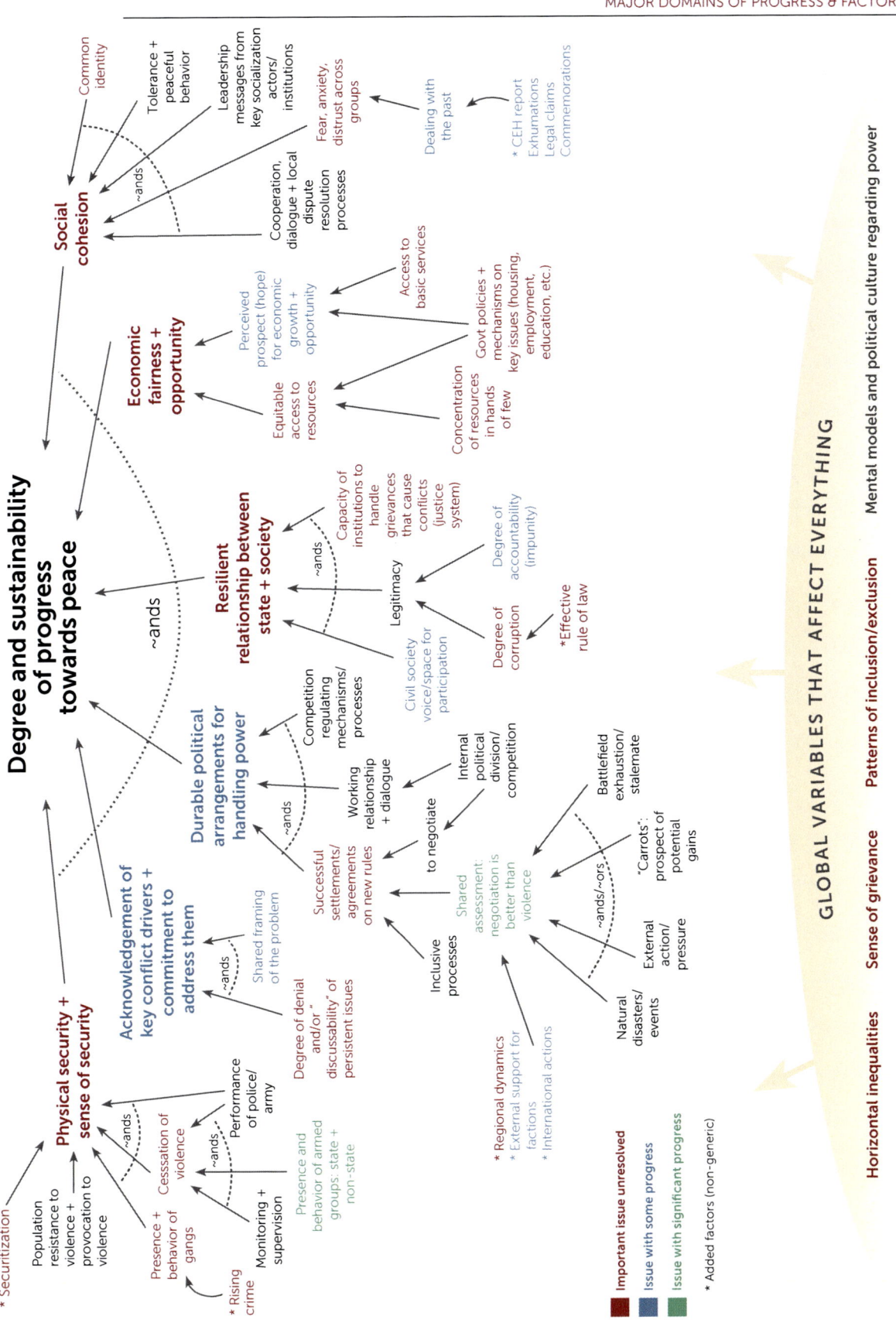

Figure 2.9: Example Peace Progress Factor Tree Coded to Show Degrees of Progress in Guatemala

3

THE ROLE OF LINKAGES IN ADDING UP

The first phase of RPP (1999–2003) produced the key insight that the effectiveness of peace initiatives depends to a large degree on their strategic links to the driving factors of the conflict and their linkages to efforts at other levels of society, sectors, and constituencies. RPP found that program impacts increased when there were active linkages between efforts that stimulate change at the individual/personal level (attitudes, feelings, perceptions, skills, etc.) those promoting change at the socio-political level (societal, institutional, public), and between efforts targeting "more people" (grassroots, broad engagement in the peace process) and efforts targeting "key people" in the conflict.[69] Experience showed, however, that peace programs are seldom linked to each other in ways that improve joint effectiveness, and efforts at coordination do not necessarily result in synergies and increased effectiveness.

Most agree that we need to improve our understanding of linkages and operational methods for linking peacebuilding efforts. What do the latest RPP cases tell us about what kinds of programmatic connections promote cumulative impacts and how those connections are formed? Although this chapter will address the various dimensions of linkages and the ways that such connections support the adding up process, we will turn to the question of *collective impact* of peacebuilding efforts in Part II, Chapter 7. We should note that cumulative impacts, the focus of the RPP case studies, are somewhat different from collective impacts. The cumulative impact cases examined how various efforts somehow added up to progress toward peace, despite the fact that they were mostly disconnected. Collective impact, on the other hand, requires multiple stakeholders to deliberately align their work in the pursuit of common peace goals—which also incorporates many of the dimensions of linkage discussed here.

69 *Confronting War*, p. 64-67

What are Linkages and Why are they Important for Cumulative Impacts?

A "linkage" is a factor or relationship that connects one thing to another. The cases suggest that these connections or bonds can be:

- Relationships among people (e.g., coalitions, collaborations among peacebuilders, contacts, and dialogue across conflict lines);

- Connections or alignment among different types of peacebuilding work or interventions; or

- Ties or relationships between various issues or types of change (e.g., attitudes and political action, development and peace).

Such connections can be formal, structured and visible (such as the National Peace Accord in South Africa) or informal and less noticeable. They may involve direct relationships between people, as in a formal network or collaboration between different agencies, or may be achieved in the absence of direct coordination, communication or joint planning by peacebuilding agencies.

Drawing on the case evidence, we found that linkages facilitate cumulative impacts of peacebuilding efforts by:

- Providing a core coherence to programming that can be seen in shared goals and understandings of the conflict;

- Creating a "density of activity" that can enhance the importance and weight of peacebuilding activities;

- Expanding the reach of peacebuilding and people's engagement in and ownership of the peace process, often transforming "targets" into "actors;"

- Enhancing the scale of change—by connecting fragmented activities to build a critical mass for collective action;

- Creating synergies among different types of work, issues or components of peace work, so that efforts build on each other and promote greater momentum towards peace.

Linkages and Systems Thinking

Linkages are a natural extension of the systems thinking themes of this book. Systems thinking promotes the notion that important factors are interrelated and that there are ongoing dynamics among elements of conflict and peace. The factor trees introduced in Chapter 2 exhibit the idea of connections among key factors, showing an upward cascade of interrelated elements that can be maximized to promote lasting peace—as well as global variables that cut across the full range of issues. We have also emphasized that there are linkages across the six major domains in the factor trees. Economic factors influence social cohesion (and vice versa). Security issues affect state-society relations. And so on. The challenge in any particular situation is to discover the important associations among factors, especially those that threaten new or renewed violence, and then to address them. On the other hand, it is important to identify important factors that are not currently linked and to create new connections that will enable positive changes or break negative dynamics. This chapter will explore different kinds of linkage and how to support them in the adding up process.

How Connections are Formed and Mechanisms that Promote Linkages

The case material shows that specific factors encourage the creation of linkages, although concerted effort is usually needed to make them operational. And, there are factors that limit the alignment of initiatives, including proliferation of groups, competition for funds, ignorance of what others are doing, and government disinterest or outright suppression.

Conceptual linkages

When groups come to understand how their efforts might be "conceptually linked," even when the groups do not coordinate directly, elements of alignment can occur. The case studies illustrate ways that concepts have been linked.

- **A shared conceptual framework** may allow people to see the conflict or their roles in a new way that permits mobilization of additional energy for peace or to see how different efforts can work together to greater effect. In Northern Ireland, a paper analyzing how efforts in various domains relate to each other was instrumental in mitigating competition among peace efforts.

- **A policy framework** for reform, reallocation of resources, or redress of grievances key to the conflict can be helpful, such as the National Peace Accord in South Africa, that established peace and development structures at local, regional, and national levels to address violence and promoted interaction between them.

- **A shared vision** for a desired future state can present a rallying point for multiple actors. Shared values, visions, and principles are only effective, however, when they are not too general or vague. A shared commitment by NGOs in Mindanao, for example, to accountability, governance, and human rights did not lead to more mutually supportive work, because they viewed these concepts differently and formed competing networks of organizations.

Whether a linkage reinforces relationships among people or groups or creates synergy among uncoordinated efforts, the more it is centered on key driving factors of the conflict, the more likely it is to be effective.

Using the same "platform" for different kinds of work

The cases offered several examples of development programming becoming a "platform" for an expansion of the agenda into peacebuilding work. Similarly, peacebuilding initiatives have sought to integrate development activities into their work with groups as a means of promoting sustainability of the efforts. It has been noted that the proliferation of groups working in the same community, and the participation by the same people in multiple different groupings have frequently operated as detractors from linkages.

Individuals acting as connectors

Civil society organizations and particular individuals have often provided mechanisms for linkage, including both secular NGOs and religious organizations. They have connected national movements and processes with local communities by providing channels of communication and consultation, as well as developing linked strategies for their work at both levels. For instance, the Solomon Islands case exhibits strong cooperation among a number of community-based organizations, both church-based and secular. Church leaders were in a position to connect local efforts to national structures.

Networking and coordination

The cases relate numerous instances in which lack of coordination undermined cumulative impacts: from the existence of uncoordinated, parallel forums for dialogue that led to confusion about the roles of dialogue processes (Aceh) to the lack of effort or vision connecting third parties' efforts to each other (Cyprus) and the lack of coordination among efforts in different sectors (e.g., DDR and SSR in Haiti).

Practitioners emphasize that relationships, collaboration and synergy among diverse agencies and stakeholders pursuing a common goal can be an important mechanism for linkage.[70] Yet, while coordination can help bring about greater programmatic alignment, the cases indicate that coordination has failed to lead to linkage at least as often as it has facilitated it. Feedback workshop participants emphasized that linkages cannot be forced, but are more effective when they are "voluntary and incidental," that is, they grow out of the situation. Although they cannot be forced, participants stressed the need for "strategic" connections that:

- Respond to a problem, and are based on a clear mutual understanding of the issues and how they relate;

- Address key driving factors;

- Are voluntary, in the sense that each member/participant is willing to work with others to resolve the problem;

---

70 See, for instance, *Multi-Stakeholder Processes for Conflict Prevention and Peacebuilding: A Manual*, Global Partnership for the Prevention of Armed Conflict, 2015.

- Are based on clear objectives and a clear, shared vision;

- Recognize and bring different and synergistic skills of agencies to bear on the problem (mapping of peace efforts can help to overcome isolated efforts); and

- Develop trust among the members and bridge differences.

In some cases, outside events (such as the tsunami in Aceh, or impending EU membership in Cyprus) have triggered opportunities and motivations for establishing such connections.

What Kinds of Connections Promote Cumulative Impacts?

While practitioners agree that linkages are important to effectiveness, there is little clarity about what an effective linkage is. Are linkages the same as relationship, alliance, or partnership? Are they broader? Several kinds of connections appear to be important for ensuring that peace efforts "add up." These types are not mutually exclusive, and, where there are cumulative effects, many kinds of linkages seem to be at play.

We will explore three different dimensions of linkages:

1. Linkages from individual-personal change to socio-political change.

2. Horizontal linkages across different kinds of issues, sectors or constituencies.

3. Vertical linkages from grassroots/community levels (what we call "peace writ little" or *pwl*) to higher levels, including national and regional processes (or "Peace Writ Large"/*PWL*).

Each of these dimensions is explored further below. We will give primary attention to the vertical dimension, as this has generated the most discussion and was most salient in the RPP cumulative cases.

Links from individual-personal change to socio-political change

In its first phase, RPP found that individual awareness, skills, interpersonal bridges or personal empowerment, while making important contributions, were not necessarily sufficient to contribute to the larger peace process, unless an explicit connection was made to broader issues of social norms/values, institutional structures, and even cultural change. In other words, linkages between individual-personal change and socio-political change in peacebuilding efforts help them to "add up" beyond the effects of individual programs.[71] These linkages connect changes in attitudes, skills, or conditions of individuals or even large groups to changes in public behavior or norms, or changes in social institutions, policies or structures.

---

71 See *Confronting War, pp. 55-58.*

Two programs with which RPP engaged in Israel/Palestine illustrate this principle. One program tried for many years to build connections among Israeli, Palestinian, and American young people, based on the theory that the relationships established would serve as social capital in efforts to improve perceptions and cooperation between groups. Recently, however, they determined that a more concerted effort was needed to build on the good work at the individual change level and to initiate more explicit program work at a political level among "alumni" of the earlier youth work.

In a similar case, another organization aimed to empower Palestinian youth, training them to become nonviolent activists for change in their own communities. The program was focused primarily at individual skills and local level changes. Following an evaluation and planning process, the program shifted to working with former participants and others interested in more explicit engagement in political change within the Palestinian communities.

In the years since the publication of *Confronting War* and its strong statements about the need to push beyond individual-personal change to socio-political change, there has been a general acceptance of this principle within the peacebuilding community—although this acceptance is not always matched by changes in programming. The cumulative case studies confirmed these findings of the first phase of RPP.

> In Northern **Cyprus,** those who had been trained in conflict resolution methods and skills in an individual capacity became active in civil society organizations to mobilize mass support for a "yes" vote on the United Nations' peace plan. In the South, by contrast, "the focus of these activities on producing a mental shift, rather than having a political goal" restricted the visibility and effect of the bi-communal activities.
>
> In **Mozambique,** the Organization for Conflict Resolution (OREC) provided training for local leaders, including youth groups, women's associations, and sports organizations and established conflict resolution nuclei in several districts. They used this base, and their membership in the Electoral Observatory, to play a role in monitoring and defusing post-election violence. Another NGO organized training for demobilized soldiers and subsequently helped them formulate a coordinated strategy for negotiations with the government. [p.37]

In many cases, organizations did not take on more political or institutional work themselves—as they lacked the particular expertise and focus for that kind of work. However, they either built upon previous work by supporting participants to organize themselves to engage at the socio-political level, or connected with other organizations working at other levels and helped their participants to connect with appropriate change processes. For instance, it is likely that organizations working on trauma healing should maintain that specialty and expertise, while, at the same time, make the link to initiatives that promote social justice and reconciliation at the community level and beyond, for those participants who are ready for such involvements.

Horizontal linkages

Horizontal linkages across peace efforts in different sectors, constituencies, or issues enhance the cumulative impacts of peace initiatives. Five kinds of horizontal linkages, explored below, are important, based on the case evidence.

Coalitions/Movement. People from different groups form coalitions (platforms, networks, consortia…) to advocate for change/peace, based on shared goals, common interests, or a shared vision. The broad coalitions that ousted Marcos and Estrada in the Philippines, the 2006 People's Movement in Nepal (against the king), and the 2003 movement in Northern Cyprus under the banner of "This Country is Ours," all brought together disparate civil society and political groups for a common, concrete and achievable goal. Many of these coalitions involved civil society, trade unions, business and political actors. In most cases, they have proven useful for achieving short-term, specific goals (such as a violence-free election), but often do not last once the specific short-term goal is reached, because they have been formed around a "negative unity"—that is, agreement on what the groups are *against*.

Nonetheless, in several situations, a "latent" ability and commitment to (re)mobilize the coalition is established when the need arises. For instance, in the Philippines, the coalition that came together to mobilize against Marcos then remained a loose and dormant structure for sixteen years until they came together again to oust Estrada from office. In South Africa, local peace committees were, in some cases, less effective when they met regularly, but members mobilized for action when there was a threat of violence.[72] Similarly, civil society in Kenya mobilized swiftly to respond to post-election violence in Kenya in 2007-8—and then undertook a concerted campaign to resist violence in the subsequent elections in 2013 and 2017.[73]

Collaboration/coordination toward a common goal. Collaboration and coordination among agencies working toward a shared purpose often leads to linkage, but not always. For instance, in Abkhazia, donor-driven coordination of all *outsiders* who came in to facilitate projects across all levels minimized competition and led to long-term cooperation and some breakthroughs in linking local level efforts to the larger political conflict resolution process.

> In **Burundi,** civil society and the media worked in mutual reinforcing ways to ensure a nonviolent election in 2005. Civil society served as a source of information while putting pressure on the state, and the media served to transmit and amplify the message. Civil society and media put pressure on relevant actors to develop proposals for an election law to bring the political transition to an end. Informational meetings were organized, and a network was developed to advocate among the political class for passage of key legislation. Also, the Citizens' Electoral Education Program—a collaborative endeavor between civil society and the media—was established to train electoral observers, monitor the electoral code of conduct and document and report voter registration irregularities. [p.30]

---

72 RPP South Africa case, p. 33-34
73 For the 2008 period, see *Citizens in Action: Making Peace in the Post-Election Crisis in Kenya,* George Wachira with Thomas Arendshorst and Simon M. Charles, NPI-Africa, 2010.

Not all networks, however, lead to effective linkages. In southern Thailand, for example, although agencies were working toward a common goal, the influence of donors created a competitive environment among civil society (Track 2 and 3) actors. The lack of effort to map who was doing what in different communities and how the different efforts fit together undermined the collective effects of their efforts, as each CSO worked on its own particular issue, with isolated impact.[74] Similarly, in Aceh, while the broad peace goal was shared, more specific shorter-term objectives were not. This led to a lack of synergy among efforts.[75]

Sufficient convergence: multiple initiatives on the same issue in different domains. This involves initiatives focusing on different dimensions of the same issue in different sectors, domains, and constituencies. For example, as already noted, in Northern Ireland, Fair Employment legislation, trade unions' confrontation of discrimination in the workplace, and development of integrated education and ecumenical activities by some churches, all converged to facilitate progress on important driving factors of the conflict there, as each of those efforts addressed different aspects of discrimination. In Aceh, the mediation process intervened at a political level, and was linked closely to the Aceh Monitoring Mission's mandate and activities in the security domain at local levels (an example of linking across domains as well as different levels).

In Burundi, the role of civil society and media organizations working on different initiatives, with different constituencies, at different levels, converged in their common goal of promoting "shared spaces of expression and communication" and played a key role in supporting the political transition. Studio Ijambo radio covered the Arusha peace process, while the United Nations led a number of awareness-raising activities through local NGOs, and the Catholic and Episcopal churches developed sensitization programs on tolerance, justice and dialogue. These activities reinforced public support for the Arusha process, which had been strongly opposed by segments of society resistant to dialogue with what they saw as "genocidal groups."

Development, peacebuilding, and human rights. The case studies revealed linkages among development, humanitarian assistance, human rights, and/or peacebuilding groups that led to broadening or sustaining of engagement in peacebuilding work. Development activities have been used as a platform for an expansion of the agenda into peace work. In one case reported in the RPP Nepal feedback workshop, a women's group used the platform of a microfinance program to begin talking about the problem of violence against women and to organize a women's peace committee that developed effective strategies to reduce gender-based violence in their communities. Linkages between development and peacebuilding work has helped keep people engaged with peace efforts.

---

74 Personal account from participants in Bangkok Feedback Workshop 2011.
75 RPP Aceh case, p. 36.

In **South Africa,** small community organizations established to deal with "bread and butter issues, around water, electricity, school fees" tended to "escalate very quickly into more ideological discussions of the larger ideals." Civil society organizations, such as the Black Sash, assisted these small CSOs, provided training and development assistance, and connected with their discussions. Because of the high level of trust, organizations such as Black Sash were able to communicate the Track 1 process to the communities. [p.29]

Building on the work of others: deepening and broadening engagement. Even if groups do not cooperate directly, they can have a greater effect if they identify and supplement what has been accomplished by others. When initiatives build on others' gains, either by deepening the level of work or expanding the agenda, they can achieve larger-scale impacts. For example, the Hume-Adams talks in Northern Ireland built on contact made between the clergy and Republicans. The British and Irish governments built on these talks to engage in secret contact with the Republicans themselves. In Mozambique, church organizations (both international and local) built on humanitarian work to educate about peace and to support the peace process.

Vertical linkages across levels

Confronting War differentiated between two basic strategies for promoting peace: "more people" efforts that try to engage or change wider groups in society, including the grassroots and broader publics; and "key people" approaches that focus on influencing those with power to decide for or against peace or other needed changes. The earlier phase of RPP also found that linking "more people" and "key people" efforts tends to enhance impacts on Peace Writ Large—and, in some cases, the failure to make those linkages undermined peace efforts. A striking case of this failure was the peace process leading to the Oslo Accords between Israel and Palestine, in which observers suggest that the leadership on both sides got too far ahead of their bases of support and had to back away from the emerging agreements.[76]

The case evidence in this phase of RPP reinforces this finding and points to two main kinds of vertical linkages that appear to help efforts at different levels to achieve cumulative impacts:

• Connections between "tracks" (Tracks 1, 2, and 3) during negotiation processes, especially where official (Track 1) peacemaking efforts are ongoing or stalled. This also includes alignment of work at different "levels" of society in a post-agreement peacebuilding environment. Linkages with grassroots efforts in several cases ensured popular engagement in peace processes and widespread support for the agreements reached at official levels. (The South Africa example cited above is a good illustration.)

76 RPP Israel/Palestine case, p. 28.

- Linkages between *peace writ little* (community or grassroots efforts) *and Peace Writ Large* at higher levels. In some cases, reconciliation and negotiation processes among local communities were connected to national level processes, and vice versa.

Vertical Linkages Across "Tracks" to Enhance Negotiation Processes

The importance of vertical connections is most evident in places where peace processes have stalled—such as Sri Lanka, Israel-Palestine, Mindanao or Cyprus.[77] In all these cases, negative effects or lack of progress was at least partly attributable to *lack of linkages*, often described as a "disconnect" across levels, in particular between Track 1 (high-level/ official or political) efforts and Track 2 and 3 (civil society and grassroots) efforts.

DISCONNECTS BETWEEN "TRACKS" OF PEACEMAKING AND PEACEBUILDING PROCESSES

In **Cyprus,** peacemaking was described as being "conducted in a tight-knit circle, and there was not a great deal of linkage of civil society into that process." [p.37] In **Sri Lanka,** the limited release of information about the negotiation process in 2003, and the lack of a powerful mechanism to take the peace message to the population, undermined the peacemaking process, while civil society fell short "in terms of reaching out to community-based organizations and to the grassroots, thereby inadvertently perpetuating a perception of peacemaking as an elite activity." [p.47] In **Israel-Palestine,** people described the Oslo peace process as an "exclusively political process" in which much was invested in gaining key political actors' support, but little was done to prepare people for the consequences of decisions taken at the top levels. [p.28]

Even in the cases where progress has been made, the fragility of the process is attributed, at least partly, to the lack of connection between work at different levels. The Solomon Islands case study illustrated this dynamic, as there were many efforts by civil society groups (primarily church and women's groups) at a grassroots level, but these were detached from national level efforts. At some key moments, civil society groups were actively discouraged from participating in official negotiation processes, which were held out of the country, undermining popular support for the process. Studies regarding efforts to achieve violence reduction in neighborhoods of Port-au-Prince in Haiti emphasize the difficulty of gaining strategic coherence among international organizations (UN and IN-GOs), national government entities, and local community groups.[78] Some patterns have emerged across the cases regarding what constitutes *effective* linkage in each of these categories.

---

77 Since the development of the RPP cumulative cases, there have been dramatic changes in Sri Lanka and a successful negotiation process in Mindanao culminating in a signed agreement in 2014. In fact, the most recent peace process in Mindanao illustrates the importance of linkages. While there was a 2009 military victory in Sri Lanka by a repressive regime (2005-2015) and then election of a more liberal government, it remains to be seen what the long-term prospects for peace will be.

78 Timothy Donais and Geoff Burt, "Vertically Integrated Peacebuilding and Community Violence Reduction in Haiti," CIGI Papers No. 25, February 2014, Centre for International Governance Innovation.

Participation in/interaction between civil society and "Track 1" processes. Direct interactions between Track 1 (official level) and Track 2 (unofficial dialogue and problem solving) and Track 3 (people-to-people and grassroots efforts) processes and actors can constitute effective linkages. For instance, in Liberia, the Poverty Reduction Strategy planning process encouraged a number of Liberian civil society groups to provide input on important peacebuilding topics; their participation helped put important issues on the PRS agenda. A Norwegian Refugee Council program that encouraged local dialogue, mediation and technical assistance on land issues connected the grassroots level with county initiatives and national institutions of land management, and lobbied with policymakers. These multiple initiatives and connecting interventions, although they did not resolve the fundamental issues of land tenure, did led to the resolution of several hundred local-level land conflicts, prevented escalation of inter-ethnic tensions and contributed to the discussion of land reform at the national level.[79]

In **Tajikistan,** those interviewed for the 2008 case study generally agreed that the unofficial Track 2 Inter-Tajik Dialogue (ITD) prepared the ground for the official Track 1 talks, starting in 1993 and continuing after the 1997 peace agreement and into the 2000s. The ITD served as a safe space where important ideas and options were discussed before being raised at the official negotiation table. One researcher interviewed the ITD organizers, participants and political analysts about how the ITD contributed to the peace process.[80] She concludes that the ITD:

- Provided inspiration for peace by creating a sense that negotiated settlement is possible;

- Addressed local manifestations of conflict and ceasefires;

- Prompted the opposition to organize politically and formulate its interests and positions;

- Prepared concrete recommendations and proposals for consideration by decision-makers (for instance, refugee returns, political change, disarmament, and economic regeneration);

- Provided an informal channel for opposition leaders to test ideas and convey messages to the Government;

- Influenced, to an extent, the wider society in Tajikistan through participants sharing their ideas and insights with the general public, as many of them held positions at universities, media, and civil society groups.

In retrospect, participants in both the official talks and the Track 2 efforts agree that these meetings provided extraordinary opportunities for key political and civic leaders to hone their negotiation and dialogue skills, which are crucial for democratic participation. Some suggest that the ITD helped to develop a culture of political dialogue that continued after the 1997 peace agreement. However, such processes have not always been able to cope with the considerable challenges in recent years, and a younger generation has not been exposed to these methods of dialogue in the same way. [p.34-35]

---

79 See "Searching for Soap Trees: Norwegian Refugee Council's Land Dispute Resolution Process in Liberia," A thematic report from the Norwegian Refugee Council, January 2011.

80 Summary from Anna Matveeva, "Tajikistan: Peace Secured, But the State of Our Dreams?" in Across the Lines of Conflict: Facilitating Cooperation to Build Peace, Michael Lund and Steve McDonald, Columbia University Press, 2015.

A national policy framework or structure operating at many levels and providing channels of interaction between them. The National Peace Accord in South Africa, for example, was a national interconnected structure involving civil society and the full spectrum of political opinion, with national, regional and local structures. In Aceh, it was noted that the agency for rehabilitation and reconstruction (BRR) that was established following the tsunami was far more effective than its post-conflict homologue, the agency for reintegration (BRA), because of its strong mandate and institutional support from and connections to the highest levels of government in Indonesia.

Public communication and information dissemination about the peace process. In many of the case studies, communication initiatives made information about the process widely available and helped people feel that they were a part of the process. These were important to the process of "adding up." Shared information and discussion then became a basis for broad public engagement in the peacebuilding process. Transparency and open public debate, including television debates and discussions and outreach to the village level, for example, is credited with helping to bring about acceptance of the UN-mediated settlement plan in Northern Cyprus.

In South Africa, communication initiatives, including workshops, meetings, and mass communication made people feel they were a part of the process, understood it, and had a role in it. As noted in a text box above, organizations such as the Black Sash, which operated at both Tracks 1 and 3, were "able to communicate the Track 1 processes to the communities" and promote "a broad dissemination of knowledge and, consequently, a broad ownership of the process," which facilitated acceptance of the results.[81]

In several cases, intra-party linkages between the policy level and the field were important to progress in peace processes. In Aceh, for example, the GAM leadership was funded to hold meetings with field commanders and civil society to provide feedback on developments in the peace negotiations. These meetings provided a forum for those actors, who were otherwise not included in the negotiations, to feel that their perspectives were incorporated into the talks. This linkage enhanced GAM's ability to deliver on its commitments in the negotiations.[82] In addition, the MOU that was concluded in Aceh "might have remained only a vision of the elite, had the AMM [Aceh Monitoring Mission] not provided a stabilizing presence, supervised implementation of the security arrangements, disseminated information to the middle and bottom levels of the pyramid through Timsos [Socialization Team] and provided a forum for dialogue and dispute resolution."[83]

Convergence of work on similar issues at different levels. The cases suggest that different initiatives to address the same issue in different ways, carried out at different levels with different constituencies, converged to create a cumulative impact, even when there was no coordination. For example, in Northern Ireland (cited above for horizontal

---

81 South Africa case, p. 29.
82 Aceh case, pp. 33-35.
83 Aceh case, p. 37.

linkages), contacts and relationships built by the Catholic clergy at the community level provided a foundation for the British and Irish governments to make contact with the Republicans to initiate negotiations. While civil society groups began to prepare the ground for this step, many different kinds of peace initiatives at different levels aimed strategically at similar results converged. In Mozambique, as direct negotiations became likely, the Catholic and Protestant churches used homilies, sermons, and songs to educate and mobilize the population. As negotiations progressed, they worked at the community level to prepare people for peace through training and mobilizing of a group of "social integrators" who provided education, brokered local ceasefires and defused community tensions.

> In **Nepal** in 2010, six donors and INGOs worked at different levels on different aspects of one cause—land rights—with some working with a high commission working on policy while grassroots movements were organizing to secure titles. The organizations facilitated linkage by taking members of the high-level commission to the villages, by supporting the creation of village-level movements to advocate for action to deal with obstacles to land ownership, and by bringing village residents and government together to talk about rules and policies. [Participant report from Nepal feedback workshop 2010.]

International-local linkages. Effective linkages have involved connecting work within a country or at the local level with work on international dimensions, such as international advocacy, work with diaspora groups. International-local linkages have been valuable means for civil society actors to influence those at higher levels. In Somalia, networks of doctors were able to get their perspectives heard with the help of outsiders, who benefitted from the local knowledge and analysis they gained from the connections. In Myanmar/Burma, civil society organizations developed strong ties with international NGOs and regional organizations—which then advocated for changes in policies among Western governments and other international actors. In the Haiti case, international engagement with local agencies as "full and equal partners," as occurred between MINUSTAH and the police, enhanced the impacts of the efforts.

Vertical Linkages between the Community Level ("peace writ little") and Higher Levels ("Peace Writ Large")[84]

Linkages between "tracks" refer to connections between efforts engaging people at different levels of society—top-level (elites), middle range leadership (religious leaders, academic/intellectual leaders, civil society leaders), and grassroots—usually connecting official peacemaking or policy-making with unofficial or complementary processes.[85] The *"peace writ little" (pwl)-Peace Writ Large (PWL)* linkage is similar, but involves

---

84 The findings on the relationship between peace writ little and Peace Writ Large were summarized and published as a briefing in the Journal of Peacebuilding and Development in 2015. See Ernstorfer, A., D. Chigas & H. Vaughan-Lee. "From Little to Large: When Does Peacebuilding Add Up?" Journal of Peacebuilding and Development, Vol. 10, No. 1: 72-77 (2015). This section expands on the conclusions summarized in that article.

85 See Lederach, J.P. Building Peace: Sustainable Reconciliation in Divided Societies. Washington, DC: USIP, 1997. This framework for understanding levels of leadership and engagement has come to be known as the "Lederach triangle" or "Lederach pyramid."

connections between sustainable peace impacts at the local or community level, or within a limited geographic scope or sector (such as schools, youth, police-community relations), which we have come to call "peace writ little"[86]—and at the macro level, or "at the broader level of society as a whole,"[87] or Peace Writ Large.

Characterizing the local level efforts as "little" is not intended to minimize them or question their value—these are important, even crucial, initiatives. However, in relation to cumulative impacts, the critical question remains how they connect with the larger, societal level conflict. That is, if initiatives have important impacts on "peace writ little," the questions remain whether, when, and how they also have level impacts on Peace Writ Large. In order to influence Peace Writ Large, such local efforts and impacts would need to create effects at a higher level (sub-national, national, or whole-of-conflict, etc.). This is one dimension of the larger question regarding effective "linkages."

Theories of change: the idea that "a lot of pwl will add up to PWL"

In the first phase of RPP, it became evident, as *Confronting War* notes, that "often peace practitioners *only assume* that good programmatic goals, because they are good, will in some undefined way lead to or support Peace Writ Large"—in other words, "the connection is *assumed* [emphasis added]."[88] Many community-level peacebuilding efforts proceed on the broad assumption that "a lot of peace writ little will add up to Peace Writ Large." Variants of this basic theory of change include the following:

1. "If we can achieve a lot of peace writ little, it will add up to Peace Writ Large." (Critical mass/tipping point theory.)

2. "If we can contain or mitigate local conflicts, we will prevent eruptions of violence that would spread to other areas or reignite fighting. (Containing contagion theory.)"

3. "If people from contending groups can cooperate together on local projects of mutual interest, this will increase friendships, reduce hostility and result in lower overall frequency of violence. (Contact theory and mutual problem-solving approach.)"

4. "If we can demonstrate that conflicts can be resolved nonviolently, other people and areas will be convinced to try nonviolent means. (Demonstration effect theory.)"

Each of these constitutes a macro-level theory of change that is not generalizable across contexts—either because the link between local and national level conflicts is weak, or because the peacebuilding work itself often fails to make a relevant link. While we found

---

86 The term "peace writ little" (pwl) was formulated by practitioners participating in RPP initiatives who were concerned that the imperative to be accountable for their contribution to Peace Writ Large (PWL), a key finding of the earlier phase of RPP, was unrealistic for small agencies working at the community level—whose impacts on macro-level peace would be nearly impossible to detect. At the time, however, RPP did not conclude that each peace program must achieve the larger peace by itself, but rather that programs, even individual programs or projects, should address drivers of conflict and make explicit how their more modest and limited work will help achieve PWL, over time and in combination with efforts by other actors.

87 Confronting War, p. 12. "Writ" is an archaic English term meaning "written." Today It is only used in the expression "[something] writ large," meaning "[whatever element] in broad terms." Thus, a commentator might say, "While there remain many problems in the housing market and key industries, in terms of the economy writ large, the country is doing well."

88 *Confronting War, p. 12.*

in the cases a number of local-level initiatives that did contribute positively to or even added up to PWL, there were an equal number that did not. A comparison of Kosovo and Aceh with Burundi and Solomon Islands illustrate the point.

In **Solomon Islands,** community-level reconciliation processes were vital to the reintegration of combatants and revitalization of community life. The combination and integration of traditional community dispute reconciliation processes with longer-term development outcomes and organic-community-led approaches to restoring peace, demobilizing combatants and enhancing community resilience were successful at creating the conditions for peace. As the case found, given the ongoing and historical absence of any form of nation building or national unity, peace writ little efforts (that is, the intra communal and intra-village processes of reconciliation) were as vital as the larger peacebuilding attempts (p. 25-26). Thus, the healing, restorative justice and reconciliation efforts practiced at the community level, supported by infrastructural and community development activities, represented the most practical and efficacious approach, while government at the national level was still struggling to re-invent itself.

In **Burundi,** by contrast, the link between local and national conflicts is fairly weak, based on our own observations from repeated visits over more than seven years and the reflections of colleagues with even deeper involvement.[89] Burundian national politics are characterized by sharp competition among political parties associated with various elite groups and organized, with few exceptions, along ethnic lines. These struggles for power are, by and large, divorced from local level concerns or the needs of local people. The existence of conflicts at the local level does not have strong impacts at the national level, in most cases. Efforts to improve the ability of local mediators (*bashingantahe*) to resolve land disputes and interpersonal conflicts are worthwhile in themselves—but not because they reduce the likelihood of conflict at the national level. On the other hand, in the past, national level politics have proven quite influential on local level dynamics, as politicians have been able to manipulate local people to attack neighbors of different ethnic groups. Thus, in the graphic above, we would show a strong downward influence from national to local but only a weak influence from local to national. This example relates to the theory regarding the containment of violence. While the work is effective at reducing violence and discontent at the local level, this appears to have very little influence at higher levels.

In **Aceh and Kosovo,** peacebuilding efforts failed to make an adequate link that would allow more local-level initiatives to contribute to PWL. In **Aceh,** interviewees noted health, education, housing, and livelihoods programs operating at the grassroots level did not link to the political level. The programs operating in individual communities did serve the needs of that community, but did not contribute to the broader peace, and may have undermined progress toward Peace Writ Large by creating pockets of aid—that is both individuals and communities who have received aid as well as those who have not. This fueled both intra- and inter-group conflict. While the impact of

---

89 Note that the reflections in this paragraph are not based directly on the Burundi cumulative case study, but on personal observations and interactions with local and international colleagues.

each individual project may have contributed to peace writ little, the sum of these efforts seems not to have contributed, or to have contributed negatively, to Peace Writ
Large. (p. 37)

In **Kosovo,** the RPP study[90] showed that some of the communities that experienced the
most violence during the 2004 riots were those that had received considerable peace
programming in the previous years. This means that community-based inter-ethnic
programming did not result in less violence. Indeed, some of the communities that
had experienced the greatest amount of progress experienced the greatest amount of
violence, while some that were resistant to any inter-ethnic contact did not—suggesting that village or town-based contact and bridge-building neither influenced other
communities, nor acted as a brake on inter-ethnic violence originating outside their
community.

When can pwl efforts have PWL effects?

Under certain circumstances, it appears that *peace writ little* efforts can produce effects
at the Peace Writ Large level, as discussed below.

1. **When community-level conflict is an important part of the PWL equation and
   therefore influences conflict dynamics at the subnational/national level.**

   Local-level conflicts may worsen violence or polarization along "master cleavages,"[91] causing them to escalate quickly into broader conflict. Or, local conflicts
   can be affected by or mirror larger societal conflict dynamics—which can result in
   spread of violence. Our findings support the conclusions of other studies exploring
   the influence of local conflict in civil wars: that that violence often emerges from the
   interaction of dynamics at all levels, or between the political and private spheres,
   giving rise to the need to address local conflicts alongside national-level factors.[92]

   For example, in **South Africa,** pwl efforts made a direct contribution to PWL par-
   tially because of the "complex relationship between the national political process
   and local conflict systems" in which the political influenced the local, and the local
   expressed itself politically.[93] Violence between local communities and the security
   forces was often triggered by local dynamics,[94] while "bread and butter issues"
   being addressed at the local community level often "escalated very quickly into

---

90 The Kosovo study was not originally part of the cumulative case process, but was included in the case analysis, since it ad-
    dressed similar issues. It proceeded with different terms of reference focused on explaining why the 2004 riots erupted in some
    communities and not others. Multiple towns were studied and compared, and the results presented in the publication: Chigas,
    Diana et al. *Has Peacebuilding Made a Difference in Kosovo? A Study of the Effectiveness of Peacebuilding in Preventing
    Violence: Lessons Learned from the March 2004 Riots in Kosovo.* Case Study, CDA Collaborative Learning Projects and Care
    International, 2006.

91 Kalyvas, S. *The Logic of Violence in Civil War.* Cambridge: Cambridge University Press, 2006, p. 382.

92 See Odendaal, A. *A Crucial Link: Local Peace Committees and National Peacebuilding,* Washington, DC: United States Insti-
    tute of Peace Press, 2013; Autesserre, S. *The Trouble with the Congo: Local Violence and the Failure of International Peace-
    building,* New York: Cambridge University Press, 2010; Kalyvas, *The Logic of Violence in Civil War;* Darby, J. The Effects of
    Violence on Peace Processes, Washington D.C.: United States Institute of Peace, 2001.

93 Odendaal, A. "South Africa's Infrastructure for Peace." In Mitchell, C. & Hancock, L. Eds. Local Peacebuilding and National
    Peace. London: Continuum Publishing, 2012, p. 96.

94 Id., p. 98.

more ideological discussions of the larger ideals."[95] In these circumstances, the work of the regional and local peace committees established under the National Peace Accord (NPA) touched on issues and dynamics of national significance.

2. When the nature of specific communities produces symbolic effects.

This was the case in **Mozambique,** where local mediation, dialogue and conflict resolution training efforts focused on areas considered to be "crucibles of conflict." The symbolic significance of averting violence in these areas helped mitigate macro-level conflict that often had been provoked nationally when violence occurred there.[96] Rubber plantations in **Liberia** carried similar symbolic significance. When the government regained control of the rubber plantations, which had been occupied by armed militia groups, even several years after the end of violent conflict, this had a positive effect on morale and confidence at the national level. Lack of command of the rubber plantations had held symbolic significance, as it demonstrated the inability of the government to exercise control over key resources.

3. When community processes are connected to larger processes, including structural connections, and help resist provocations to violence.

Efforts that address macro-level drivers of conflict that are significant at the local level, as part of community-level processes, can have PWL impacts, even if they are visible only at the local level. A 2010 conflict analysis in **Liberia,** for example, suggested that there were strong existing links between local communities and national-level politicians and other influential persons, including some associated with armed groups suspected to remain present just outside of the country. At the local level, one of the primary sources of conflict in Liberia is land, including issues regarding access, ownership/tenure, concessions to corporations, expropriation, and communal vs. individual ownership. Given the enmeshed political relationships, volatile land issues did have the capacity to ignite local violence, which could spark more widespread violence, especially if formerly demobilized elements rearmed, or suspected ongoing armed groups mobilized and took action. In this context, one agency's program to provide alternative dispute resolution mechanisms in local communities for land disputes was singled out as contributing to PWL, because the program focused on local manifestations of a key driver of conflict in Liberia, along with its efforts to link with other local and international NGOs and government to promote broader and sustainable national capacities for addressing land disputes.[97]

In **Mindanao,** similar complex dynamics between national politics (and politicians) and local level conflict made *peace writ little* work highly relevant to PWL. Elite powerbrokers at the regional and provincial levels maintained strong ties with national-level officials (including the military and the presidency) and supported the

---

95 South Africa case, p. 28.
96 Mozambique case.
97 Liberia case, pp. 30-33.

rule of feudal dynasties that exert strict control over political and economic life at the local level. These connections created a powerful linkage between national and local dynamics. While no one would suggest that there has been any fundamental movement away from the feudal power system, the efforts succeeded in preventing local level conflicts from escalating into wider violence, as well as averting violence provoked by national policies and developments. The case study highlights the impact of local level efforts, such as zones of peace, or Culture of Peace (COP) training that was provided to thousands of people. After years of training at the local level, the COP training program was adapted specifically for presentation to field level troops and commanders, which resulted in noticeable changes in how the military treated local-level incidents, especially those involving inter-family feuds (*rido*). In addition, civil society engaged in successful efforts to prevent communities from engaging in violence in response to a threatened failure of peace talks in 2011 and launched a campaign to pressure the government and rebel groups to return to the negotiating table.

Conclusions Regarding Linkages

Local-level or community-based work is often (although not always) "More People" work. In the language of *Confronting War,* this means that it works with large numbers of people at the local level. Such efforts do not necessarily engage "Key People." or those who can say "yes" or "no" to violence or peace. The cumulative cases support the findings reported in *Confronting War* that peace writ little work must engage, influence, or link to Key People, or to other activities that engage or influence Key People, if it is to have an influence on Peace Writ Large.[98] These "Key People" are not always found at the national level or in official positions of authority. However, they must be able, as noted above, to have a significant influence on the course of conflict or peace.

The cumulative cases provide additional insight into the types of linkages that help efforts "add up" and how analysis and planning may need to be adapted to encourage incorporate such effective connections.

Linking pwl to PWL: Performing another kind of analysis

There is no "checklist" of advice that can be offered regarding vertical linkages. As Figure 3.1 indicates, the relationships among the unofficial and official tracks and among various geographic levels (community, province/state, national sub-region, nation, region) are not straightforward; rather, they differ from context to context, and are complex and non-linear. Actions aimed at achieving whole-of-conflict or Peace Writ Large impacts must be based, therefore, on an analysis that examines how political, economic and social factors of conflict are interrelated across different levels (local, subnational, national...) and across different sectors, constituencies or geographic areas.

---

98 *Confronting War, pp. 65-70.*

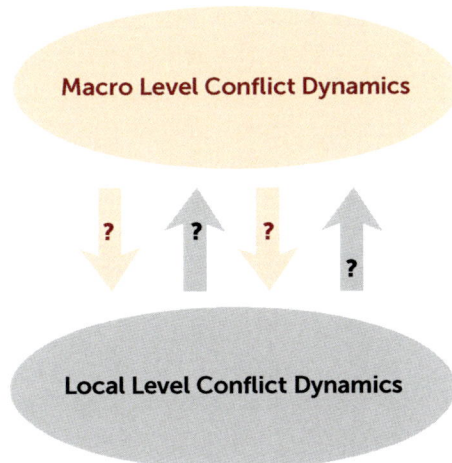

Figure 3.1: Relationship between Local and Macro-Level Conflict Dynamics

This suggests that to be effective, conflict analysis must incorporate questions regarding the relationship of *pwl* to PWL, such as the following:

1. How do local-level conflicts affect societal-level conflict dynamics, especially key drivers of conflict at that level? How do larger societal dynamics affect local social relations and political processes?

2. What is the strongest *direction* of influence between the local and societal levels? Do local level dynamics exert a strong influence on higher levels—or do higher levels influence local levels more strongly?

3. If we resolve local conflicts using nonviolent means, will this influence the way that conflicts are handled at higher levels (sub-national, national, regional)?

4. If important conflict dynamics are transformed at higher levels, will this have an impact on how conflicts are dealt with locally?

5. If local level conflicts are not addressed and flare into violence, what will be the effects on larger levels in the society?

In order to determine whether or not local dynamics—and their better resolution—can affect conflict dynamics at a higher level, we need to understand whether and how the two levels are connected. By diagnosing how the connections function at different levels, we should be able to determine what kinds of local level interventions might produce changes at a higher level.

Linking work across levels, sectors, and constituencies

While there are many indicators of missed opportunities and disconnects between the local and national (or other) levels, feedback workshop participants also cited careful work to establish effective linkages, with good results. Participants in Kenya recounted efforts to better understand the post-election violence in 2008, and how national level politics resulted in massive violence at the local level—and subsequent initiatives to make communities less susceptible to manipulation in the future. The later, relatively peaceful 2013 election demonstrated the effectiveness of these initiatives undertaken at multiple levels, even though they did not address the underlying, long-term drivers of conflict.[99]

Some feedback workshop participants suggested that it is necessary to identify key people who can act as connectors across levels, by linking people and organizations working at the different levels to ensure that efforts have greater collective impact. As one participant stated, "Act where you can at whatever level you can, but keep the larger picture in mind in order to make sure efforts add up to transform the conflict." This underlines the conclusion from the first phase of RPP that it is necessary to align work across levels for greater effectiveness. And, as noted earlier in this chapter, establishing programmatic linkages across sectors (especially from peacebuilding to development and humanitarian assistance) can increase the effectiveness of each. Generally, single-constituency work and efforts that only address personal change, while important foundational work—will have few impacts at broader societal levels—unless bridges, connections, synergies, and complementarities can be forged with other efforts. We will return to linkages as one dimension of efforts to achieve collective impacts in Chapter 7.

---

99 Indeed, as we finalize this text in 2017, election-related violence has again emerged.

4

HOW OUTSIDERS SUPPORT OR IMPEDE THE ADDING UP PROCESS

For many years, CDA has been concerned with international actors and their effects, both positive and negative, on situations where they operate.[100] People who leave their home countries, families, and familiar situations to intervene in other people's conflicts, address development challenges and deal with humanitarian emergencies have a responsibility to maximize their effectiveness and minimize the harm they might cause—even inadvertently. The current study regarding the cumulative effects of peacebuilding adds to our understanding of the relationship between "insiders" and "outsiders" within conflict areas. We have examined the case evidence to identify the useful—and potentially harmful—effects of external peacebuilding actors on the contexts of conflict and on the process of adding up to peace.

International actors—governmental, inter-governmental and non-governmental—continue to play important roles with respect to the reduction of armed violence, both within and between countries. In most cases, international actors make efforts to promote peace, although some individuals, companies and nations also pursue their own agendas for personal, commercial, or political gain. Those agendas do not necessarily align with peace goals and sometimes actually benefit from continued hostilities. As we shall see, even those with the best intentions can impede progress towards peace and undermine the cumulative effects of other efforts.

External Actors and Local Ownership/Leadership

In recent years, there has been increased emphasis on supporting local ownership, agency, and leadership in peacebuilding for reasons ranging from moral imperatives

---

100 CDA's Do No Harm Program addressed the impacts of humanitarian and development actors in conflict zones; the Reflecting on Peace Practice Program advocated more effective peacebuilding practice; the Corporate Engagement Program promoted responsible business operations; and the Listening Program elicited the perspectives of people at the receiving end of international assistance and their appreciations and criticisms of the aid system. See the CDA website www.cdacollaborative.org for information on these efforts.

to purely practical considerations regarding what works.[101] At the same time, critiques of external actors have increased, including a lively debate about the imposition of the "liberal peace" recipe for security, democracy, market economies and the rule of law (etc.).[102] Despite ongoing admonishments that "context matters" and genuine efforts to ensure processes are locally driven, external actors are often criticized for importing solutions that may have proven effective in one setting but are not always appropriate in other circumstances.[103] Many of the concerns of "insiders" reported in Confronting War in 2003 remain true in 2017, about the ways "outsiders"—mainly international actors—undermine or weaken their contributions and effectiveness, from lack of understanding of local realities, to crowding out space for local actors and imposing external models.[104]

At the same time, it is worth considering what is meant by "local" continues, and to develop nuanced considerations of degrees of "outsider-ness."[105] In conflict contexts, the local setting is, almost by definition, characterized by competing forces and diverse perspectives. Those who are committed to supporting local leadership are, therefore, confronted with dilemmas about which forces and voices to support, which usually involves building and maintaining productive relationships. In most conflict situations, there are sharp distinctions between national elites and grassroots communities, as well as between governments and their citizens, particularly when certain groups have been systematically excluded from access to social, economic, and political power. In such circumstances, it would be all too easy to reinforce conflict factors simply by supporting certain local initiatives that reflect those deep divisions in society.

Despite substantial criticism of outside actors, there is also acknowledgment that they can sometimes play crucial roles, especially when peace processes are stuck or frozen. As we discuss below, outside forces can prove decisive when regional or international forces are helping to sustain conflict, either through direct support for the combatants or by using local forces as proxies in broader political struggles, as suggested by the roles of Russia and Uzbekistan in Tajikistan and the influence of the United Kingdom and the Republic of Ireland on the struggles in Northern Ireland. For this reason, RPP has highlighted the need to analyze regional and international dimensions of conflicts (and peace) as an element of effective conflict analysis.[106] Regional groupings have also increasingly exerted influence to bring parties to the table and to facilitate or mediate agreements, as in Burundi, where African neighbors brought parties to the table and brokered a deal in Arusha that helped end the civil war, and in Solomon Islands where

---

101 See, for instance, Chandler, D. *Peacebuilding: The Twenty Years' Crisis, 1997-2017* (Rethinking Peace and Conflict Studies). Palgrave Macmillan, 2017; Autesserre, S. *Peaceland: Conflict Resolution and the Everyday Politics of International Intervention.* Cambridge: Cambridge University Press, 2014; Hellmüller, S, & Santschi, M. (Eds.), *Is Local Beautiful? Peacebuilding between International Interventions and Locally Led Initiatives.* Springer International Publishing, 2014; McGuiness, K. Ed. *Local First: Development for the twenty-first century.* Peace Direct, 2012.

102 For a good summary of the state of the debate, see Mac Ginty, Roger and Oliver P. Richmond, "Where now for the critique of the liberal peace?" Volume 50, Issue 2, pages: 171-189, 2014, Nordic International Studies Association.

103 Autesserre, *Peaceland.*

104 *Confronting War,* p. 40.

105 *Confronting War* (pp. 40-41) pointed out that, in much of the Global South, someone from a middle class urban family may be as much an "outsider" to a rural village as someone from another country

106 *Confronting War,* p. 47.

regional powers pushed for a negotiated settlement. While such initiatives are subject to charges of strong-arm tactics and power plays, the results, nonetheless proved critical to movement towards peace.

What are useful roles outsiders can play in facilitating "cumulative impacts," and how can they undermine them? We turn to this below.

How External Assistance Supports Cumulative Impacts

Confronting War noted that peace requires involvement of leadership from local stakeholders, and that solutions rooted in local realities (vs. externally imposed) are likely to be more sustainable.[107] Outsiders can bring power, resources, knowledge, influence, and, often, access to international policymaking arenas to support peacebuilding. *Confronting War* identified a number of ways that outsiders bring value and can enhance effectiveness in partnership with local peacebuilders, including:

- Advocacy and awareness-raising internationally on the causes of conflict and on peace initiatives by insiders;

- Influence and pressure on national political authorities;

- Increased security of insiders, through on-site presence, monitoring, and reporting;

- Contribution of comparative experiences, new ideas and techniques from other settings;

- Hosting of "safe spaces" where all sides of a conflict can come together; and

- Mobilization of resources.[108]

These contributions complement the strengths of "insiders," who bring passion and long-term commitment from daily experience of the conflict, as well as in-depth knowledge of the context and internal resources for peace, trust and credibility with local constituencies, social networks, and the ability to follow up.

Our findings from the cumulative impact cases reinforce these findings from *Confronting War*, not only in the context of specific partnerships between local and international, or "outsider" agencies for peacebuilding work, but in the broader process of "adding up." However, these roles do not always contribute to cumulative impacts, even when they are done well and are successful in themselves. For cumulative impacts, one needs to look not only at the specific achievements of "outsiders," but also the sustainability of the impacts and the ripple effects to other areas or domains and further progress. This insight from the cumulative cases is consistent with a view of conflicts as complex adaptive systems. A systems view emphasizes that "systems change best when they change themselves."[109] In other words, as systems thinker Margaret Wheatley notes, "We never

---

107 *Confronting War*, p. 43.
108 *Confronting War*, p. 38-39.
109 Ricigliano, R. *Making Peace Last*, p. 63.

succeed in directing or telling people how they must change."[110] Efforts for change, including peacebuilding, are more effective when they build on institutions, structures, or practices existing in the system that constitute positive movement, or when they identify existing energy for change and reinforce it.[111]

Exerting influence and pressure on key actors in the conflict. Several of the case studies noted actions by external parties that were considered "game-changing" events, involving peace initiatives, and even agreements, by influential regional or global actors that fundamentally changed the structure of the situation. One salient example was the Anglo-Irish Agreement, which fundamentally changed the relationship of the United Kingdom and the Republic of Ireland to the contending parties in Northern Ireland. At the time, people from all sides of the struggle in Northern Ireland felt betrayed by their "sponsors." Over time, however, each side came to realize that the relationship between the UK and Ireland would no longer allow unquestioning support for the Unionist or Republican cause—and that the parties needed to get on with reaching an accommodation.[112]

> The conflict in **Tajikistan** is an instructive example of the decisive influence of external geopolitical actors on internal conflict dynamics. In the early 1990s Russia shifted its policy towards Tajikistan from supporting the democratic opposition to supporting the government based on the fall of democratic parties in Russia. Uzbekistan supported the pro-government People's Front as a means to promote the interests of the local Uzbek minority. The rise of the Taliban and concern over the United Tajik Opposition's cooperation with terrorists shifted Russia, Uzbekistan and the Commonwealth of Independent States to favor a speedy resolution to the conflict. The resulting pressure and coordination by outsiders is credited with bringing about the peace agreement. [p.25-26]
>
> In **Mozambique,** the collapse of communism in the late 1980s and early 1990s prompted international actors to pay attention to Mozambique, whereas during the Cold War major world powers and the UN showed a lack of interest in peace in Mozambique and took actions that perpetuated hostilities. By the time international conditions changed, most of the conciliation work, both at top and grassroots levels, had been done by the religious community, preparing the ground for parties to seize opportunities created by these events. [p.15]

Such "game-changing" influence by outsiders can open opportunities for accelerating change, when they realign outsider-insider relations and coalitions in ways that make negotiation or cooperation more attractive than continued violence or stalemate.

Outsider pressure on key actors and recalcitrant parties can also be important in contributing to progress, especially in the domains of security and political arrangements,

---

110 Wheatley, M. *Finding Our Way: Leadership for an Uncertain Time.* San Francisco: Berrett-Koehler Publishers, 2007, p. 132.

111 This approach is closely related to the notion of identifying and supporting "positive deviance," which assumes that, within any context, some natural innovators will have developed successful strategies for overcoming a problem. While the concept of "positive deviance" was originally developed in the health field, it was expounded by Richard Pascale, Jerry Sternin, and Monique Sternin, in *The Power of Positive Deviance: How Unlikely Innovators Solve the World's Toughest Problems.* Cambridge, MA: Harvard Business Review Press, 2010.

112 Northern Ireland case, p.23.

to end violence and in peacemaking; in this sense, the cumulative cases mirror examples found in many conflicts, of international pressure pushing parties to conclude agreements or implement policies.

In **Burundi,** regional powers (prominently Tanzania and South Africa) put pressure on the elite power brokers to engage in negotiations—which met with stiff resistance from members of the elite who feared to even acknowledge the legitimacy of the opposing forces. And once representatives came to the negotiating table, the regional mediators acted quite forcefully to gain a workable settlement. In **Aceh,** the mediator, former Finnish President Martti Ahtisaari, also exerted considerable pressure on the parties throughout the negotiations. Regional organizations or loose groupings of neighbors played similar positive pressure or support roles in reaching peace agreements in Liberia and, more recently (since the writing of the CDA case study), in **Mindanao.**

In **Solomon Islands,** the success of the Regional Assistance Mission to Solomon Islands (RAMSI) early in the intervention was due in large part to its overwhelming physical presence, with 325 police and 1,800 military personnel, including 450 combat troops. This created enough fear among militants and their supporters to motivate them to comply with RAMSI demands, including handing over weapons (p. 21).

Despite the usefulness of unilateral or coercive initiatives by outsiders in these cases for achieving peace agreements, or demobilization, peacebuilders should exercise caution in generalizing conclusions about the contribution of external pressure to "adding up." Regional actors' peace initiatives can equally entrench the existing structures, making peace efforts or positive peace more difficult. In the Solomon Islands (see boxed text above), the role of RAMSI, dominated by Australia and New Zealand, was seen as supporting an elite process disconnected from grassroots communities that had been suffering from violence. In Cyprus, the European Union, by offering membership to Cyprus without requiring an agreement first, undermined the prospect of the peace settlement brokered by Kofi Annan. The EU action changed the calculus of the Greek Cypriot side, as they felt that they no longer needed the Turkish Cypriots to gain accession to the EU, and could potentially use their position within the EU to extract greater concessions from the Turkish Cypriots in later negotiations.[113]

Other examples illustrate the double-edged nature of external pressure. The negotiation process in Guatemala was supported and funded by the international community. Several Western governments also pushed for a range of commitments to change in support of human rights for minority groups. The government agreed to these provisions at the table but apparently had no intention of fulfilling them. The resulting agreement has not been fully implemented, although it remains a reference point for those advocating change, and the continued attention of international groups make it more difficult for government to intimidate or marginalize civil society groups.

---

113 Cyprus case, p. 44.

"Game-changing" opportunities often arise in response to geopolitical shifts and shifts in interests, and cannot be orchestrated. Similarly, external pressure can bring about an end to armed violence, a peace agreement or a policy change, but if it occurs in a context where there is no acknowledgment of the fundamental drivers of conflict, nor sufficient coalitions for progress in other domains, the progress toward positive peace may be stymied. In these cases, careful conflict and stakeholder analysis could help identify whether and how unilateral or coercive actions will catalyze favorable structural change or progress.

Providing security and space for dialogue. "Outsider" roles in providing security have contributed significantly to cumulative impacts. Outsiders have enhanced the effectiveness of efforts to end violence and maintain security, both physical and psychological—as peacekeepers or in peace enforcement operations, as ceasefire monitors, witnesses, monitors, and reporters of human rights violations, conveners and protectors of space for dialogue across conflict lines, etc.

The cumulative case studies found, in most cases, that local people appreciated the stabilizing influence of peacekeeping forces and feared the consequences of premature withdrawal. In Aceh, as in Solomon Islands, for example, many of those interviewed felt that the uncertainty regarding the term of the mandate of the peacekeeping forces undermined confidence in the peace process. In Aceh, people felt that peacekeeping forces left too soon and without either adequate provision for ongoing security or effective processes for sustained implementation of the peace agreement. At the same time, contribution to "adding up" depends also on outsiders linking their efforts to and partnering with indigenous actors and processes, as this helps ensure that their contribution to security will continue beyond stabilization (or pacification) and provide a bridge to longer-term progress toward positive peace.

> In **Solomon Islands,** in 2003, the Regional Assistance Mission in Solomon Islands (RAMSI) defense, police and civilian personnel intervened in the Solomon Islands to end the cycle of violence that persisted following the 2000 Townsville Peace Agreement; unarmed monitors, civil society actors and the police, which was in disarray, had not been able to influence the militants to end violence and turn in their weapons. There is consensus in Solomon Islands that the 2003 intervention, initiated at the request of the Solomon Islands government, stopped the lawlessness and contributed to the restoration of order and stability. This was in part because of the overwhelming armed presence of RAMSI, which could effectively counter that of the militants, and the advice and support of local monitors from the indigenous National Peace Council (NPC). The NPC monitors were able to facilitate RAMSI entrance into more difficult communities, provide logistical and advocacy support to spread the message of RAMSI; as they were trusted in communities, they were able to act as a de facto intermediary between RAMSI and the communities in which RAMSI intervened. [pp. 20-21]
>
> In **Aceh,** the Aceh Monitoring Mission (AMM) was identified as playing an "important and stabilizing role" following the Memorandum of Understanding (peace agreement, or MoU). People felt it did an "impressive job" of supervising the process of disarming and

demobilizing the non-state armed group, GAM, and relocating Indonesian troops and helped to build confidence amongst the population of Aceh during the initial stages of implementation of the MoU. It also signaled to Acehnese that the international community was committed to monitoring the peace process, thus reinforcing confidence. The AMM also convened regular meetings of the Commission on Security Arrangements—comprising Indonesian government and GAM representatives—at the provincial and district levels. These provided an effective forum for communication and trust-building between Indonesian military, police and GAM field commanders, and between the parties and the local communities. [pp. 13-14]

In **Israel and Palestine,** the World Council of Churches' Ecumenical Accompaniment Programme in Palestine and Israel (EAPPI), with a mission to accompany Palestinians and Israelis in their non-violent actions, provide monitoring and reporting of violations of human rights and international humanitarian law and offer protection through non-violent presence, among other things. The presence of EAPPI monitors at checkpoints and in popular protest has been important in decreasing incidents of harassment at checkpoints and attacks by neighboring settlements, and increased the sense of security of people crossing checkpoints.[114]

In addition to the security dimension, external entities (civil society/NGOs, UN agencies, bilateral government/diplomatic entities) have also provided safe space for dialogue, whether informal and off-the-record or formal and public. As discussed in Chapter 3 regarding linkages, such dialogue processes take place among influential citizens connected to decision makers (Track 2) or among key representatives of warring factions themselves (Track 1). The case studies cite a wide range of activities organized and often facilitated by external entities that promoted dialogue as a step in progress towards peace.[115]

The **Inter-Tajik Dialog** (ITD) is an example. Led by a joint American-Russian team led by Harold Saunders (former U.S. Assistant Secretary of State for Near Eastern and South Asian Affairs) and Prof. Vitaly Naumkin (Director of the International Center for Strategic and Political Studies in Moscow), ITD organized a Track 1.5 dialogue process that fed directly into the formal negotiations, offering concrete policy options, many of which were adapted by the official negotiators. Until the beginning of the UN-sponsored official negotiations, ITD was one of the few unofficial channels of communications between the opposition and the Government. People noted that the ITD team brought a high level of skill and expertise to the process, but they "were important because of their political ties." (p. 24). In other words, they had influence that facilitated the translation of the ideas generated in the ITD to the official process, but also protected the space for the ITD to continue.

In **Mozambique,** the Rome-based Catholic Community of Sant'Egidio provided a private, neutral, and non-judgmental space for discussions among representatives of the

114 Palestinian Counseling Centre, Evaluation of the WCC Ecumenical Accompaniment Programme in Palestine and Israel (EAPPI). Jerusalem: Palestinian Counseling Centre, 2008. Available at https://norad.no/globalassets/import-2162015-80434-am/www.norad.no-ny/filarkiv/ngo-evaluations/1a-evaluation-of-the-impact-of-the-wcc-ecumenical-accompaniment-programme-in-palestine-and-israel-eappi--2.pdf (accessed December 16, 2017). See also http://eappi.org/en (accessed December 16, 2017).

115 Again, see Chapter 3 for these examples.

> two main warring factions. This space was essential for facilitating the start of official negotiations and helping the parties to settle some significant differences and to reach a political accommodation; it is widely credited for breaking the stalemate. Backing by the Italian government, and deep ties to the local churches in Mozambique, which in parallel engaged in activities with their constituencies, reinforced Sant'Egidio's ability to provide safe space—both enhancing the legitimacy of the process and protecting it against efforts to undermine it.

As with outsider roles of pressuring key parties or shaping incentives and structures of stakeholder coalitions, provision of security and safe spaces for dialogue and interaction does not always "add up." For example, MINUSTAH's (UN Stabilization Mission in Haiti) crackdown in 2007 on criminal gangs that controlled major urban areas did establish a fragile, but real, stability and improved conditions of security. While there is broad consensus regarding this positive contribution, the crackdown remains controversial. Even before the 2010 earthquake and subsequent outbreak of cholera traced to the UN, not everyone shared the view that MINUSTAH operation created stability, and the conditions that allowed for success in establishing security are instructive.[116] The success of "Operation Baghdad," as the 2007 MINUSTAH security operation to clean difficult neighborhoods was called, succeeded in part because of the caution MINUSTAH exercised, and the attention paid to the importance of gaining public confidence, their willingness to engage the police as "full partners," and the inclusion of municipal and neighborhood-focused initiatives (i.e. linkage to community initiatives).[117] At the same time, this MINUSTAH also was perceived as tilting the balance in favor of certain groups in the struggle for power for the Haitian state, of addressing the symptoms but not the underlying causes and did not go deep enough to address the causes of Haiti's instability and violence.[118] In the realm of security, people saw progress as stymied due to MINUSTAH's narrow securitized approach and the lack of progress on "institutionalization" of a police force enmeshed in politics.[119]

Undertaking advocacy, lobbying, and support for internal processes. We observed many instances where international agencies brought local voices into international policy-making arenas, bringing international attention and action to local perspectives on peacebuilding needs and processes that helped them in "adding up."

One effective role of international actors is to undertake advocacy to galvanize international pressure on human rights. A wide array of supporters in the international community brought the South African situation into the policy realm in Western capitals and the UN, lobbying for boycotts and sanctions against the apartheid regime, and pushing international corporations operating in South Africa to support change. While the peace process in South Africa was driven internal actors, the pressures placed on

---

116 Haiti case, p. 19.

117 Haiti case, pp. 42-44. See also Muggah, R. "The Effects of Stabilisation on Humanitarian Action in Haiti," *Disasters* 34, No. S3 (2010).

118 Haiti case, p. 41; Lemay-Heber, N. "United Nations Stabilisation Mission in Haiti." In Koops, J. T. Tardy, N. MacQueen and P. Williams (Eds.) *The Oxford Handbook of United Nations Peacekeeping Operations. Chapter 61. Oxford: Oxford University Press, 2015; Muggah, R. "The Effects of Stabilisation on Humanitarian Action in Haiti."*

119 Haiti case, p. 41.

South Africa by the international community in response to this advocacy—including economic sanctions, trade sanctions, an arms boycott, cultural isolation, sporting and political isolation—had a dramatic effect on the South African economy, and was a significant factor in pushing the National Party government to negotiate.

Partnerships between "outsider" and "insider" organizations can also help to bring missing local voices into nationally- or internationally-led peacebuilding processes. Regional and international networks of civil society, such as the Global Partnership for the Prevention of Armed Conflict, for example, have worked in collaboration with local organizations in Burundi and Sierra Leone to ensure that local perspectives on the peace process were heard by the UN Peacebuilding Commission (PBC). They not only arranged meetings with PBC delegations in country, but also brought representatives of civil society to testify at Commission meetings in New York.

International agencies have helped to bring community and grassroots voices and experiences into national peace processes. This was illustrated in the Solomon Islands case study, among others, where international NGOs and UN organizations advocated for and funded the establishment of a Ministry of National Unity, Peace and Reconciliation that was tasked with extending local dialogue processes to inter-communal dialogues and connecting local and national peace processes. This helped to provide a mechanism for the regionally-supported national peace process to connect with and sustain community-level negotiation and reconciliation processes.[120]

> Six donors and INGOs in **Nepal** worked at different levels on different aspects of one cause: land rights. Some worked with a high commission working on policy, while grassroots movements organized to secure titles. The organizations facilitated linkage by taking members of the high-level commission to the villages, by supporting the creation of village-level movements to advocate for action to deal with obstacles to land ownership, and by bringing village residents and government together to talk about rules and policies.[121]

Mobilizing resources and providing expertise and comparative experiences. An important and valued role for international actors has been to mobilize resources for local efforts and to share expertise and experiences from elsewhere. The cases highlight external support as a key factor especially for the quantitative and qualitative strengthening of civil society engaged with peacebuilding. In Cyprus, peacebuilding efforts outside the official negotiation process were mostly funded and run by outside third parties. International funding made possible the development of a "flourishing of special bi-communal interest groups,"[122] which challenged the official narratives that Greek Cypriots and Turkish Cypriots could not live and work together, and were creating new ideas for resolution.

---

120 Solomon Islands case, p.29-31.
121 Report of consultation on cumulative cases, Kathmandu, Nepal, May 6, 2010 (internal report).
122 Cyprus case, p. 17.

Similarly, in Burundi, the number of civil society groups multiplied many times from the early 1990s through the mid-2000s, through constant support and capacity building from INGOs and funding from international donors. International support helped civil society organizations, which at first were characterized by the same ethnic cleavages that plagued society as a whole, become more diverse and engage effectively in peacebuilding. As the case notes, "Burundian civil society grew increasingly plural and diverse, transcending its initial weakness to play a primary role in driving the society's development."[123] This was especially true in the media, where international agencies supported the development of independent and outspoken new media organizations that were seen by people interviewed for the case to have played a critical role in Burundi's 2005 elections. During the 2005 election, such civil society groups played an important role in ensuring that the campaign and voting were accomplished without significant violence. Unfortunately, the Burundi situation has deteriorated significantly in recent years, including disturbing closing of spaces for civil society and an independent media.

UN organizations and international NGOs also provide technical expertise and bring experiences from other settings that can be adapted to local conditions. The Cambodia and Cyprus cases reflected that outside support helped local groups gain skills and confidence through exposure to concepts and experiences from other countries.

In **Cambodia,** in the early 1990s, a core group of local people participated in a training program provided by Responding to Conflict, a UK-based NGO, in cooperation with the Cambodian Centre for Conflict Resolution (CCCR). CCCR operated under the auspices of the Cambodian Development Resource Institute and introduced the first conflict resolution training program in 1997. CDRI was a special contributor to the leadership of local actors working directly for peace.

The first core group trained by the CCCR formed themselves into a national networking organization called the Alliance for Conflict Transformation (ACT). Many of the key peacebuilding NGOs have been established and guided by this core groups of individuals. ACT's contributions include capacity and skills development, technical support in the area of peacebuilding to other sectors, and advocacy for policy changes, through workshops, conferences, networking, and research. Significantly, the CCCR, known today as Cambodia Peace and Development, has also provided training courses to commune councils in what are known as the "reconciliation zones," former Khmer Rouge–controlled areas. It is believed that the trainings in peace and conflict transformation provided many officials with the skills and concepts to transform their approaches to conflict and provided opportunities to influence change without violence. [p.37]

In **Cyprus,** conflict resolution trainings initiated by outsiders and bi-communal initiatives beginning in the 1970s led to increased local ownership of the work and the beginning of Cypriot-started organizations like the Peace Centre Cyprus. One interviewee said, "[The] training of trainers was a powerful step in the right direction for what would become multiplier groups, and ultimately became what some consider the beginning of the citizen-based peace process itself." This work preparing the ground is credited

---

123 Burundi case, p. 28.

with helping to catalyze the dinner meetings between Clerides and Denktash to discuss the Annan Plan. These dinner meetings were widely perceived by both sides to be a step forward, as they were not held in a neutral UN sanctioned or foreign-hosted meeting place. [p.33]

How External Assistance Can Undermine Cumulative Impacts

The acknowledged importance of "outsider" resources, expertise and experience for cumulative impacts is not without its negative aspects. Some of the same activities and roles that help can also undermine cumulative impacts—and sometimes simultaneously. Critics point to the creation of "project societies" and "pocket NGOs," in which the lure of funding generates proliferation of organizations that lack a real base or constituency and cannot be sustained when funding dries up. In Cyprus, the authors of the case note, international sponsorship of peacebuilding activities limited their reach and opened them to accusations of being guided by "foreign interests," which led, in part, to participants being marginalized in their own communities.[124] Clearly, *how* outsiders engage in peacebuilding and how they support local initiatives and efforts affects whether they contribute to, or undermine, cumulative impacts. We turn now to the ways that outsiders prevent or undermine "adding up."

Dependent relationships undermine local ownership and initiative. Outsider support for civil society has often caused dependence on international funding sources, which can distort peacebuilding strategies and undermine local initiatives and development of locally-driven agendas and planning for peace.

In **Tajikistan,** financial support and expertise in the early stages of development of local civic groups were important contributions from outsiders, but questions about the sustainability and focus of externally funded initiatives arose. Local groups were dependent on foreign funds and, in response to shifting donor priorities, developed proposals to continue receipt of external funding. The arrival of international agencies with narrow mandates or priorities introduced problems. An example was what people referred to as "disproportionate" attention to border issues, which reflected the foreign policy priorities of external governments concerned with terrorism. One head of a local NGO working on reconciliation issues commented, "If local groups are unable to present their own ideas for funding to donors, then these initiatives, however well-designed and implemented, will lack local ownership and commitment on the part of staff and participants." [p.38-39]

Similarly, in **Mozambique,** civil society grew through international support and technical assistance, yet financial dependence left them at the mercy of donor agendas to sustain their operations, and they were "unable to implement what they believe is best for the country." [p.28]

---

124 Cyprus case, p. 53.

CDA's *Listening Project* noted that one effect of increasing adoption of business principles and practices by aid providers has been that "people in recipient societies become askers rather than doers."[125] And while people in recipient countries acknowledge and accept the fact that outsiders have their own agendas, in the eyes of many people in recipient communities, outsiders decide priorities and pursue agendas without consultation, adaptation or negotiation that aid recipients can influence. This tends to limit local actors to the role of implementers of programs designed by external agencies, rather than as the primary initiators or drivers of peace processes—a passive rather than active function.

These dynamics have made peacebuilding processes vulnerable to distortion by donor agendas, priorities, timelines and understandings of the conflict. In Sri Lanka, people spoke of the development of an NGO "workshop culture," driven in part by the availability of funding, combined with a lack of outsider understanding of the context and a focus on "quick fixes" that distorted the peacebuilding agenda, undermining its relevance to the issues driving conflict in the country.[126] As the case authors note, "The importance of ensuring public participation and building local legitimacy of the peace process, rather than relying purely on international assistance is one of the lessons to be learned from the failure of the [Cease-Fire Agreement 2003]."[127]

Dependent relationships can subvert the legitimacy of organizations and peacebuilding efforts. Financial dependence often leads civil society organizations to suffer from weak levels of legitimacy, through the importation of "cookie cutter" programs with little regard for context and vulnerability to perceptions that they are implementing foreign agendas—as peacebuilding initiatives often become responsible to international funders first and constituents or governments second. Guatemala, for example, saw a sharp rise of local organizations during the development of the Peace Accords, transforming the nature of social organizations in the country. But they were fragmented, had low levels of legitimacy in the eyes of the general population, and depended almost entirely on funding from international agencies.

> In **Cyprus,** despite calculated UN restraint from meddling in internal affairs with regards to direct advocacy for the 2004 Annan Plan, both Turkish and Greek Cypriots expressed the sentiment that Cyprus is often a pawn in the self-interested agendas of international players. The Annan Plan, which was drafted largely by outsiders, was met with considerable resistance and backlash, contributing to its defeat by referendum on the Greek side. It was perceived by the leftist, AKEL party as too "Anglo-American," which did not serve the interests of the Cypriot people but rather the larger interests of geopolitics. Even some Turkish Cypriots expressed suspicion about the motives of the international community concerning the Annan Plan, which is of note, because of the strong support and mobilization on its behalf on that side. [p.11]

---

125 Anderson, M., D. Brown and I. Jean. *Time to Listen: Hearing People on the Receiving End of International Aid. Cambridge, MA: CDA Collaborative Learning Projects,* 2012, p. 42.

126 Sri Lanka case, p. 45. The authors argue that the framing of the conflict as a "two-party process" (p. 34) ignored the complexity of contradictory interests and groups in Sri Lanka, and limited the inclusivity of the process, to negative effect.

127 Sri Lanka case, p. 39.

In **Sri Lanka,** one interviewee, commenting on the international community's engagement, observed: "Some came with textbook solutions. For example, Getting to Yes was practiced frequently in workshops. Even internationally reputed conflict resolution experts came to Sri Lanka for three-day workshops and no long-term commitment. These quick interventions gave a bad name to the whole community." [p. 47]

In **Israel and Palestine,** the post-Oslo rise in the number or organizations and projects applying for peace funds has been referred to as the "peace industry" in Israel, and, to a lesser extent, in Palestine. Increased competition for funds affected cooperation among Israeli and Palestinian NGOs and resulted in a loss of trust and legitimacy, as the power dynamics embedded in the conflict itself were mirrored in externally-funded peace programs, and led to Palestinian perceptions that "people to people activities have turned into business relationships" dominated by Israelis. While this "peace industry" was seen to have "cleared out" after many external donors pulled out and others tried to change their policies after the second Intifada, these concerns still remained. [pp. 24-26].

Evidence from CDA's Listening Project, as reported in *Time to Listen,* suggests that even though the international assistance community is committed to participation of aid recipients in planning and implementation of projects, and has developed procedures to encourage this, these are not working as well as intended; people report that they rarely feel listened to or truly involved in the critical decisions about the assistance they receive. Aid agency staff and people in recipient societies point to funding procedures as one driver of limited participation: proposal writing processes that require agencies to make critical decisions before they put staff on the ground, lack of financial resources or time to allow for meaningful participation in initial decisions about program direction and priorities, and flaws in execution of consultative processes that do not facilitate meaningful engagement by participants.

There are examples of internationally-supported initiatives that managed to avoid these pitfalls. In Solomon Islands, churches, with international funding, actively promoted peace activities, from psychosocial support to funding of inter-and intra-community processes. Many externally-funded infrastructure and community development processes have survived because the church—a stable and locally-embedded institution that, in communities where government presence or service delivery was negligible, was the main service provider and community support agent—was an active participant. In Liberia, the Norwegian Refugee Council's (NRC) program to assist communities in resolving land disputes was cited by many as particularly successful, and that NRC was trusted by all sides. This was due to the fact that the program addressed a key issue in conflict for communities. In addition, a number of features of NRC's funding and its relationships with authorities and partners facilitated its success, including: research and demonstration of a deep understanding of the issues, linkages with officials and traditional authorities, close partnership with local NGOs who were also supported in setting up local peace councils that would be able to settle disputes themselves, and the fact that, as reported by interviewees, they never imposed a solution from above.[128]

Local and international agendas are not always aligned. The effects of international agendas on local dynamics are an important part of understanding insider/outsider relationships in relation to cumulative impacts. Often, international agencies set the agenda entirely because they hold the purse strings, and insider participation is minimal. Lack of alignment can undermine cumulative impacts by undermining linkages or diverting local efforts to areas or programming that are less relevant to the drivers of conflict. Local perceptions that donor agendas are imposed from the top down and override "insider" priorities is exacerbated by frequent shifts in priorities—which affects the potential to make sustained progress.[129]

Outsider agendas have significant impacts on peace efforts, with implications for cumulative impacts. A city official in Davao, Mindanao noted, "the pervasive attitude is that beggars can't be choosers. In many cases, we don't have much say in what gets funded. These programs usually benefit the donors in meeting their funding priorities. What we suggest often doesn't fit their menu of options. After much back and forth, we end up asking them, 'What do you want to fund?' And we adjust."[130] Nonetheless, some local organizations have, on occasion, turned down funding because it is not consistent with local priorities.

> As already noted in Chapter 2, interviewees in **Mozambique** offered a useful distinction between spaces that are created by insiders and those created by outsiders without insider participation. Interviewees made a distinction between "offered space," created and funded by international agencies, in contrast to "conquered space," created by local civil society and arising out of a commonly identified need. Civil society organizations feel ownership of spaces that are conquered but are skeptical of offered spaces. [p.59]

> In **Aceh,** funding for "post-conflict" efforts was less than four percent of the post-tsunami reconstruction budget (as of 2008), and aid was not allowed to enter unless donors guaranteed that they would not spend funds on conflict-related programming. The resulting uneven distribution of aid caused people in coastal areas to report that the peace process was a success and people in the mountains to maintain that tensions remained high. "The terms "post-tsunami" and "post-conflict" were a creation of the international community and have now been adopted into local vocabulary. Such language falsely creates the notion that post-tsunami reconstruction can operate independently from conflict and post-conflict peacebuilding activities. This has enabled organizations to implement humanitarian and development programs absent of any consideration for the conflict context." [p.21]

> A local NGO director in **Cambodia** said that they need to change their mission every five years to keep up with donors and continue to get funding. The leader of a local NGO in Phnom Penh noted, that the danger is that in many areas it is not possible that

---

128 Liberia case.
129 See Anderson et al., *Time to Listen*, p. 59-61.
130 CDA Collaborative Learning Projects, Listening Project Field Visit Report: Mindanao, Philippines. Cambridge, MA: CDA Collaborative Learning Projects, 2009, p. 18; Anderson et al. *Time to Listen*, p. 61.

"the impact can be felt in just three years of support." The NGO leader advised that "donors shouldn't change their minds frequently."[131]

Many interviewees in **Liberia** were critical of the government's hiring of many expatriates – in donor-funded programs, but also relying on Americans of Liberian descent and other members of the large Liberian Diaspora community. One interviewee suggested that the Liberian government had largely "borrowed manpower," and that its interests were not the interests of ordinary Liberians. Several informants felt that donor money was often spent to meet the interests of those small elites with ties abroad rather than to truly invest in Liberia's future. [p. 42]

Some observers point to what might be called an "analysis deficit" in explaining the mismatch between local and international agendas. Many international agencies (UN and INGOs alike) focus on technical expertise rather than deeper knowledge of the local context and conflict dynamics. International staff are cycled through multiple assignments in conflict zones and arrive with often simplistic assumptions regarding the nature of the conflict and ready-made programs. While exposure to other conflict areas could be seen as a strength, if such knowledge is not adapted to local social, political, and cultural conditions, program approaches will not align with local realities and are likely to fail.[132]

Dependence creates fragmentation and weakens linkages. Outsiders have undermined cumulative impacts by inadvertently promoting fragmentation and competition and weakening horizontal linkages among "insiders." As the Liberia case study noted, the fragmented, small-scale and short-term nature of most peacebuilding efforts, may be one reason peacebuilding initiatives fail to tackle deeper issues needed for progress toward positive peace.[133] This occurs when:

- There is reliance on the project mode of funding and delivery in peacebuilding. Project-based support means that assistance and engagement come in the form of relatively short-term, discreet efforts. Yet projects do not "add up." In Kenya, for example, people commented that international assistance is a series of disjointed, one-off efforts to meet isolated needs, provided in ways that left incomplete, unsustainable results, rather than holistic interventions with long-term impacts.[134] In Aceh, agencies reported that they implemented activities on a project basis, doing whatever they could to get funding, rather than determining projects based on a comprehensive post-conflict peacebuilding strategy. These disconnects and lack of coherence among donors, multilateral institutions and local and international NGOs are not intentional, yet they represent a systemic problem that has proven difficult to change. The project mode often leads to piecemeal interventions that are not strategic, often are cut short by changes in outsider agendas and priorities, and do not, within the short timeframes given, support sustainable systemic change.

---

131 Anderson et al. *Time to Listen.* P. 61.
132 Autesserre, *Peaceland.*
133 Liberia case, p. 51.
134 CDA Listening Project, Kenya Listening Exercise, p. 10.

- "Outsiders" promote competition among local actors. Financial dependence has prevented local NGOs in Mozambique from collaborating, and has bred distrust and undermined their ability to create linkages. More generally, funding procedures often unintentionally foster competition among local civil society organizations (and, indeed, international NGOs), leading to fragmentation and lack of synergy among individual programs.

- Shifts in outsider agendas leave "orphaned" peace actors and promote fragmentation. In Cyprus, for example, after the failure of the referenda to bring about an agreement on the Annan Plan (the UN-sponsored plan to reunify the island) in 2004, external funders shifted focus from dialogue, rapprochement and exploration of federal options to CSO strengthening and sustainable development. This was partly in reaction to intense criticism by the Greek Cypriot government and accusations leveled at international actors (especially the UN) of bias and inappropriate advocacy for the Plan. It was also partly in response to the weaknesses of the peacebuilding efforts that had been conducted throughout the 1990s. However, this sudden shift of strategy and partners left a large part of the local peace community in limbo, causing further fragmentation among peacebuilding actors.

> In **Aceh,** cumulative impacts have been hindered by the narrow, project-based focus of many activities, along with what people perceived to be a lack of a comprehensive post-conflict strategy and intense competition between external donors (and their partners) to "obtain a piece of the peacebuilding pie." The Agency for Reintegration (BRA) strategy document itself notes: "One of the reasons a comprehensive strategy for sustainable peace is needed is because the majority of peacebuilding activities following the MoU have had a narrow and more immediate focus." A number of additional problems were perceived by interviewees: politicking and jockeying between organizations that has undermined programmatic benefits, with most people feeling that donors' "strategic" initiatives had had little impact to date on peace at the grassroots level; and negative conflict sensitivity outcomes, as both inter-group and intra-group tensions were perceived to have been exacerbated because of the focus on cash payments to individuals, as well as the uneven distribution of aid by the government and international organizations among both individuals and communities. [pp. 32-33, 37]

Lack of linkages between local and international actors undermines cumulative impacts. The case studies reveal a lack of linkage between international and local agendas in conflict contexts that can result in missed opportunities and even undermine local CSO efforts.[135]

> As of 2010, lack of communication and coordination between UN and local NGO work on judicial reform in **Mozambique** reduced the effectiveness of local NGO work and inhibited cumulative impacts overall. The UN abandoned participatory methodologies in favor of more traditional, top-down approaches to development after 1994, and local civil society groups focus on developing conflict management capacities at multiple

---

135 See further discussion of this dynamic in Chapter 3 regarding linkages.

> levels. Interviewees reported a lack of local ownership of UN activities, as well as a major disconnect between it and local initiatives like Justapaz's work with police at high levels that enjoyed strong national ownership. "Local peacebuilding NGO's technical knowledge is not used or legitimized by the UN, and NGOs feel that the UN might be reinforcing the propensity of the government to see the NGO sector not as a partner but as a competitor, and is itself not fostering cross-sectoral collaboration on judicial reform." [p.25-26]

Lack of linkage can also result from a lack of a nuanced understanding of the context in polarized societies.

> In **Kosovo,** the promotion of the internationally defined and imposed agenda of multi-ethnicity, intended to promote inter-ethnic bridge-building, actually exacerbated ethnic tensions. The Albanian community experienced the encouragement of inter-ethnic dialogue as "coercive and unwanted conditioning." Since most donor funding required a component of multi-ethnicity, participants went through the motions of co-operation, when actually these efforts were superficial in nature. Without contextual knowledge of these dynamics, international donors heralded many of these projects as great successes and in some cases increased funding. [p.86]

> Similar pitfalls have exacerbated tensions in **Tajikistan,** due to lack of joint strategy between donors and international agencies and poor knowledge of local context. There is evidence that regionalism within the country, a key driver of conflict, has not been addressed systematically or adequately in programming. One senior program staff person said, "We are not even sure how to work on this issue or around it. While we have field offices in most regions and some of our projects bring together representatives from all regions, we are not sure if this indeed addresses the clan regionalism issues and what kind of impact we are having." Thus, the lack of a nuanced understanding of a key local dynamic has exacerbated tensions. [p.39]

International actors, often in partnership with national governments, can hinder progress on addressing unfinished conflict business by committing to "road maps" that do not adjust to changes in circumstances. For instance, in Guatemala, the government, INGOs and CSOs still use the Peace Accords as a basic framework to judge the progress of Guatemalan society, despite it being defeated in a referendum and being widely regarded as too far-reaching. The weak state and an explosion of social violence, make the Peace Accords increasingly difficult as a road map to reconstruction, yet donor funding is still largely tied to its framework.

Freezing the process. In some circumstance, the international community has, however reluctantly, "accepted" less than ideal conditions, often choosing security as a higher priority than a deeper, more sustainable peace. In many situations, post-conflict assistance and support has been directed to supporting elite power structures that perpetuate social, political and economic marginalization and exclusion—a tactic that may provide a degree of security in the short-term but will likely lead to renewed violence over time. In Cambodia, Liberia, and Tajikistan, elite power structures exclude significant portions of society. In Burundi, Mozambique, Tajikistan, and Cambodia, single-party dominance is increasing, yet a weary population (and international community) are seemingly willing to accept the situation rather than return to active political struggle. Indeed, political violence did return to Burundi during the 2015 elections and beyond.

> A majority of **Liberians** interviewed in 2008 believed that, while the war was clearly over and the formal institutional make-up had changed, the root causes of the conflict had not been addressed. Not only had exclusion and marginalization of large parts of the population continued (with development and investment focused in Monrovia and suburbs), but people felt that outsiders—members of the diaspora whose links to Liberia were tenuous, or foreigners—continued to control a disproportionate share of government positions and economic assets. [p. 50] The lack of fundamental change in political and economic power structures was perceived as a lack of commitment on the part of the government—and its international supporters—to address these drivers of conflict.

Conclusion

The discussion above could be taken as a sweeping indictment of the failures of international assistance in general and of peacebuilding efforts by outsiders in specific. The story is not so bleak, however. We have seen many instances in which external actors have provided constructive support to peace processes—some of them cited earlier in this chapter. The essential findings are that support for local leadership and initiatives must come first, and that efforts by external peace practitioners must complement internal efforts and, at a minimum, avoid undermining local partners or otherwise making matters worse (the Do No Harm principle). And, there are times when peace processes are not moving at all, and well-designed interventions by external actors can help to overcome gridlock or stalemates.

5

THE ROLE OF LEADERSHIP IN ADDING UP

Leadership for Change

Leadership represents an important resource or capacity in the system for change, which can be exercised at all levels, from local communities to the national arena to regional and even international relations. Some leaders occupy formal, even elected, positions, while others exercise leadership in informal ways, based on moral authority, support from a particular constituency, influence within specific sectors, or connections to powerful people. John Paul Lederach, in presenting his "pyramid,"[136] suggested a differentiation between top-level leadership, representing powerful military and political elites; mid-range leadership, including highly respected individuals or people with formal leadership positions from civil society, business and religious communities, who are connected to both elites and to grassroots constituencies; and grassroots leaders, who often are people involved with local communities, members of local CSOs working with or part of the larger population.[137]

In all of the cases in our study, leadership has been used to escalate the conflict, divide people further, or to block peacebuilding. This negative leadership needs to be identified and addressed if there is to be progress. The focus of this chapter, however, is on the way leadership *contributes* to "adding up." Leaders have played an essential though not exclusive role in promoting progress towards peace—in particular by tying together the different strands of progress to promote cumulative progress toward sustainable peace. Leaders contribute significantly to "adding up" directly by explicitly acknowledging the fundamental causes of conflict and communicating that change is possible. More often, they demonstrate this implicitly through their actions. In these ways they inspire hope, confidence, and support for an ongoing peace process. As we

---

136 John Paul Lederach, *Building Peace,* 1997.

137 This formulation corresponds in most ways, with RPP's distinction between "key people" who have the power to decide for or against peace, and "more people" representing the lager population—with intermediaries connecting to both "key" and "more" groups.

shall see, the concept of leadership must embrace not only the named, elected, and visible leaders, but also the relatively unknown citizens who take initiative through mobilizing civil society and encouraging those with power and authority to take action for peace.

Leadership Takes Many Forms

There are many, often competing ways of framing the concept of leadership that can provide useful lenses for this discussion. Among others, key theories of leadership include:

- The "great man" theory of leadership[138] assumes that leadership qualities are inherent and that great leaders were born and not made.

- The "traits" approach to leadership focuses on individual personality, ability, and other specific characteristics. In this case personality traits – for instance adaptability, confidence, charisma, etc.—that enable leaders to inspire others to follow them, are connected to a leaders' effectiveness.

- Behavioral theory identifies and analyzes the behaviors of successful leaders and assumes that leadership can be taught, and that it is not a quality that individuals are born with.

- Transactional leadership is an exchange that takes place between leader and follower, often favoring the interests of one group over others and perpetuating the status quo.[139]

- Transformational leadership is characterized by leaders who engage with their followers in a way that raises both to higher levels of motivation and morality, often transcending factions and changing the way people view what is possible.[140]

- Adaptive Leadership theory sees leaders as "giving the problem-solving work back to the people by getting them to face reality, learn, discover, solve problems, take responsibility for the work they must do to generate real progress."[141] Leadership can be exercised anywhere, and is not just a formal title conferred on the elite few.

The RPP cumulative cases—and the Peace Progress Factor Tree analysis presented in Chapter 2—support the idea that leaders interact in important ways with their followers or constituencies. They can provide transformational leadership that promotes a transcendent vision for change towards peace. This, in turn, requires a clear statement of reality (i.e., the problems to be solved) and engaging multiple stakeholders in

---

138 The debate over Great Man theory versus the assertion that leaders are enabled by factors in their environment has been going on since the 19th century, with thinkers like Thomas Carlyle, Hegel, Kierkegaard, Nietzsche and others. supporting the sense that leaders (or heroes) are born with the requisite traits, and others, such as Herbert Spencer (Tolstoy, William James...) claiming that leaders are a product of their times and circumstances.

139 Bass, BM (1997) From transactional to transformational leadership: Learning to share the vision. P 20

140 Ibid.

141 Heifetz et al. (2009) *The Practice of Adaptive Leadership*.

seeking mutually acceptable solutions. At the same time, as Reychler has argued, and cumulative cases reinforce, there is a need for a "critical mass of peacebuilding leadership," including those with both formal and informal authority at all relevant levels of society (elite, middle and grassroots), as well as internationally, across the different domains of peacebuilding.[142] Mari Fitzduff and her colleagues also suggest that we should not concentrate exclusively on local leaders as the means to end conflict and build peace, but also on the potential influence of the international leaders and organizations to effect change and influence local leaders, especially at the peacemaking stage, as they often lack administrative capacity and may have little power over grand issues of conflict and peace.[143]

Positive leadership clearly contributes to the adding up process. Rothstein writes, "Societies with strong leadership on both sides are more likely to make agreements which will be sustainable...Societies with weak leaders on both sides are more likely to continue to maintain the status quo within their society since their political positions continue to be assured."[144]

The study of specific leaders and their traits is a natural entry point for this issue. In societies that experience conflict or are in transition, focus on elites and their ability or missed opportunities to exercise leadership is important, because elites often have the power to bring about peace processes or continue violence. Looking at the conditions and events that allow leaders to emerge and lead, as well as the missed opportunities in places where peace continues to be elusive, can also be useful for framing leadership issues. Often, leadership may not actually come from an individual or a small group of individuals, but rather stems from the structural conditions that enable or hamper individuals from assuming leadership roles. In this sense, leadership is embedded in the broader conflict system that can either promote or frustrate the exercise of vision and practical problem solving.

Leadership as a Contributing Factor in Adding Up

Leadership is relevant and important across all the domains of the Peace Progress Factor Tree presented in Chapter 2 domains of progress. One of those is closely related to leadership—namely the key factor of "acknowledgment of key conflict drivers and commitment to address them"—a factor that is relevant to progress across all of the domains, as well as on its own. While the factor does not identify *who* is supposed to engage in such acknowledgment and commitment, it is clear that it is at least partly a leadership function to promote a common understanding and recognition of key

142 Reychler, L. & A. Stellamans. "Researching Peacebuilding Leadership." Paper presented at the Conflict Resolution and Peacebuilding Commission at the International Peace Research Association in Sopron, Hungary, July 2004. Available at http://lucreychler.com/wordpress/wp-content/uploads/2012/11/Cahier71_ReychlerStellamans.pdf (accessed December 16, 2017).

143 Peake, G., C. Gormley-Heenan & M. Fitzduff. *From Warlords to Peacelords: Local Leadership Capacity in Peace Processes*. INCORE Report, 2004. Available at http://citeseerx.ist.psu.edu/viewdoc/download?doi=10.1.1.489.9098&rep=rep1&type=pdf (accessed December 16, 2017).

144 Robert L. Rothstein ed., *After the Peace: Resistance and Reconciliation* (London: Lynne Rienner, 1999) p.9-10, as quoted in Gormley-Heenan, Cathy, (2001) "From Protagonist to Pragmatist: Political Leadership in Times of Transition," INCORE, p. 22-24.

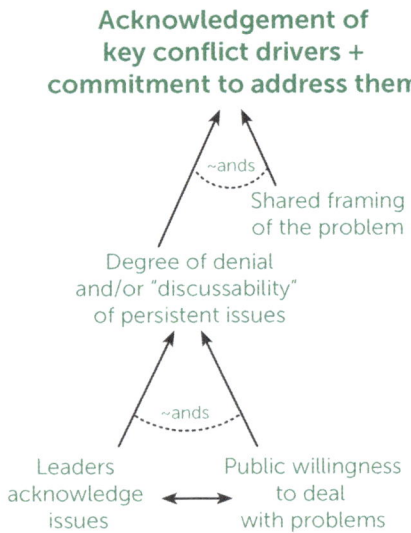

**Acknowledgement of
key conflict drivers +
commitment to address them**

~ands

Shared framing
of the problem

Degree of denial
and/or "discussability"
of persistent issues

~ands

Leaders
acknowledge
issues

Public willingness
to deal
with problems

Figure 2.4

conflict drivers—and to mobilize people and resources to address them. Of course, the process goes both ways; members of the public and civil society organizations can urge leaders to acknowledge and address conflict issues.

A crucial component of the leadership function for those in positions of authority or influence in the peace process is the education of the broader population, as well as allies and opponents in the political sphere. National leaders with authority are often obliged to garner financial and political support from international donors and allies in order to obtain the necessary backing to challenge persistent assumptions, especially if change requires certain powerful individuals and groups to cede or share power.

The factors lower on the "tree" include explicit mention of leaders, and there is a clear relationship between leaders and the public. Each can influence the other in important ways, which echoes the earlier RPP finding regarding the linkage between "more people" and "key people."[145] If the public is mobilized to work for change, they may be able to agitate for actions (changes in policies, allocation of resources, etc.) by those in power. On the other hand, leaders may be motivated to acknowledge fundamental drivers of conflict, which can influence public attitudes towards conflicts and other societal problems.

> In **Haiti,** at the national level, there was the perception that leadership was lacking in terms of skill, political will, and character. Yet, deep unhealed divisions within the society and entrenched self-serving patterns of governance also hampered leadership. Well-communicated messages—a vision—about clear progress in the areas of development, reform and governance on a national level would go a long way to catalyze local peace initiatives; build national unity, public confidence and momentum for positive change. [p.49]

> One of the main themes that emerged from the interviews is that many people in **Aceh** were frustrated that there seemed to be a gap between activities at the political level and activities at the grassroots level. Many people commented that activities that were taking place at the political level did not impact what was going on at the grassroots level, and did not address the concerns of many at the grassroots level. [p.36]

Leadership from the Powerful

> "[**Burundi**'s history of] poor governance can be associated with absence of vision, or visionary leadership. Most often, this absence of leadership is characterized by a failure to understand the medium and long-term consequences of certain actions and

---

145 See the RPP Matrix in *Confronting War* and in RPP Training Manual available on www.cdacollaborative.org.

to act accordingly to prevent them. According to a number of observers, this lack of visionary leadership has served to obscure the country's problems and has facilitated a general denial of certain truths. [p.7]

The RPP case material points to a number of important functions of leadership from those who have the positions and authority to move a society or nation towards peace—or away from it.

Communicating commitment to change. A paradigm shift can occur when leaders show regard for the other side—not necessarily in the form of an agreement—but perhaps in the acknowledgment of the legitimacy of a set of interests or a symbolic act that represents a thawing of relations. These events were often identified by interviewees as key turning points, even if they represented one step forward followed by two steps back (as in Cyprus).

> In **Tajikistan,** in the mid-1990s, meetings held between President of Tajikistan Rahmonov and Chairman of the UTO, Said Abdullo Nuri, in Northern Afghanistan was an extraordinary example of their willingness to find common ground—and is credited with leading eventually to the 1997 peace accords. As experienced and informed leaders, they understood the consequences of continuing the military confrontation and worked hard to get buy-in from their constituents, even if they were not ready for compromise. In the spirit of compromise and in recognition of the interests of the UTO, President Rahmonov pressed parliament to adopt amendments to the constitution allowing the activities of "parties based on Islamic values" in Tajikistan. These amendments were considered a cornerstone for the peaceful coexistence between secular state and political Islam in Tajikistan. [p. 29]

When leaders break with past behaviors or patterns, they offer hope for a different future. There are examples of leaders that honored their transaction with those who put them in power by subordinating their own self-interest. Such events can build confidence among constituencies in the durability of the law and the possibility of forward movement. In some cases, these acts of leadership might not contribute to overall peace consolidation, but represent significant steps that help build confidence in the peace process—often encouraging others to promote change as well.

> In **Burundi,** after the Arusha Accords were signed, Pierre Buyoya was forced to abide by his pledge to cede the seat of president to his designated successor in 2003. Despite his reluctance to leave power, his departure had symbolic importance, because it showed that previous engagements needed to be respected, laying the groundwork for a culture of respect for communities and, in a certain sense, regarding them and the law itself as binding. [p. 16]

> In **Mozambique,** in 1990, towards the end of the Cold War, Mozambique's political leaders began reconsidering their approach to governance. The country's leaders adopted a new Constitution in 1990, two years before the signing of the peace agreement, which called for a multiparty state. This constitution is widely

considered to have been an important cornerstone for peace. It provided evidence that the regime was willing to change substantively, thereby serving as an important confidence-building measure. This was a confidence-building measure that represented steps towards democratization. [p. 19]

In **Cyprus,** in the run-up to the 2004 referendum on the Annan Plan, leaders on both sides were influenced by the gathering strength of the citizen-based peace movement and set up a series of dinner meetings among leaders for discussion of the Plan. "This type of informal meeting in a relaxed atmosphere gave the appearance of a gradual move towards friendship and reconciliation, because it was not held at a formal, neutral, UN sanctioned meeting place. The whole of Cyprus as well as the world saw the first glimmer of hope in these affairs because the news was covered island-wide and internationally." Clerides and Denktash reopened the issue of missing persons from both sides, an issue that had been stalled for fourteen years. [p. 33]

Shaping understanding of the conflict and the possibilities for change. Despite some situations in which leaders risk pushing their constituents too far or losing them completely, presenting new ways of thinking about solutions can shape people's understanding of the conflict as well as of what kind of change is possible.

In **Northern Ireland,** in the late 1980s, John Hume introduced the unpopular idea of engaging with the IRA in the Hume-Adams talks, a risky decision, though one that created long-term positive change. At a time when neither the British nor the Irish government was willing to talk with Sein Finn, the IRA's political wing, John Hume pursued his own agenda of drawing Republicans into political discussions. The Hume-Adams talks, which continued into the early 1990s, were unpopular, but helped assist republicans to move towards a more political approach. "His concepts and visions, which often seemed far-fetched at first, captured paradoxes and dilemmas that later turned out to encapsulate the way the situation needed to move, and tended to become the dominant discourse about the situation and the way people understood the conflict." [p.1]

Initiating events that represent conceptual shifts can change minds and narratives. In Burundi, despite strong opposition to even participating from many political leaders, the Arusha process had a huge psychological effect on the population—even though the Accords themselves had major shortcomings and are often called "the peace agreement with no peace." It was the first time that Burundian society had come together to discuss key drivers of conflict and "the accord itself served as training ground for dialogue, tolerance, and search for compromise. Arusha marked crucial achievement not so much in terms of content, but of process it set in motion."[146]

Leading intra-community or intra-party consensus building. The cases showed situations in which leaders were responsive to the demands of their constituencies, as well as situations when leaders set a new course and shaped a new understanding of what is possible. Sometimes leaders sense the readiness of constituents, and sometimes constituents need to be brought along and make difficult choices and compromises for

---

146 Burundi Case p 10

the larger goal of peace. The concept of "elastic band leadership" describes the potential hazards of leaders getting too far ahead of their constituencies. "The leadership is expected to stretch its constituents in the interests of peace, all the while remembering that if the elastic band is stretched just a little too far there is always the danger of it snapping."[147] *Leaders creating consensus within their own party or constituency can often be more important as a step towards peace than reaching out to so-called enemies.*[148]

In **South Africa,** the ANC leadership carried out extensive internal consensus building work to bring along radical elements and consolidate their base before reaching across group lines during the late 1980s and early 1990s while Mandela was still in prison and prior to formal negotiations.

In **Tajikistan,** both President Rahmonov and UTO leader Said Abdullo Nuri pushed their constituencies to take part in the peace process, even though many politicians and field commanders refused to recognize the peace agreement and were highly skeptical of the process. Their willingness to compromise and push their constituencies led to the signing of the peace agreement in 1997.

In the **Middle East,** the Oslo peace process, leading to the signing of a first accord in 1993 and a subsequent agreement in 1995, was marred by leaders who lacked an understanding of the attitudes of their constituents and not doing the necessary work to build internal consensus. As a result, negotiation processes came to a halt because of lack of ownership and buy-in or an understanding of the agendas among the constituencies on both sides. A joint Israeli-Palestinian research team concluded that the Oslo peace process failed in part because the negotiators were not seen as representing the interests of the people on either side of the divide; The Israeli population had been educated about the costs of peace but not the options or how to choose among them; and there was a lack of ownership on the part of everyday people and no understanding within the larger population what the destination was. There was also no public education on either side for a common future. One Palestinian peace advocate said he saw leaders and committed individuals who "lost their constituencies... there has been a loss of hope. There's no hope for an agreement in the near future." [p.20]

Gormley-Heenan's 2001 study of the evolving nature of the "culture of leadership" in South Africa, Northern Ireland and the Middle East presents examples in which political leaders on both sides were ready to make an agreement, but their constituents were not, or when leaders failed to convey the significance of a concession made by the other side, missing opportunities to create bridges between parties.[149] Getting too far out ahead of constituencies can cause leaders to lose credibility and cause peace processes to stall, as noted in the Middle East example above.

Leadership in official negotiations: Breaking taboos. In some cases, leaders are able to catalyze negotiation processes. John Hume engaged with Sinn Fein at a time when no one else would talk with them. The Italian organization Sant'Egidio opened pre-

---

147 Gormley-Heenan, C., "From Protagonist to Pragmatist: Political Leadership in Times of Transition," INCORE, Londonderry, 2001, p. 12.
148 Gormley-Heenan, p 11-12.
149 Gormley-Heenan, p 9.

liminary talks between the Burundian government and one of the rebel movements in the mid-1990s, well before official negotiations began. A South African newspaper editor and a civil society leader went to Zimbabwe with exiled ANC leaders in 1985, at a time when such contacts were illegal. These initiatives broke taboos and opened a process of engagement with those excluded from discussions. These steps prepared the ground for subsequent engagement of key actors in negotiations, and for public acceptance of the need for negotiations.

Challenges and Constraints on Leadership

Even leaders with apparent power cannot always act effectively. Political pressures, expectations of constituents and allies, and unpredictable events get in the way of taking necessary action.

Pressure and coercion by third parties. The evidence is mixed on the effectiveness of coercive leadership, in which international or regional powers or powerful individuals take decisive action without seeking the consent of conflicting parties. During the negotiations leading to the 2000 Arusha Accords for Burundi, Nelson Mandela "impose[d] solutions where parties did not agree," and in Northern Ireland, the Anglo-Irish agreement was imposed on the parties in 1985. Despite criticisms, these coercive moves were acknowledged as critical positive turning points for the peace processes—creating structural changes in the situations that the parties could never have negotiated on their own. In Cyprus, by contrast, perceptions of coercive tactics by the United Nations, indeed quite similar to Mandela's in Burundi, were perceived negatively and were partly responsible for the failure of the last round of negotiations.

Leaders often promote the status quo, particularly in uncertain times. Leaders in a divided society are often caught in a dilemma; while they might want to reach out to their opponents, political tensions may not permit such actions. In Cyprus, politicians on both sides promoted a divisive culture and deepened ethnic divisions and fears, in order to maintain the status quo and their positions of power. Papadopolous portrayed the Annan Plan (2004) as pro-Turkish, deepening Greek Cypriot fear of a "yes" vote and entrenching the status quo. The renewed border crossings momentarily helped smooth out old stereotypes and misconceptions, while creating new and different relationships, but the post-referendum political climate was one of renewed mistrust and fear and betrayal on the side of Turkish Cypriots. There was a deep lack of faith in their own leadership, as many Greek Cypriots perceived that many politicians built their careers on the Cyprus conflict. This did not help bring more group cohesion either, as those forces worked against whatever "yes" movement was beginning to develop there. Confrontations between pro-settlement GC political factions on the left and right resulted in the politicians becoming the obstacles, and issues of compromise were not part of any party's official policies. This led to general feeling that the status quo was acceptable.

Leadership and persistent issues. The RPP case evidence shows that in some places, post-peace agreement—despite differing degrees of reform and modernization—power continues to be held in ways similar to those that operated before the conflict. Yet there is little complaint from the general population about the perpetuation of this status quo. In Cambodia, Tajikistan and Liberia, each country has achieved relative peace, stability, and change in other areas, and has been praised by the international community: "Cambodia's progress has involved tinkering with the status quo rather than fundamental structural change: power, leadership and governance continue to be based on family ties, connections and "client" relationships, without change or questioning from the broader population."[150] This has caused wealth to accumulate in the hands of a small circle and a loss of scrutiny by those close to the top.

Similarly, in Tajikistan, President Rahmonov, suppressed all political opposition and left major parts of the peace agreement unimplemented (in particular with regards to power sharing). The system of government is identical to what it was pre-conflict, only with a different clan holding monopoly power. Despite this, he has managed to maintain popular levels of support among the general population (called "the unifier of all Tajiks") and is heralded by the international community for his contributions to the peace process.

Finally, in Liberia, many interviewees said that little had changed and that the political system is as corrupt as ever and patron-client relationships that characterized pre-war Liberia persist. "Many interviewees stressed that they found the conditions in post-war Liberia to resemble pre-war Liberia and that the root causes of war had not been properly addressed... widespread poverty, underdevelopment and exclusion in parts of the country and the marginalization of parts of the population have remained unchanged."[151] Despite criticism by many interviewees, the leadership in these countries maintain a level of popular support that ensures they will stay in power, and the relative stability, despite persistent unaddressed issues, keeps violence from recurring.

It should also be acknowledged that leadership carries risks—and leaders that get too far out front of popular opinion or the views of more extreme elements of their own party or faction, risk their reputations, lives or other sanctions.

Leadership from "Below"

As noted in the Lederach pyramid, not all leadership is exercised by those in powerful positions. Civil society leaders are often in a position to advocate for peace—and, in many case, have greater flexibility to make demands, push for productive talks, condemn ongoing violence, and/or make specific recommendations regarding potential solutions to key problems. They can work both "up" to governmental elites and "down" to grassroots communities. Despite their apparent power, government leaders are typically constrained by internal politics or international pressures. They may

---

150 Cambodia case, p. 45.
151 Liberia Case p 41

even feel compelled to declare a return to "peace" and "normal" conditions—often, then, denying the fundamental causes of war and violence that usually persist after the fighting stops and a peace agreement is signed—as noted in the paragraph on Liberia above. Even international bodies find themselves hampered from taking strong action, due to the structures and rules determining their interactions with governments. Civil society groups may be in a position to make informal contacts with hard-to-reach parties in ways that might be illegal or politically risky for national or international officials.

The RPP cases provide notable examples of civil society leadership that influenced the adding up process. Specifically, when there was a lack of political will or political legitimacy at the government level, civil society and community level actors had catalyzing effects. Also, linkages between the community and national levels became important for violence reduction at the community level, making community leaders particularly crucial.

Shaping understanding of the conflict and the possibilities for change. This is not only the purview of political leaders as in the "Leadership from the Powerful" section above. Civil society leaders, especially those from major "socialization institutions,"[152] can have tremendous power to shape understanding, as can the media. In some divided and post-war societies, broad civic coalitions also contribute to shaping important national debates and agendas and offer a platform for sorting out the competing ideas and visions circulating in the socio-political sphere. Some civic coalitions and their leaders attempt to change the direction of the political debates by daring to express previously unacceptable terms and visions and demanding new or reframed solutions to the conflict. Conversely, in other places, collective civil society actions are determined through the influence of external factors and actors, largely having to do with donor agendas and priorities and availability of funding.

> In **Burundi,** radio stations assumed a crucial role in keeping the population informed and supporting the democratic transition following the Arusha Accords in 2000. They organized public debates on key political issues and challenges, fostered a media climate favorable to negotiations and dialogue, supported reconciliation initiatives, and promoted good governance in interaction with civil society. At the same time, the stations' ongoing vigilance helped limit state abuses through denunciations. The debates organized between various political figures and parties generated a palpable shift in people's outlooks and attitudes, thereby facilitating a change in individual and collective behavior. [p. 31 + 37]

When constituents want to shift the status quo, acts of leadership can take place outside of formal political spaces. Social movements can create change in response to what is happening in the government with respects to the conflict, and often has significant effects on creating positive change for peace. In the Philippines, the success of the People Power Revolution in 1986 in toppling the Marcos regime strengthened

---

152 Paffenholz, *Civil Society*

the legacy of nonviolence as a social change mechanism. One academic notes that, "the democratic transition brought about by the people power revolution created the conditions for building national consensus on the need for social and political reforms that would break down the repressive apparatus of the martial law regime and address gaping social inequities."[153]

Unfortunately, constituencies sending clear messages to political leadership about the intolerance of the status quo does not always result in long term change. In Cyprus, the Turkish Cypriots found that while they were serious about a solution, their leaders were not. The 'Revolution from Below' is an example of constituents showing the way, when leaders might have preferred to maintain the status quo. This mass mobilization to promote the referendum on the 2004 Annan Plan "...reflected the "maturation of the next generation of leadership... rallies opened the doors for people to express their desire for something different."[154] It was supported widely by civil society, businesses and unions (in particular the Chamber of Commerce), played a key role in uniting the Turkish Cypriot agendas and forced the Turkish military and Turkish Cypriot leadership to open some check points across the green line which allowed a freedom of movement not seen since 1963, and led to the defeat of Denktash in 2003, bringing pro-solution forces to power in the north. The Turkish Cypriot mobilization for a "yes" vote represented a significant shift, but competing interpretations (and misrepresentation by media and political leaders) of the Plan caused a "no" vote on the Greek Cypriot side, reversing progress and deepening divisions.

Connecting parts of the system that need to be connected. "Adding up" can be undermined by fragmentation and lack of linkage. Leaders can take initiative in linking people, connecting levels and actors (see Chapter 3, on Linkages). Frequently, this linking or bridging leadership is undertaken by civil society. In several contexts where civic coalitions were formed across ethnic and political lines, they played an important bridging role that political parties and government institutions could not. It is highly impractical to expect that political elites, in the wake of a bitter conflict, can instantly embark on a "nation-building" effort and create common bonds, foster common values and manufacture a common political culture that would define a new peaceful and democratic nation. In some cases, like South Africa, Mozambique, and Burundi, influential civic leaders invested considerable energy in building ties between political elites as an important step toward accommodation. Particularly in transitional times, coalitions often "filled a political dialogue gap" and ensured continuity of democratic consolidation processes when the state itself was still fragile.

In **Mozambique,** local peacebuilding organizations and the Election Observatory worked directly with political party candidates to ensure peaceful elections. The work of improving relations between political factions made an important difference to

---

153 Miriam Coronel Ferrer, *Framework and Synthesis of Lessons Learned in Civil Society Peacebuilding.* (Manila: UP Center for Integrative and Development Studies, 2005). P. 7
154 Cyprus case, p. 37.

peace consolidation in Mozambique by injecting a higher level of civility and tolerance in the most recent election in 2004, compared to the 1998 and 1999 elections, as well as connecting civil society and government institutions.

In 1991 in **South Africa,** the negotiation process for the National Peace Accord (NPA) which brought together opposing parties was an initiative of civil society, whose members realized that the political parties themselves were not going to get it done. NPA was deliberately established as a national structure managed at all levels by civil society and parties representing the full spectrum of political opinion in the country. It was felt that a multilateral agreement involving all political parties, civil society, the government (and particularly the police) was more likely to result in peace than a bilateral agreement between the ANC and the NP. Ultimately, NPA created an important political space for the parties to negotiate and deal with each other more effectively.

Civil society leadership provide linkages that contributed to adding up. Maha Ghosananda was seen as a key civil society peace leader in Cambodia, most notably for starting the Dharmayeitra for Peace and Reconciliation walk through war torn parts of the country to promote peace. In 1993, he led the second walk through areas of open civil war, encouraging citizens to overcome fear of political violence and intimidation to exercise their right to vote. Ninety percent of the Cambodian electorate voted in the 1993 elections and many interviewees attribute the success of the elections to Ghosananda.

The National Peace Council in Solomon Islands was a group of councilors and advisors representing each of the nine provinces and had field monitors that served an essential role in traditional reconciliation ceremonies and helping RAMSI and the IPMT access to communities through their contextual knowledge and relationships, creating an essential linkage. One NPC Advisor reflected, "In the absence of inspired political leadership, or will within government, or of consistent or coherent leadership from churches, or an effective civil society, NPC created and occupied a unique space between government and the civil sector. At the same time, it had greater influence and contact with government than other civil society organizations."[155]

Competent, community-level leadership, intra-community bonds and social networks. These elements were among the most significant resources that communities drew upon to avoid or resist violence and kept communities from being pulled to extremes.

CDA's Steps Project[156] explored evidence of community resistance to violence and to what extent leadership was a contributing factor to such resistance. Evidence showed that leadership was an important contributor, but not the sole determining factor, of processes and outcomes in communities that resisted violence. Steps Project findings also contradicted several common assumptions about the role of leadership. In particular, the project found that:

---

155 Solomon Islands case, p.19.
156 See Mary B. Anderson and Marshall Wallace, *Opting Out of War: Strategies for Preventing Violent Conflict*, (2013), Lynne Rienner Publishers, Boulder

- Strong, charismatic leadership is not necessary to motivate people to resist violence;

- Particular ideologies or visions are not required to resist violence; and

- The leadership required to enable a community to choose an extraordinary path of conflict prevention does not itself have to be out of the ordinary. Thus, new and non-traditional leadership and leadership structures are not required; existing structures and persons can rise to the occasion.

In Kosovo, in all cases of successful avoidance of or resistance to violence during the 2004 riots, individual leaders in communities took a clear stand and mobilized community action. Or, in the case of communities that did not react prematurely to reports of violence, leaders sent a clear message to stay calm and not to provoke. Not only were timeliness and clarity of message important, but in some communities, leaders took public stands against violence and failed to forestall attacks. Leadership that was listened to was seen to be credible and connected to the community and could command attention and disseminate information quickly to their communities. In Mindanao, community efforts at establishing ceasefire mechanisms and longer-term resistance to violence were successful, as persons caught in the crossfire understood that by networking with others outside their communities, they could have a positive impact on the violence thrust upon them. This reinforces the critical importance of establishing links between community leaders and national leaders.

Leadership for the Long Term

While individual leaders can certainly exert influence, leadership is embedded in political, social and cultural structures. When promoting improvements at this structural level of leadership, it is key to understand that change is long-term. Augmenting structural conditions for good leadership can take twenty or thirty years and may require a shift of mindset brought on by a new generation. This is particularly true if the leadership culture is institutionalized, and poor leadership is the norm rather than an exception.

In working on systemic factors of leadership, traditional leaders can play a vital role. Such leadership may have strong influence over political elites, as well as represent communities and the general public. For structural change in leadership to be effective, however, the entire chain of leadership needs to be influenced, from traditional and grassroots settings to the national level. Without a comprehensive approach, structures will not change in sustainable ways.

Leaders must have the courage to acknowledge, unequivocally and openly, the fundamental drivers of conflict—and to chart a realistic pathway to change. If not, important issues of equity, justice and access to resources and power will persist, and lead to renewed cycles of violence. Unfortunately, too many leaders are entrenched in resilient—and often corrupt—systems of power and influence that constrain positive leadership for change.

PART II

IMPLICATIONS FOR PRACTICE

6

INTRODUCTION TO PART II:
CHALLENGES IN THE PEACEBUILDING FIELD

The Focus of Part II

Part I of this book focuses on the findings from the RPP cumulative case studies, which includes many references to the case material itself. Part II takes up the implications for peacebuilding policy and practice—or what we like to call the "so what?" question. This section will, therefore, be much more prescriptive in suggesting stronger practices, with fewer direct references to the cumulative case materials.

Our recommendations are based partly on the findings discussed in Part I, but also draw on almost fifteen years of applying and refining the earlier RPP lessons, as well as the combined experience of the authors, two senior peacebuilding practitioners, and our colleagues at CDA. As noted in the acknowledgments, we are also indebted to hundreds of colleagues who have shared their experiences, including, most importantly, dedicated peace workers struggling to achieve justice and security in conflict zones around the world. We have also benefitted from the insights of stalwart practitioners from the international community who are trying to support local partners. While we have learned from them during a variety of engagements in the field and international headquarters, the conclusions presented are our own.

Before we turn to the implications for practice, we will address what we term the "dysfunctions and challenges of the peacebuilding field." This analysis provides a broader picture of the global peacebuilding context that our suggested courses of action seek to address. After presenting that analysis, the remaining chapters in Part II will provide a framework for collective impact in peacebuilding, discuss the challenge of developing shared analysis in situations of conflict and fragility, and then summarize a series of conclusions, drawing on the previous chapters of the entire book.

Dysfunctions and Challenges in the Peacebuilding Field

Peacebuilding is broadly defined to embrace violence prevention, peacemaking, peace keeping, and post-war reconciliation and consolidation of peace. These efforts are, in many ways, part of an ancient undertaking, which includes venerable practices of diplomacy, informal and formal go-betweens, inter-group mediation, and other forms of conflict resolution that are as old as human civilization. Yet peacebuilding is young as a professional and academic field. The field is also quite diverse, embracing individuals and groups from quite local civil society organizations, national-level NGOs, international NGOs, regional organizations, transnational networks of peacebuilders, and people based in multilateral institutions, such as the UN and World Bank, among others. It is difficult, therefore, to offer assessments that apply equally and fairly to all of these organizations and individuals.

Many have offered critiques of the peacebuilding field, questioning the effectiveness of a range of initiatives and programs and even challenging whole subsectors and associated theories of change—or criticizing how international peacebuilders function. [157] The internal and external critiques have been asking whether the peacebuilding professional field is reaching its full potential—and, if not, why not? Perhaps because our ambitions are lofty, but also because our professional tools push us to be self-critical, peacebuilding practitioners tend to engage in regular questioning of our effectiveness, both in terms of achieving results in specific conflict contexts, but also asking whether our efforts are attaining sufficient scale and influence to make a significant and lasting difference in peoples' lives.

In analyzing our case material and developing this book, as we approached the "so what?" question, the issues associated with effectiveness have naturally surfaced—as this has been the central preoccupation of the Reflecting on Peace Practice Project since its inception. In Part I, we presented findings related to key domains of progress, persistent issues, the importance of creating linkages, the appropriate roles of outsiders in attempting to support local peace initiatives, and the functions of leadership in the adding up process. Each of these issues intersects with an analysis of the broad challenges that face the peacebuilding field.

A Systems Thinking Approach to Challenges and Dysfunctions

Readers who have reached this point in this book will not be surprised that we have applied systems thinking to the question of challenges in peacebuilding—in order to understand how multiple forces interact to create both positive and negative effects. The resulting systems map is presented in Figure 6.1. In developing this overview of

---

157 In exploring the critiques of peacebuilding, we have looked back at several key pieces, including, among others, "Towards a Strategic Framework for Peacebuilding: Getting Their Act Together: Overview Report of the Joint Utstein Study of Peacebuilding," Dan Smith, Royal Norwegian Ministry of Foreign Affairs, 2004; "Just Wasting our Time? Provocative Thoughts for Peacebuilders," Simon Fisher & Lada Zimina, Berghof Research Center for Constructive Conflict Management, 2009; *Peaceland: Conflict Resolution and the Everyday Politics of International Intervention.* Séverine Autesserre, Cambridge University Press, 2014.

key factors operating in the peacebuilding field, we drew on and benefitted from the analyses of colleagues already cited (noting changes and improvements over time). We also discovered that our friend and colleague Rob Ricigliano of the Omidyar Group and Nichali Ciaccioa, a graduate student at the University of Wisconsin-Milwaukee, had been developing a similar map in parallel. We have compared our analysis with theirs, finding a substantial amount of overlap, especially with respect to the most salient issues. While our map might appear somewhat complex, theirs has even more detail complexity, far more than we needed for this basic overview.

The "Challenges in the Peacebuilding System" presented in Figure 6.1 is in the form of a causal loop diagram,[158] based on the information in the cumulative cases, our review of multiple authors who have offered critiques (see first footnote in this chapter), as well as our own observations. The purpose of such a diagram or "map" is to show how a range of factors interact to generate a series of effects. The advantages of such a graphic are that a) it can be presented in a fairly condensed fashion, with an accompanying explanation; b) it avoids the trap of trying to establish whether a particular single factor is *the* determining factor (rather, it promotes an understanding of dynamic interactions among multiple factors); and c) it provides the basis for discussing how to transform the system, by looking for "points of leverage" and ways to support elements of positive change already underway. We will now turn to an explanation of the map.

---

158 This form of systems analysis is discussed in detail in Chapter 8. See also Robert Ricigliano, *Making Peace Last: A Toolbox for Sustainable Peacebuilding*, Routledge, 2012; David Peter Stroh, *Systems Thinking For Social Change: A Practical Guide to Solving Complex Problems, Avoiding Unintended Consequences, and Achieving Lasting Results*, Chelsea Green Publishing, 2015.

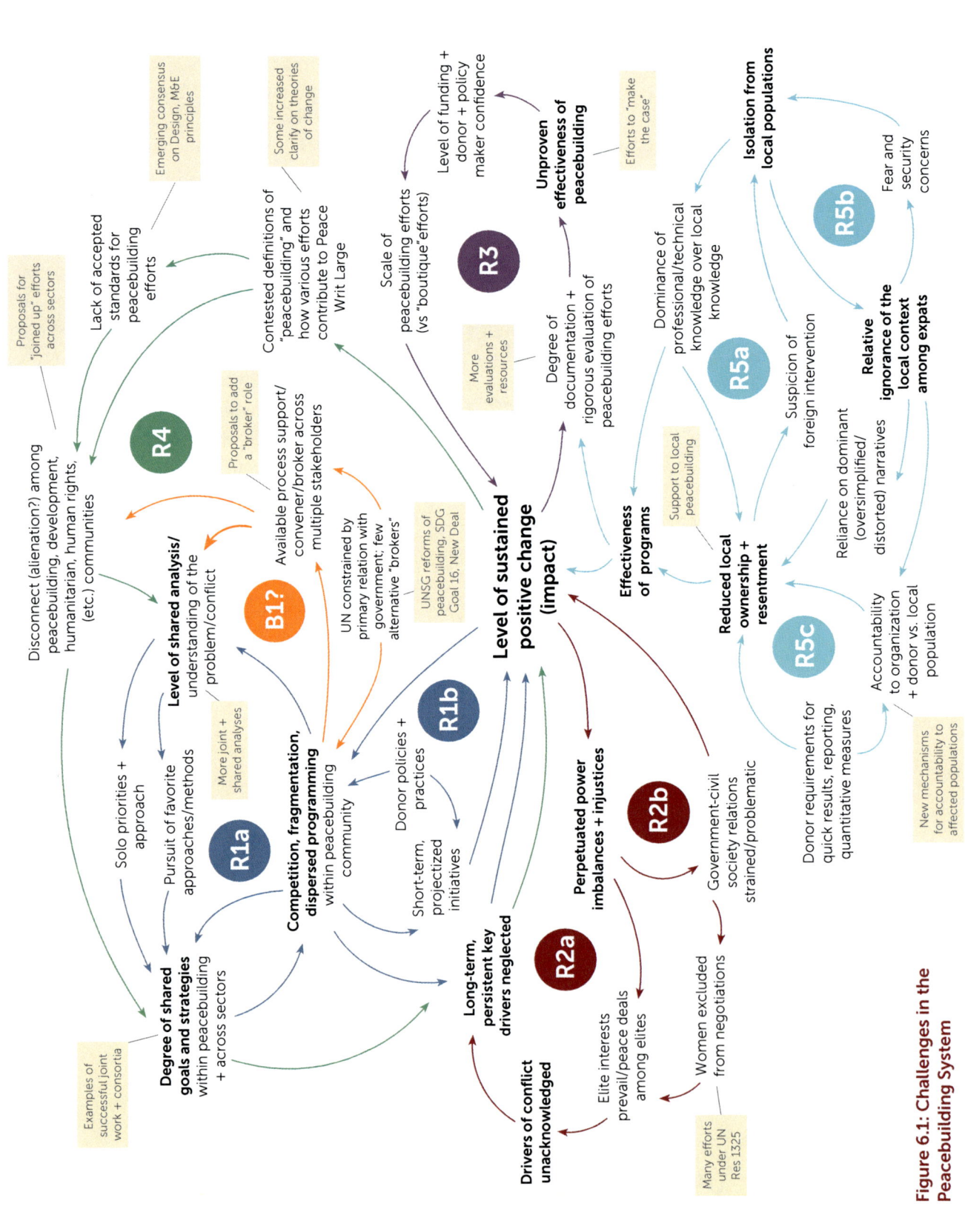

Figure 6.1: Challenges in the Peacebuilding System

Proposals for "joined up" efforts across sectors

Emerging consensus on Design, M&E principles

Some increased clarify on theories of change

Level of funding + donor + policy maker confidence

Efforts to "make the case"

Isolation from local populations

Fear and security concerns

R5b

Lack of accepted standards for peacebuilding efforts

Contested definitions of "peacebuilding" and how various efforts contribute to Peace Writ Large

Unproven effectiveness of peacebuilding

R3

Disconnect (alienation?) among peacebuilding, development, humanitarian, human rights, (etc.) communities

Scale of peacebuilding efforts (vs "boutique" efforts)

Dominance of professional/technical knowledge over local knowledge

R5a

Relative ignorance of the local context among expats

R4

Degree of documentation + rigorous evaluation of peacebuilding efforts

More evaluations + resources

Suspicion of foreign intervention

Proposals to add a "broker" role

B1?

Solo priorities + approach

Available process support/ convener/broker across multiple stakeholders

UN constrained by primary relation with government; few alternative "brokers"

Support to local peacebuilding

Reliance on dominant (oversimplified/ distorted) narratives

Level of shared analysis/ understanding of the problem/conflict

UNSG reforms of peacebuilding, SDG Goal 16, New Deal

Level of sustained positive change (impact)

Effectiveness of programs

Reduced local ownership + resentment

R5c

Pursuit of favorite approaches/methods

Accountability to organization + donor vs. local population

More joint + shared analyses

R1a

Competition, fragmentation, dispersed programming within peacebuilding community

Donor policies + practices

R1b

Short-term, projectized initiatives

Perpetuated power imbalances + injustices

R2b

Government-civil society relations strained/problematic

Donor requirements for quick results, reporting, quantitative measures

New mechanisms for accountability to affected populations

Examples of successful joint work + consortia

Degree of shared goals and strategies within peacebuilding + across sectors

Long-term, persistent key drivers neglected

R2a

Elite interests prevail/peace deals among elites

Women excluded from negotiations

Drivers of conflict unacknowledged

Many efforts under UN Res 1325

The map of Challenges in the Peacebuilding System shows a series of interacting loops—mostly what are called "reinforcing loops" in systems thinking terms—essentially similar to vicious circles. There is at least one "balancing loop" that has potential for providing a counter-balance to a negative dynamic, which we will describe below. Each of the loops is marked with a label: R1, R2, R3... (and one B1). The explanation below will follow those labeled loops. As you will see, many of the factors in the map are expressed as things that can either increase or decrease: thus, the "level of X" or "degree of Y." However, in some cases, for clarity, we have included clear indications of the "lack" of something or persistence of a negative dynamic. Also, the map includes (in blue) a series of efforts underway that represent attempts to mitigate or eliminate some of the challenges.

R1a and R1b: Competition and fragmentation within the peacebuilding community. These two interconnected loops depict dynamics within the peacebuilding field and among peacebuilding organizations.

> **R1a** shows that a pervasive factor of **competition, fragmentation and dispersed programming** leads to lack of a shared analysis among practitioners. The deficit in a shared understanding of the conflict or problem, results in organizations undertaking their own priority efforts and utilizing their favorite approaches—methods that they feel comfortable with, rather than what might be most urgent in the situation. From these "go-it-alone" stances and focus on favorite methods, the result is a limit in the amount of shared goals and strategies, which reinforces the fragmentation and competition, bringing the reinforcing loop back full circle. In terms of helpful efforts, we have seen, in recent years, more joint analyses performed among peacebuilders in specific locations, as well as examples of more effective collaboration through consortia, platforms, etc. However, such collaborative efforts are not yet the norm, as we will discuss further in the next chapter in relation to collective impact.

> **R1b** addresses the issue of the **neglect of fundamental drivers of conflict**. This loop presents a second set of factors that reinforce competition and fragmentation. Prompted partly by donor policies and practices, and exacerbated by competition/fragmentation, practitioners and their organizations undertake short-term projects and neglect long-term efforts to address deeper conflict drivers. As a result, they are unable to generate sustained positive changes, which, again, reinforces competition and dispersed programming—rather than more collaborative efforts concentrated on long-term key drivers of conflict. The **B1** element represents a potential (hence the question mark: B1?) enhanced initiative and role consisting of process support that would facilitate shared analysis and development of shared goals among peace practitioners (and, as we shall see, with other sectors and stakeholders as well). The UN Security Council (see Resolution 2282), General Assembly and Secretary General have made commitments to achieve greater coherence among United Nations

agencies and actors—which could provide greater ability to bring peace actors together. At the same time, proposals have been put forward for a relatively neutral "broker" or convener role that would promote more focused and joined-up initiatives to make a significant difference in key conflicts.[159]

R2a: Perpetuation of power imbalances and injustice. R2a shows how the neglect of long-term, persistent conflict drivers impedes sustained positive change, which, in turn, perpetuates power imbalances and injustice in conflict zones. Those in powerful positions are able to shape peace agreements to ensure that the resulting bargains maintain the interests of political and economic elites. As noted in Chapter 2, those in power are rarely induced to acknowledge the key drivers of conflict—especially where they are privileged by the status quo, even though that situation contains the root causes of conflict. Thus, the key drivers of conflict remain unacknowledged and largely unaddressed by governments, even though civil society and international organizations continue to advocate changes.

R2b: Disconnect from civil society and women. In a related dynamic, R2b suggests that the perpetuation of power and injustice undermines the relationship between government and civil society—that is, they are not included as partners in addressing important conflict issues—resulting in less movement towards positive change. At the same time, women and women's groups (a key component of civil society) are often excluded from negotiations—whereas they have been shown to provide a compelling voice for more equitable solutions and more open acknowledgment of fundamental conflict issues.

R3: Failure to make the case for peacebuilding. R3 focuses on the issues of effectiveness and scale of peacebuilding efforts. The low level of sustained positive changes that can be attributed to peace efforts, results in a lack of rigorous evaluation and documentation, leading to unproven effectiveness of peace efforts—even if the reality is that they are quite valuable. The (perceived) unproven effectiveness of peacebuilding influences the levels of funding for this work and undermines policymaker confidence in the efficacy of peacebuilding. As a result, in many cases, peace work is constrained to relatively small scale or "boutique" projects that do not achieve the magnitude of effort needed to make a significant positive impact. We have noted that the peacebuilding field is making great strides in conducting more consistent and higher quality evaluations (for both learning and accountability) and peace practitioners and their leaders are mobilizing to "make the case" for this young field more forcefully and backed by evidence to policymakers and donors.

R4: Dearth of alliances with other sectors and stakeholders. The analysis notes that the very definition of "peacebuilding" is contested, including debates about how a range of programming contribute to Peace Writ Large (the larger societal peace). Due partly to this lack of clarity, it has been difficult to establish accepted standards for

---

159 As of early 2018, the "Pax Spiral" idea is being developed under the leadership of the Centre for Peace and Conflict Studies, and others are pursing similar initiatives.

peacebuilding efforts (in terms of program analysis and design, theories of change, program logic, etc.). As a result, other sectors operating in the same conflict zones

are often unsure how to relate to the peace efforts, including those engaged in longer term development, humanitarian assistance, human rights, and atrocities prevention, among others.[160] This represents a lost opportunity, as potential synergies are rarely grasped, feeding the dynamics noted in R1a regarding lack of shared analysis and goals, and resulting in the neglect of long-term drivers of conflict and reduced positive impacts. On the positive side, we are seeing more proposals for collaborative efforts across sectors—as well as more joint analysis and shared goals in multi-stakeholder groups and greater openness to collaboration in some multilateral organizations, such as the World Bank. At the same time, the peacebuilding field is beginning to achieve more definitional clarity and standards for design, monitoring, and evaluation are emerging.

R5a, R5b, and R5c: Disconnect between local and international peace actors. This area of the analysis presents concerns regarding the relationships between local people and "outsiders"—as discussed in Chapter 4, and as described by Séverine Autesserre.[161] The essential argument (R5a and R5b) is that some outsiders who arrive with good intentions and want to help the situation find themselves in an international system that discourages meaningful interactions with local populations, and instead relies on technical knowledge rather than local insights. Such outsiders come to accept simplified explanations for conflict and other problems, leading local people to feel suspicion and withhold cooperation with peace initiatives. Meanwhile, (R5c) accountability is often oriented towards donors who typically demand quick results reported in quantitative terms, which further exacerbates the problem. Together, these dynamics result in reduced effectiveness of programs and, therefore, less sustained positive change.

On the positive side, we have seen, within the peacebuilding community and among some donors, greater emphasis on working closely with local leaders and taking the lead from local partners—and there are certainly many examples of effective partnerships between external and internal actors, as discussed in Chapter 4. At the same time, all sectors of international assistance, both donors and operational agencies, have shown a surge of interest in mechanisms for eliciting feedback from "affected populations"—and acting on the information received.[162]

---

160 An exception to this dynamic should be noted: "multi-mandate" organizations (such as CARE, CRS, World Vision) work across development, humanitarian relief, peacebuilding, and, in some cases, human rights. Some of those organizations have managed to integrate peacebuilding into other programming, recognizing that a huge percentage of development and especially humanitarian work takes place in fragile and conflict affected areas. The World Humanitarian Summit of 2016 also acknowledged the close link between conflict issues and relief assistance. At that event, the Peace Promise was signed by 25 UN agencies, humanitarian, development and peacebuilding NGOs, including the World Food Program, UN Development Program and UNICEF, the World Bank and the UN Peacebuilding Support Office. The Peace Promise presented a set of commitments and practical ways to support peace.

161 Autesserre, *Peaceland*.

162 As a follow-on effort to its Listening Project and the *Time to Listen* book, CDA has been providing technical support to the development of feedback loops and accountability to affected populations.

Implications of the Systems Analysis

Although the peacebuilding system still experiences some challenges, it has made progress in the period since some of the earlier critiques from Dan Smith, Simon Fisher and Lada Zamina.[163] As noted in the analysis above, a series of significant initiatives are underway to mitigate some of the negative dynamics—and proposals are being considered for additional actions. On the other hand, many of the dynamics described above and shown in the systems map are structural issues that are difficult to change, since they are embedded in organizational routines and donor policies, as well as the conscious and unconscious habits of interactions between insiders and outsiders. Changing those elements will require open acknowledgment of the issues and joint efforts between donors and their local and international partners.

The deeply-rooted systems of power imbalance, injustice, marginalization, and exclusion that are found in most conflict-affected societies represent knotty long-term problems that will likely require approaches to change associated with nonviolent action and social mobilization that are not the usual tools of the peacebuilding community—although a healthy dialogue between peacebuilding practitioners and nonviolent action experts has begun.[164] Such approaches to change are seldom amenable to direct outside intervention, although external support and solidarity have proven helpful. In the final chapter of this book, we will return to the question of how the peacebuilding community can build stronger and more effective alliances with development and humanitarian actors, as well as with those promoting nonviolent change.

Where to from Here?

Chapters 7 and 8 will address two important issues: how to promote better collaboration among multiple stakeholders to achieve collective impact and how to undertake more useful—and shared—conflict analyses that can be used as the basis for developing shared goals and measures. Chapter 9 will present a summary of action points aimed at addressing many of the challenges described above.

---

163 Cited in first footnote in this chapter.

164 The Alliance for Peacebuilding has initiated these interchanges. For resources regarding nonviolent action, see the International Center on Nonviolent Conflict, Nonviolence International, Peace Brigades International, and Nonviolent Peaceforce, among others.

7

A FRAMEWORK FOR COLLECTIVE IMPACT IN PEACEBUILDING [165,166]

Introduction

As we worked to identify the cross-cutting factors and recurring patterns that would help us understand the notion of cumulative impacts—or factors that contribute to the "adding up" process—we searched the literature for helpful frameworks and concepts. While there is an extensive literature—and theory—about the "coordination" of peacebuilding initiatives (as well as humanitarian and development efforts), we found very little that specifically addressed the mechanisms that promote the adding up process.

We did, however, come across the work of the Collective Impact team at FSG who have been working with organizations in the United States and around the world regarding "better ways to solve social problems."[167] The FSG team has produced several publications that document the experiences of coalitions and campaigns for change, identifying the factors that enable those groups to achieve collective impact.[168] While many of the FSG cases involved domestic U.S. campaigns or coalitions for change, some were larger scale international efforts across several countries, and the same

---

165 This chapter is an adaptation of a paper developed in cooperation with Humanity United, "Framework for Collective Impact in Peacebuilding," Peter Woodrow, CDA, January 2017. As of this writing (January 2018), CDA is engaged in field testing of the framework with partner organizations in several conflict zones, and documenting the actual experienced of coalitions, networks, platforms or consortia for peace, under a grant from Humanity United.

166 While this paper refers to collective impact in "peacebuilding," this term should be understood broadly to include conflict prevention, efforts to promote peace in the midst of war/violent conflict, and post-war consolidation of peace and the prevention of further cycles of violence. It is our assumption, also, that "upstream" conflict prevention efforts ultimately must address the same factors as atrocities prevention. However, the crisis intervention modes in relation to conflict and atrocities may look somewhat different.

167 "FSG is a 501(c)(3) nonprofit consulting firm specializing in strategy, evaluation and research...FSG was originally founded in 2000 as Foundation Strategy Group, and today works across all sectors in every region of the globe...." About FSG (from cover of their publication).

168 Kania, John and Mark Kramer, "Collective Impact." *Stanford Social Innovation Review*: 36-41, 2011. "Embracing Emergence: How Collective Impact Addresses Complexity." John Kania and Mark Kramer, Stanford Innovation Review, January 2012. "Channeling Change: Making Collective Impact Work." Fay Hanleybrown, John Kania, and Mark Kramer, *Stanford Social Innovation Review*, January 2013

principles appeared to apply. We were interested to see how FSG's conditions for collective impact might correspond to achieving cumulative impacts towards peace—or how the FSG concepts might be adapted to situations of intense conflict and inter-agency competition. Much of this chapter is devoted to adapting the basic FSG approach to the peacebuilding context.

Before we delve more deeply into the necessary conditions for collective impact, we should acknowledge an important difference between *collective* impacts (per FSG) and *cumulative* impacts, the focus of the RPP cumulative impact case studies. FSG has been examining the results from groups that self-consciously decided to harness the work of multiple organizations to achieve a common set of goals. Although such coalitions often involved many different types of organizations, they were able to agree on the elements necessary to achieve shared goals. On the other hand, cumulative impacts (as explored in the RPP cases) may be attained, over time, by groups working independently without any reference or even awareness of each other. Work in separate realms of action somehow adds up to progress towards peace, despite relative incoherence among actors. In fact, this mysterious "adding up" process was the main motivation for undertaking the study.

In most of the situations we analyzed through the case studies, there was no agreed-upon agenda. In fact, the very nature of conflict suggests competing agendas—even among those dedicated to reducing war and violence. In most conflict settings, many groups were working towards an ill-defined goal of "peace," including government entities, UN bodies, the business community, and a myriad of NGOs and civil society organizations. These groups rarely worked in concert, except for limited objectives during short periods. For instance, we have seen examples of successful concerted action lasting several months to achieve an open, transparent and violence-free election, such as in Burundi and Kenya. However, in most cases, even the first condition for collective impact is not met, as the "common agenda" for peace is understood only in vague terms. The groups working for peace seldom define it in the same ways or even come to agreement on the important drivers of conflict.

Despite the differences between the relatively incoherent, even chaotic, processes of cumulative impact/adding up to peace and the more self-conscious, organized and deliberate efforts for collective impact, the framework suggested by FSG has proven useful for examining the adding up process. In fact, we would contend that there is an urgent need for groups dedicated to peace in specific settings to work in a more coherent and aligned manner to achieve the desired collective impact of peacebuilding as a field. We will return to this issue in the final chapter of this book, in which we return to the broad challenges confronting the peacebuilding endeavor as described in Chapter 6.

Proposed Model or Framework for Collective Impact

Models can be dangerous. If misused or misinterpreted, they can suggest that there is a formula or set series of steps that, if followed faithfully, will lead to predictable results. In the peacebuilding and conflict prevention arena, this is an absurd notion. Conflict contexts are extremely varied and dynamic, requiring constant renewal of analyses and adaptive management in response to changing conditions and learning in response to actions for peace. In fact, the overall "model" for effective peacebuilding should embody adaptive management in relation to constantly updated and systemic analysis of the key drivers of conflict. We suggest that the concept of a "framework" implies greater flexibility than a "model"—and have used that language in this chapter.

This proposed Framework aims to achieve a clear goal: greater impact from collective efforts towards a specific set of shared peace goals. That is, even if peace practitioners improve the effectiveness of their individual programmatic actions, collectively, they are not likely to achieve sufficient impacts at a systemic level. Hence the need for a framework for collective impact to help ensure that disparate actions by multiple dedicated actors become mutually supportive and create effective synergies to accelerate and sustain progress towards durable peace. We should note, however, that we do not expect that a large number of organizations will voluntarily join collective action efforts. The Framework would apply to those groups that do agree to work together towards shared, attainable goals.

As noted, in developing this Framework for Collective Impact in Peacebuilding, we started with the Collective Impact model provided by FSG in a series of articles in the Stanford Social Innovation Review.[169] In doing so, we recognize that the FSG approach has certain limitations, while it also benefits from many years of experience among networks dedicated to justice and peace in many dimensions, mostly within the United States context plus a few international examples. Some experienced experts in coalition building and networking have offered critiques of the Collective Impact model—and we have accounted for those critiques in offering this Framework for Collective Impact in Peacebuilding.[170]

As we shall see, the Collective Impact model needs significant adaptation and adjustment to make it applicable to the peacebuilding context, as even the minimum criteria or preconditions for collective impact, as suggested by FSG, are rarely entirely met in conflict zones. We also completed a literature review to identify other possible approaches to collective action and/or coordination that could complement (or contradict) the FSG framework.[171] While the available research and commentaries are

169 See previous footnote.

170 See, for example, Tom Wolff, "Ten Places Where Collective Impact Gets It Wrong," *Global Journal of Community Psychology Practice,* March 2016.

171 See Marin O'Brien Belhoussein, "Developing a Model for Collective Impact for Conflict Prevention and Peacebuilding: Summary of Initial Findings," CDA Collaborative Learning Projects, May 2016.

neither extensive nor deep, some useful ideas and cautions emerged—and these have been incorporated into the Framework as presented below.[172]

Who might use this Framework? As we elaborate the elements of a Framework, we imagine a range of entities that might use it, including:

- An emerging coalition or network of local organizations wishing to increase the results of their peace efforts.

- An international peacebuilding NGO, private foundation or coalition/consortium intending to support local actors and organizations to undertake complementary actions and/or to supplement official peace processes.

- A donor or group of donors wishing to increase the effectiveness of their grantmaking and/or the impacts of grant recipients.

- A UN official, UN agency, or regional intergovernmental organization (e.g., a Special Representative of the Secretary General or UN Resident Coordinator or UN Peacebuilding Fund/Commission) wishing to a) improve the impacts of the UN "family" itself; and/or b) increase effectiveness of the international community as a whole or regional initiatives in relation to a peace process or post-violence peacebuilding efforts.

- A government peace commission or ministry tasked with consolidating peace or preventing future violent conflict.

Each of these entities faces a common challenge: how to harness the energies and initiatives of multiple groups and individuals towards achievement of the shared goal of durable peace. While applications of the framework by these different groups must differ in important respects, the fundamental tasks remain similar.

Fundamental Principles Supporting Collective Impact in Peacebuilding

Before delving further into the Framework for collective impact, we offer the following summary of key principles that should inform any effort to promote greater collaboration and cooperation among peace actors. These are consistent with principles that have evolved from CDA's own involvements over twenty years—and have been validated in the lively discussion among practitioners and academics during our consultation on the draft Framework.

1. **Local actors and organizations must drive and control collective impact efforts.** The role of external organizations is to provide support and reflections from other experiences. *Pay attention to issues of power, privilege, and control.*

---

172 As a key step in developing this Framework, we shared a draft with a range of colleagues and convened a one-day consultation in Washington. This current Framework incorporates feedback received.

2. **All organizations, especially "outsiders," must recognize their own interests, motivations, and agendas**—*and be as transparent as possible about them.* Coalitions and networks that are able to discuss values and culture openly will be stronger.

3. **Legitimate and inclusive bottom-up processes** are more likely to achieve sustained successes than initiatives driven from the top or externally.

4. **Vertical and horizontal linkages, must be built into collective initiatives,** both within and outside of a network.[173]

5. **Learning processes must provide the core of collective impact processes.** Flows of information, analyses, and responses are crucial activities across participating organizations.

6. **How funding is provided and how accountability is structured both influence the ability to promote collective impact.** Accountability should be to those most affected by war and violence. *Longer-term commitments to key issues are important.*

7. **Inclusivity must be a consideration from the beginning**—balanced with ensuring the ability to act and achieve a "sufficient" group of organizations operating from a common agenda. A group that is too large and represents divergent interests may not achieve adequate agreement on shared analysis and goals. A somewhat smaller group with clear common objectives may be more effective.

8. **Participatory analysis must include as many perspectives as practical and be updated regularly**—using systems tools and supporting an adaptive and learning approach to programming.

9. **Efforts must be must be motivated by the importance of the issues, durability, sustainability, and achievability**—rather than "urgency," which can lead to short-term and transitory efforts with no lasting effects on fundamental drivers of conflict.

10. **Incremental building of the collective action is advised**—with room for reconfiguring (adding and dropping organizations) over time and phases of action.

11. **Identify the incentives for participating in collective impact** for peacebuilding. Apart from the preliminary considerations, preconditions and five core conditions for collective impact discussed below, adherence to these principles is paramount.

---

173 See Chapter 3 for a thorough discussion of linkages.

Preliminary Considerations

Overall proposed approach

The proposed Framework assumes application of two essential approaches to achieving collective action and impact in peacebuilding:

A systemic understanding of conflict dynamics and how to change the system. Conflict analysis must push beyond traditional frameworks and tools to add a systems dimension taking into account the complexity and interaction among conflict factors. We have most frequently used systems thinking and tools for ongoing and repeated mapping of conflict, although other tools are available. Conflict mapping/analysis is necessary but not sufficient; tools for identifying points of leverage and ways to induce positive change in conflict systems are also needed.[174] Thus we suggest use of a range of tools for ensuring that analysis is translated into robust and operational strategies. (Systems thinking tools for conflict analysis are explored in Chapter 8.)

An adaptive management approach to program planning and implementation. Colleagues engaged in the development and humanitarian relief arenas are increasingly trying to move away from rigid programming regimes (such as results-based management and the ubiquitous logframe). The need for flexible and adaptive action is even more pronounced for peacebuilding, where there are no proven methods for change, and the objects of change (conflict dynamics) are in constant flux. Adaptive management requires frequently updated conflict analysis, a regular flow of information/feedback regarding the effects and results of program activities, and program management structures that are designed to respond to conflict analysis and feedback.

Each of these principles has been the subject of considerable debate as well as recent elaboration and identification of specific tools and methods; we are simply restating them here to note that they inform the rest of the Framework.

Initial Assessment and Strategy Development

Before engaging fully in the process of collective impact among multiple organizations, several preliminary actions are needed, to ensure that a collaborative effort is well conceived, targeted and resourced. These are outlined below and include 1) initial stakeholder mapping to identify the potential range of stakeholders that could be involved; 2) identification/convening of a sufficient network, in terms of size, strength, and diversity; 3) performance of a preliminary conflict analysis; 4) initial decision

---

174 Other useful analytical tools include actor/stakeholder analysis, Do No Harm/conflict sensitivity analysis, power analysis, and political-economy analysis.

regarding the appropriate level of collective action (local, national, regional, etc.); and 5) preliminary determination of the intended focus and scope of collective impact efforts. At this stage, all actions and products are provisional; they will evolve and change over time, as the process unfolds.

1. Initial stakeholder mapping

Preliminary exploration involves identification of the important stakeholders involved, including both those actively promoting peace and those engaged in ongoing violence or who are otherwise direct parties to the conflict. Stakeholder or actor mapping identifies the parties to the conflict, their interests, demands, sources of power, and so forth. A complementary mapping analyzes the groups and key individuals working for peace, showing who is doing what, where, and addressing which issues.

This stakeholder mapping permits preliminary determination of the range of possible partners in collective efforts, including existing networks or coalitions and their strengths.

2. Identification or convening of a "sufficient" network or coalition of interested groups

Although the composition of the group(s) will likely change over time through an iterative process, it is necessary to work with a network that has sufficient reach, both vertically (local to international) and horizontally (across sectors, perspectives, and geography) to enable consideration of the questions involved in these initial stages. Subsequent discussions may result in narrowing or expanding of the network, depending partly on the chosen focus (topic, problem, issue, geographic area) and the groups that express interest in joining a collective effort. From the beginning, it will also be necessary to address issues of power and decision-making, to guarantee that, to the extent possible, local actors control the process, and that external actors and funders do not determine or undermine the agenda. In pulling together an initial grouping, it will also be necessary to assess whether there is sufficient trust to sustain the group through difficult processes and challenges.

3. Preliminary conflict analysis

The FSG framework calls for the development of a "shared understanding" of the problem (or problems) at hand. (This will be addressed below and in Chapter 8, as an important component of the FSG condition for a "common agenda.") Even before launching a new collective initiative, it will be important to understand the conflict context. In most conflict settings, there is existing knowledge that can be identified and built upon; local and international groups have performed conflict analyses, and some are willing to share those or have posted them online. If few such analyses are available or are deemed out-of-date or inadequate, a preliminary analysis engaging multiple local stakeholders will be necessary. Involving a wide range of actors from the beginning will build local ownership of the process.

4. Decisions regarding the level of collective action

CDA's own research has explored the connections between local or community level work on "peace writ little" and efforts at the larger Peace Writ Large level, which could be subnational (province, state, etc.), national, or involve international regional dynamics.[175] Collective impacts can be understood at any of these levels, although the stakeholders involved and objectives would vary at different levels.

> Coalitions or networks dedicated to promoting peace could involve a range of levels, including any of the following, or combinations of them:
>
> Local level coalitions/networks
>
> National level coalition/networks
>
> Networks or coordination efforts among international donors
>
> An international donor and its grantees
>
> Government peace efforts/commissions (with/without international support)

Quite apart from the conflicting parties themselves, any of these categories could involve civil society organizations, community-based organizations, national or international NGOs, local/international businesses, national governments, regional intergovernmental organizations, UN agencies/officials, and bilateral/multilateral donors.

Each of these levels represents a different degree of difficulty involved in promoting collective impacts. Organizing for collective impact involves a considerable investment of time and other resources—so the added value of attaining shared goals must justify the effort. Work with an entirely local group of organizations, even with support from international partners and donors, would be relatively straightforward, compared with efforts to organize a national level coalition among peacebuilding groups. Efforts among multiple bilateral donors, while involving a relatively small number of entities, would be complicated by their varied program priorities, bureaucratic and decision-making processes, and predetermined funding mandates from parliaments or the equivalent.

5. Preliminary determination of focus and scope

In addition to the level and range of stakeholders or partners involved, a preliminary question concerns the scope/scale of the core issue(s) to be addressed—and gaining agreement on them. (Note: this must be preliminary, as the process of group formation and determination of focus/scope will be iterative and emergent.)

In our experience working with groups of organizations in the field, the most effective joint efforts focus on a relatively discrete and time-bound issue—although

---

175 See *Confronting War* and Chapter 3 on Linkages.

such endeavors can be embedded in a larger and longer-term strategy towards a clear shared vision and concrete goals. Combined work on "peace" or some other lofty long-term goal usually fails due to vagueness and lack of clear outcomes. At the other extreme, efforts focused on a narrow set of activities rarely result in any systemic impact. Therefore, collective impact initiatives must identify achievable objectives that represents significant contributions or stepping stones towards Peace Writ Large, but not so ambitious as to be unrealistic or too focused on the long term.

In terms of the timeframe, in several places (Kenya, Ghana, Burundi, Guinea-Bissau) we have seen successful short-term collective efforts dedicated to achieving a violence-free election, in which organizations joined in a coalition, secured joint short-term funding, outlined a series of joint activities, assigned specific activities to different organizations, and even divided up territory to ensure geographic coverage of the country. Examples of longer-term efforts exist, but their successes have been less clear.[176] The challenge, therefore, is to undertake a series of shorter term efforts (one to three years) that are each an integral element of a longer-term vision and sustained strategy.

6. "Go/No-Go" decision

After exploring each of the five areas above, it is important to decide whether there is sufficient interest, shared understanding, and confluence of vision or goals to warrant dedication of focused energy, time and resources to an effort towards collective impact.

Conducive Environment for Collective Impact: Leadership, Funding, & Sense of Importance

FSG posits three important *preconditions* that should be established before launching a collective impact effort—which we have renamed as a "conducive environment." In FSG's terminology, the preconditions include "an influential champion; adequate financial resources, and a sense of urgency for change."[177] We have recast these as "leadership, adequate financial resources, and sense of the importance of sustained change." Even before we approach the five core conditions for impact in the next section, these elements represent real challenges for peacebuilding activities.

Leadership

In most situations of war and conflict, there is either no single outstanding champion for peace—or there are multiple competing champions. Overt leadership for peace is more likely to appear during a peace*making* phase—efforts to end violence and reach some form of settlement. In these circumstances, leadership can be provided to either

---

176 Marin O'Brien Belhoussein's review (op. cit.) provides quick summaries of ten selected examples of relatively successful coordination.
177 "Channeling Change," p.3.

build bridges between contending groups or to help articulate an emerging consensus among groups participating in various forms of dialogue or negotiation.

In the RPP cumulative cases, we have seen examples where an international/regional power or group (such as in Burundi, Guatemala and Solomon Islands) or a prominent individual has performed a key leadership role (such as Mandela in the Burundi case, and a Scandinavian businessman in the Aceh case). But we have also seen situations where such leaders ultimately fail for a range of reasons. The Oslo Accords process, involving leaders from Israel and Palestine and spearheaded by Norway, is an example where initial success was undermined by conditions on the ground. Kofi Annan spearheaded the proposed Cyprus agreement, which failed to pass a referendum on the Greek Cypriote side; he had more success in Kenya in 2008.

In some situations, the UN mounts a major peace*keeping* and peace*building* operation, as in Liberia, Kosovo, East Timor, and Haiti. However, even when the UN is playing a central role, to the point of essentially running the country (Kosovo, Liberia, East Timor), its ability to generate a common agenda, even among its own agencies, is limited. Bureaucratic instruments (including the UN Development Assistance Framework, Integrated Strategic Framework, Poverty Reduction Strategy, Peacebuilding Fund/Commission, etc.) provide the basis for building a common agenda, but those opportunities are often squandered.

In most conflict contexts, it will be useful to identify different forms of leadership in different substantive areas or to address specific key factors of conflict, rather than looking for one champion to deal with the full complex array of issues. From a systems thinking perspective, we can also consider the notion that "systems change best when systems change themselves." That is, effective systems change often involves leadership from within the system—or at least someone who can activate internal people or forces to generate and sustain change. This is consistent with the first and second principles from the beginning of this Framework that call for locally led efforts for peace, complemented by appropriate roles for outsiders.

Experience suggests that it would be effective to undertake more narrowly-focused campaigns with specific objectives to be achieved within relatively short time frames, yet conceived as building on each other within a longer-term strategy. In these cases, an influential leader could inspire groups to join a campaign and articulate how the relatively narrow goals would fit within a larger vision and strategy for Peace Writ Large.

Adequate financial resources

In conflict prevention or post-war peacebuilding efforts, a wide array of issues need to be dealt with over time—as discussed at length in Chapter 2 and depicted in the factor tree tool. Together, the key high-level elements needed for sustained peace represent an ambitious agenda for change. Unfortunately, even if donors (and governments) agree on the issues, obtaining long-term commitment of funding for fundamental change processes is difficult. Thus, this requirement represents a challenge for funding peace activities at all phases, especially for prevention.

In the run-up to a peace agreement or a series of smaller accords, most funding is channeled to *humanitarian* assistance, with only small amounts extended to building support for peace. There tends to be a burst of funding for a wide range of activities during the immediate post-violence phase of "peace consolidation." But this funding tends to be relatively short term, generally up to three years, is rarely sustained for the long term, and usually fails to address key drivers of conflict, as we have already noted.

FSG points out that, once underway, a collective impact effort "can last a decade or more...Collective impact is a marathon, not a sprint. There is no shortcut in the long-term process of social change."[178] In order to address the fundamental problems that generated violent conflict in the first place, long-term commitment is needed, and is seldom available. Therefore, funding must be sufficient in *amount* to get the work done, and sustained enough to address issues over a decade or more. This suggests that part of the collective impact process will be to generate financing processes that are not permanently dependent on external funding.

Sense of the importance of sustained change

As noted immediately above, in peace efforts, there is usually a sense of urgency to stop violence through ceasefires and development of a peace settlement or an incremental series of agreements. This sense of urgency often continues through a brief period of "peace consolidation." Typically, once the situation has reached a degree of stability, the international community feels that its work is done, attention is diverted to another crisis, and funding dries up. In some situations, the peace process falters or becomes distorted by power players, which can undermine its legitimacy and vitality. The peace commitment must be sustained beyond short-term urgency and oriented towards sustained efforts for durable change.

There is a short window of opportunity, immediately following the signing of a peace accord for about three years, when weariness with war and widespread acknowledgment of serious problems can create momentum for change and provide the conducive environment needed. At the same time, there is often a strong push for "normalcy," a sense that conditions have returned to a tolerable state, and that the government is in charge of the situation—which typically results in active discounting of key conflict drivers. Peacebuilding actors must, therefore, focus energy, not so much on urgent action, but rather on long-term commitment to addressing the fundamental causes of conflict—the unfinished business described in Chapter 1. These cannot be confronted with speed or demands for immediate results. "Urgency with patience" is needed, as the issues to be addressed are usually deeply embedded in political culture, social norms and economic systems. Preventing a new cycle of violence must be a priority.

---

178 "Channeling Change," p. 4.

The commitment to change in a post-violence period is attenuated by the desire by governments to assert control and project the image of a return to normal life. Unfortunately, in many settings, "normal" conditions include inequitable distribution of resources, neglect of large portions of the population, marginalization/exclusion, favoritism, corruption, and elite power struggles (among other things). "Business as usual" implies ignoring the factors that resulted in warfare in the first place. A challenge for peacebuilders is to promote an acknowledgment of such key drivers of conflict, and to engage in longer term prevention and development programming that addresses them.

The Five Conditions for Collective Impact

FSG presents five basic conditions that must be met in order to achieve collective impact—and these are explored below.[179] These include:

Common Agenda

Shared Measurement

Mutually Reinforcing Activities

Continuous Communication

Backbone Support

As noted, the FSG model needs significant adjustment to make it applicable in the context of conflict prevention and peacebuilding. We have determined that it is necessary to change these basic categories (and subcategories) of the five conditions to make them more appropriate and applicable to conflict prevention and peacebuilding. The following reframing of the five conditions is suggested—and incorporated into the subsequent discussion below:

1. **Collective & Emergent Understanding** (ongoing conflict analysis, assessing the degree of progress, who is doing what)

2. **Collective Intention & Action** (common agenda, level/scope of action, core strategy, mutually reinforcing activities, division of labor, common measures)

3. **Collective Learning & Adaptive Management** (seek regular feedback regarding common measures, adjust actions accordingly, emphasize mutual learning)

4. **Continuous Communication & Accountability** (continuous data sharing, exchange of experiences, reflection)

5. **Sufficient Support Structures** ("backbone" support)

An important overarching comment is needed: *There can be no generic formula for addressing these conditions; the approach, methods, and processes must be adapted to the specific political, economic and social context.* What might work in one setting

---

179 See FSG articles cited in footnote at the beginning of this chapter.

might seriously backfire in another. Therefore, while the overall categories and subtopics will be important in almost all settings, exactly how to accomplish them will vary considerably. As noted in the first principle at the beginning of this chapter, local people and organizations must drive the process—including deciding whether and how to address these conditions.

The table below presents each of the five conditions (in our revised framing), suggests potential activities for advancing that dimension, identifies potential constraints and challenges, and offers some ideas for mitigating those challenges.

Putting the Framework into Practice

This Framework draws on the FSG approach and the RPP cumulative case findings (as presented in Part I), while also building on RPP's experience working with many practitioners and organizations in the field. Nevertheless, further exploration and applications are needed to validate and refine the Framework. The authors and our colleagues will be publishing additional reflections, as we learn more, based on field applications and case studies.

Table 7.1: Exploring the Five Conditions for Collective Impact

Collective Impact Condition	Possible Activities in Peacebuilding Contexts	Constraints & Challenges	Potential Mitigating Action(s)
1. Collective & Emergent Understanding: engage in ongoing process of joint conflict analysis and tracking progress			
A. Develop a shared understanding/ analysis	Perform joint conflict analysis and conflict mapping and/or share existing analyses that identify key drivers of conflict.	The basic framing of the conflict is, itself, often contested. Not all stakeholders are able/willing to engage in joint analysis. Some analyses are not shared. Are all voices/perspectives represented in the analysis? Who "owns" the analysis?	Work only with publicly available documents. Work with contesting parties separately, then combine. Confidential third-party amalgamation of analyses.
B. Assess current conditions of progress on key driving factors and/ or elements of positive change	In addition to conflict analysis, assess the degree of progress (or lack thereof) in key areas of change needed (use of "Peace Progress Factor Tree" tool—see Chapter 2).	Different perceptions of progress and different assessments of what is most important to address, based on interests and experience.	Engage in dialogue about progress made and priorities for action as fundamental exercise in building a coalition/network.

Collective Impact Condition	Possible Activities in Peacebuilding Contexts	Constraints & Challenges	Potential Mitigating Action(s)
C. Map who is doing what—and what has already been tried, with what results	Based on the key drivers and areas of progress or lack thereof (see #1A and #1B), identify which organizations are working on which issues and where there are significant gaps in the number and/or scale of efforts for change. Analyze the success or failure of previous change efforts.	Some activities are, by necessity, confidential or off-the-record. The number of different actors is often enormous—making it difficult to gain a full picture of all efforts. There are likely contending interpretations or analysis of the success/failure of previous efforts.	Map at least the most significant efforts, taking care to note locally-driven efforts that may be less visible. Develop more complete information over time.
D. Repeat/update analysis on a regular basis	Update joint analysis regularly, as a "normal" element of group activities	Time constraints	
2. Collective Intention & Action: develop a common agenda, core strategy, action plan and shared measures			
A. Develop a shared vision and goals	Identify a common, long-term vision and a series of achievable intermediate goals or building blocks. Build relationships of trust and open communication, including willingness to acknowledge challenges and blockages.	The contrasting visions for the future and "peace" may be central to the conflict. Underlying issues regarding inclusion/exclusion, grievances, models of power holding, and equity/justice may impede a shared vision, even among peace proponents. Even if a shared vision is achieved, designation of building blocks or intermediate steps may be difficult.	Agree to principles driving a vision first, then how those would apply in the context. Determine incremental steps towards the vision, rather than major leaps—break issues down into doable parts. Plan 'backwards' from a significant achievement to how we got there. Work with those who are willing to join a collective effort.
B. Adopt a common overall approach, strategy and theories of change	Within an identified vision and goals, develop a strategy for achieving intermediate goals and an accompanying theory of change.	The system will push back or resist change efforts.	Address system pushback in planning. Ensure that "harm" is not done. Adopt an adaptive management approach to respond to progress, failures and unexpected events. (See #3D)

Collective Impact Condition	Possible Activities in Peacebuilding Contexts	Constraints & Challenges	Potential Mitigating Action(s)
C. Determine priority areas for action	Use the various forms of analysis in #1A, #1B and #1C to identify priority areas for action—especially issues or groups that have been neglected.	Determination of needed scale of efforts often a stretch for organizations accustomed to modest programs.	Engage in exercises that free up imagination and innovation. Work with donors to provide resources for scaling up.
D. Differentiate tasks/ roles	Use analytical information to identify who is best placed to do tasks, based on experience, capacities, mandates, skills, access, etc. Explore potential linkages and synergies across efforts.	Agencies may compete now or previously. May be hard to openly discuss capacities. Some may be attached to dubious theories of change (favorite methods).	Emphasis mutual learning, based on evidence (hence common measures).
E. Coordinate a plan of action, if possible	Build on the differentiated tasks/roles (above), develop an action plan: who will do what, by when, with what resources.	Organizations may resist perceived centralized control or erosion of independence.	Core purpose of coalition and goal of collective impact—requires some level of coordination and adjustment to achieve common agenda.
F. Identify shared measures, based on action plan and theories of change: ongoing monitoring	What changes can reasonably be expected from collective activities over what period of time? How can those be measured? How can we track other (unexpected / unintended) effects?	Participants may disagree about what is important to track. Issues of security and access in conflict zones may impede accurate data collection.	Use local organizations for data collection. Build local capacities for survey research and feedback. Utilize crowd sourcing and other emerging technologies. Develop baselines.
3. Collective Learning & Adaptive Management: seek regular feedback, adjust actions accordingly, adopt shared measures			
A. Engage in ongoing process of collaborative learning	Organize processes of mutual reflection/learning to inform further implementation and to capture lessons to inform other efforts.	Time constraints. Distrust or lack of openness to discuss "failures" as well as successes.	Build learning processes into programming, provide useful feedback on a regular basis

Collective Impact Condition	Possible Activities in Peacebuilding Contexts	Constraints & Challenges	Potential Mitigating Action(s)
B. Collect feedback and analyze data	Analyze together information gathered from shared measures (#2F above). Elicit perceptions and opinions from a full range of stakeholders.	Participants may disagree about expected changes—and how to interpret data.	Provide for external evaluation and/or expert review of data.
C. Evaluate regularly	Engage in ongoing monitoring and evaluation processes. Periodically gather additional information and feedback, using a mix of qualitative and quantitative methods, revealing both expected and unexpected changes. Repeat application of Peace Progress Factor Tree to track advances.	Often deemed a low priority for budget allocation or an afterthought.	Build evaluation into the overall strategy, combined with other forms of ongoing feedback.
D. Engage in adaptive management	Use monitoring data, evaluation results and feedback to discuss needed adjustments in program approaches and theories of change.	Some organizations and/or donors may be committed to specific strategies, actions or outputs.	Gain prior commitment from participating organizations and their donors for an adaptive management approach, with clear accountability mechanisms.
4. Continuous Communication & Accountability			
A. Engage in mutual accountability	Use information gathered to track progress towards mutual goals and/or to work together to adjust strategies and activities in response to feedback/data	Participants may resist mutual accountability, preferring independence. Some may question accuracy of data, especially if it contradicts their favored methodologies or approaches. Some donors may refuse to change deliverables or methods.	Address mutual accountability from the beginning of network or coalition formation: meaning, process, decision-making, use of data. Encourage experimental attitude, testing theories of change together. Avoid blame. Educate donors and make them part of the adaptive management process.

Collective Impact Condition	Possible Activities in Peacebuilding Contexts	Constraints & Challenges	Potential Mitigating Action(s)
B. Set transparent mechanisms for ongoing internal communication	Ensure a platform for open exchange among members, ongoing decision-making, addressing concerns, sharing of information, and planning.	Member time constraints. Potential for misunderstandings or miscommunication regarding important decisions. Tensions may arise between "insiders" (local entities) and "outsiders."	Use transparent processes for information sharing + decision-making. Engage in frank dialogue about appropriate roles for insiders and outsiders, ensure that outsiders support insider initiatives.
C. Set mechanisms for ongoing external communications	Identify important external stakeholders and constituencies (publics), the information they need and how it will be provided.		
D. Review plans/ results periodically	Organize occasions to examine data/feedback received and analyzed (see #2F and #3 above), and engage in further planning and adjustments needed.	Time constraints. Possible questioning of data/feedback. Resistance to adjusting plans (by partners or donors).	
5. Sufficient Support Structures (backbone support)			
A. Identify organization(s) to provide staff support for a "secretariat" or backbone function	Coordination of activities among partners: convening regular meetings; ensuring decision-making; undertaking planning, data collection, and communications; fundraising—and other activities outlined above.	Resistance to perceived central control. Competition among members for leadership role and/ or associated funding. Perceptions of bias or a hidden agenda.	Explore multiple options for this function: single organization, several organizations, a coordination group, rotating role. Keep structures light/non-bureaucratic and flexible.

8

STRIVING FOR SHARED ANALYSIS USING SYSTEMS THINKING TOOLS

Promoting Joint Analyses or Shared Understanding of Conflicts

The previous chapter on the collective impact of peacebuilding notes a need for "shared analysis" or shared understanding of the problem—as one of the requirements for achieving greater collective impact towards peace. The issue of conflict analysis—including joint analyses across multiple organizations and individuals—has been a preoccupation of the Reflecting on Peace Practice Project since the earlier phase (1999-2003). We have devoted considerable time and energy to exploring the nature of the difficulty with analytical processes, what constitutes better analysis, and how to promote shared analyses as suggested in the collective impact models.[180]

This chapter will review our essential findings on this important topic, drawing primarily on our direct experience working with practitioners in the field and in training workshops. That said, all of the cumulative cases that are the focus for Part I of this book engaged in conflict analysis—and some case writers used sytems thinking in presenting their understanding of the conflicts, based on extensive interviews in the field.

Critiques of Existing Conflict Analysis Frameworks and Analyses Processes

During the first phase of RPP, in subsequent field applications, and further elaboration of the findings (since 2003), peace practitioners raised an important dilemma that drove us to further explore systems thinking and tools for conflict analysis. This issue was reflected in the finding in *Confronting War* that there was no apparent relationship between the amount or even the quality of conflict analysis performed and the effectiveness of programming. Universally, practitioners agreed that conflict

---

180 RPP guidance on conflict analysis is provided in the Advanced RPP training program (also known as "RPP II") and "Designing Strategic Initiatives to Impact Conflict Systems: Systems Approaches to Peacebuilding. A Resource Manual." Cambridge, MA: CDA Collaborative Learning Projects, 2016. Available on www.cdacollaborative.org

analysis is crucial to the effectiveness of peacebuilding programming. After all, the more one knows, the more relevant peacebuilding efforts are, and the more likely one is to find productive avenues for promoting peace. Yet some programs seemed to do almost no analysis, yet had significant effects, while some other programs engaged in elaborate forms of rigorous analysis, yet were found to "miss the mark." We were faced with contradictory findings: analysis is crucial, but more or even better analysis does not automatically result in more effective programming. How could these two conclusions both be true?

In field applications and ongoing collaborative learning with practitioners and policy-makers during the second phase of RPP, starting in 2003, we began to understand why and how that could be the case.

Conflict analysis is partial and biased. Many organizations design programs with a favorite methodology or approach already in mind. For those organizations, conflict analysis has little impact on their program design, since they have already decided what they will do. Conflict analysis is used simply to justify their predetermined approach or to confirm their preconceived assumptions.

Conflict analysis is too comprehensive. Many people carry out *context* analysis, believing it to be conflict analysis. Many frameworks for analysis aim to be comprehensive, seeking a broad understanding of all the political, economic and social (historical, environmental, etc.) factors at play in the conflict. Long lists of factors are created, without prioritization or a sense of how the factors work together. As a result, *everything* becomes relevant for peace, and it is difficult to identify which factors influence the conflict the most (as drivers or lynchpins) or how the factors work together.[181]

There is a serious disconnect, in many cases, between analysis performed (even that which is performed well) and actual program strategy and design. Analysis processes and the resulting understandings often remain disconnected from program strategies. Even good analysis processes do not enable people to identify what to do about the situation. Or, as already noted, organizations and practitioners tend to do what they feel most comfortable doing without being guided by analysis. Thus, no amount of analysis will persuade them to do something that might be more relevant or a higher priority, if it lies outside of their comfort zone or most usual organizational approaches.

Conflict analysis is static. In many cases, conflict analysis is performed only one time at the beginning of a program or as a step in developing a program proposal for a funder. The analysis is then set aside and never revisited or updated to inform ongoing program development or adjustment, other than in quite informal ways.

Conflict analysis is often implicit, unstated, and not shared. We found that some practitioners, particularly those who had been working in a particular conflict zone for several years or who were themselves from the area, carry implicit analyses of the conflict

---

181 RPP Training Manual, Schirch, Lisa, *Conflict Assessment and Peacebuilding Planning: Toward a Participatory Approach to Human Security.* Kumarian Press, Boulder, 2013. p. 25.

in their heads. They are constantly adding to it, sifting information, and elaborating on their personal understanding of the conflict and its ongoing evolution. Therefore, some of the more effective programs were informed by such implicit analyses—due to the wisdom of these "walking analysts." However, we also found that their analyses were not always shared, even with their own colleagues. Therefore, program strategies were determined by agency heads or other influential people, without participation by other colleagues or partner organizations. As a result, program or project staff carry out activities without knowing the underlying rationale for those particular engagements and without directives to remain alert for disconfirming information or significant changes in conflict dynamics that should inform program adaptations.

Why Systems Thinking?

At the time of *Confronting War*, RPP had found that no one analysis framework or tool was better than any other—and, in fact, analysis is usually strengthened by applying several types of analytical tools. However, in the period since then, experience with and feedback from practitioners has uncovered a gap, both in the conflict analysis frameworks and tools used, and in how strategy and planning was done. Practitioners around the world felt that current tools were too limited, did not show relationships or priorities, and did not help them reach across sectors.[182] Assumptions and theories of change connecting programs to changes in conflict factors were also weak. In many cases, organizations tended to conduct analyses as though they were not a part of the conflict system, rather their needs and interests were somehow disconnected from the conflict dynamics.

Systems thinking tools appear well-suited to addressing these issues. Such tools can help practitioners move from fragmented analysis (and work) to a greater understanding of the whole conflict system, rather than just its individual parts. If done well, the resulting analysis can avoid being overwhelming or too comprehensive. Systems thinking pushes us to identify *key* factors, relationships and patterns that drive or influence the conflict dynamics, and to analyze the connections among them, and then to feed that understanding into strategy, program design and monitoring and evaluation.[183] Since 2003, RPP has been experimenting with applications of systems thinking tools, including conducting joint conflict analysis processes across multiple organizations, representing a spectrum of perspectives on the conflict in multiple conflict zones.[184]

---

182 Ricigliano, Robert, and Diana Chigas, with AMEX International. *Systems Thinking in Conflict Assessment: Concepts and Applications.* USAID, 2011, p4; Schirch, 23-25.

183 See Schirch p. 23; Ricigliano, p. 4; Stroh, David, "The Systems Dynamics of Identity-Based Conflict," in *The Non-Linearity of Peace Processes: Theory and Practice of Systematic Conflict Transformation.* D. Korppen, N. Ropers, H.J. Giessmann (eds.), Barbara Budrich Publishers: Farmington Hills, MI, 2011. p.169.

184 RPP has facilitated systems mapping of conflicts, in most cases involving multiple individuals or organizations, in Afghanistan, Burundi, Democratic Republic of the Congo, Ghana, Guinea-Bissau, Kenya, Kosovo, Liberia, Mindanao, Rwanda, Serbia, Sri Lanka, South Sudan, Syria, and Yemen. Most recently, we have applied systems thinking tools to analyze corruption in the criminal justice systems of Uganda, Central African Republic and Democratic Republic of the Congo.

The Case for Shared Analysis for Collective Impact

The previous chapter presents five major requirements that must be met in order to achieve collective impact in peacebuilding. A key consideration is *shared analysis of the problem*—in this case, joint analysis of a particular conflict in order to inform joint strategy development. Efforts undertaken during violent warfare to achieve an end to violence and, often, some form of peace settlement, must be considered in a different light from post-agreement activities, in which many groups are working more or less towards consolidating "peace," even if often defined in fuzzy terms.

During hostilities, some groups (including governments) may be active participants in violence and, depending on how they view their options and interests, may resist efforts to bring about durable peace. Based on the nature of the peace accords and the new roles of former belligerents, any successor government may or may not see it as in their interest to address the fundamental key drivers of conflict. (See the discussion in Chapter 2 regarding the need to acknowledge issues, as noted in the Peace Progress Factor Tree.) For instance, in Burundi, the government elected in 2005 was not a party to the peace talks in Arusha that ended the war, and had uncertain commitment to implementing its provisions. This made achievement of a common agenda that included a major player—the government—quite difficult.

The UK Department for International Development (DFID) typically posts its conflict analyses on its website, and the US Agency for International Development (USAID) has shared somewhat sanitized versions of its analyses. In fact, the authors were asked to assist a joint conflict analysis effort by DFID and USAID in South Sudan. The analysis was intended to inform a peacebuilding planning workshop among the partners of both donors. International NGOs, often in cooperation with their local partners, also produce conflict analyses, and increasingly do so across agencies and make the results public. One international NGO, World Vision International, has also produced a conflict analysis framework explicitly designed to be applied in joint analyses involving multiple local and international stakeholders.[185]

Unfortunately, these efforts to achieve a shared understanding of the problem have seldom resulted in anything like a joint approach to problem solving or programming. On occasion, donors who are active in a particular conflict zone have tried to attain a degree of coherence across their funding priorities, but not to the levels that seem to be necessary for collective impact, and not in any consistent manner.

Systems Thinking, Conflict Analysis and Peacebuilding Strategy

The systems thinking tools we have been working with have proven useful for achieving a shared understanding of conflict drivers. Although all groups would not necessarily take the same programming approach, working on the same key driver

---

185 *Making Sense of Turbulent Contexts: Local Perspectives on Large-scale Conflicts,* Michelle Garred, et al, World Vision International, 2015.

of conflict from different, yet still related angles, would be more likely to gain collective impacts.

Systems thinking[186] is a way of understanding reality that emphasizes the *relationships* among a system's parts rather than simply listing the individual parts. It provides language and tools for expressing what many practitioners already know about conflict contexts and about peace practice: that the "parts" of the conflict system—the issues, actors, attitudes, behaviors, institutions, etc.—interact with each other to form a complex dynamic that is not linear—or at least not as linear as suggested by the predominant frameworks and tools for analysis and program design.

Systems thinking is based on a few core principles about how systems function:

The whole is greater than the sum of the parts. Because any element or factor exists in relation to other factors, any part of the system affects and is affected by other components of the system. Changes in one part of the system are likely to produce either positive or negative impacts in other parts. Therefore, it is important to analyze, not only the elements of a system (which are generally more noticeable, because they can usually be seen, felt or heard), but also their interrelationships and the "mental models" or thought processes that accompany them.

> In **Mozambique,** as international assistance has swung from support to the non-governmental sector to focus on the state budget, citizens are concerned that foreign assistance, while intended to support the development of state capacity to provide public services, is helping to strengthen trends toward government hegemony and politicization of the state. This illustrates not only an unintended negative consequence—at a policy level—but also how a seemingly benign effect in one part of the conflict system may have damaging effects elsewhere. (p.62)

Non-linearity. Cause and effect relationships are not linear. In other words, the scale of the "effect" can be unrelated to the scale of a precipitating factor or "cause." We often think of change as a linear process, but the trajectory of change can take a different shape—like a J-curve (things get worse before they get better), a step function (long periods of apparent stagnation before a tipping point), diminishing returns (significant change early on that fades over time), among others. Delayed consequences of actions, indirect effects, and feedback effects can affect how change happens and how quickly. As a result, it is important to understand these dynamic interrelations, in order to plan effectively and gauge or interpret what is happening in the conflict.

> In **Cyprus,** the opening of the check-points at the Green Line, the ceasefire line that kept the two conflicting parties apart and divided the island into north and south, was a turning point in the conflict, "a new era for the Turkish and Greek Cypriots." (Cyprus, 12). But it had the unanticipated effect of weakening support for unification of the island. While crossings to and from North and South helped reduce some old stereotypes and

---

186 Systems thinking is part of the larger field of complexity theory, etc. See bibliography for additional references and resources.

> misperceptions, they did not lead to significant changes in the broader policy realm or a comprehensive settlement. Greater contact led to a "clearer vision of the practical and negative realities that 'there is no political will on either side'" (p.29)

Unintended consequences. Immediate consequences of people's actions are often neutralized or reversed by the long-term unintended consequences of their own actions, as well as those of others. Or, our actions may have unintended negative consequences, based on dynamic reactions in the system. Both the Mozambique and Cyprus examples in the boxed text illustrate the point. The apparently positive development of providing direct support to a more capable government in Mozambique and opening the border between the two sides of the island in Cyprus had unanticipated negative results. Systems maps can be used to project possible consequences or system "push back."

Leverage. Systems evolve and transform as a result of a few key changes sustained over time that have broader effects on other parts of the system; one does not need to address all of the parts.[187] In considering how best to produce change in the conflict system, we can look for "points of leverage"—in other words, specific factors or dynamics that appear susceptible to change, where we can make a difference, and that may stimulate additional changes.

RPP has been using an approach to systems thinking derived from systems dynamics, a highly technical approach developed by Jay Forrester of MIT in the 1960s, and made more user-friendly by Peter Senge, Donella Meadows, David Stroh, and others working in the organizational, social and environmental domains.[188] The approach provides a way to visualize how the parts of a system work together by mapping the drivers of conflict (and peace) and the interconnections among them in ways that show causal relationships.[189] Such maps are called "causal loop diagrams." Any map is not the same as the "territory" depicted; it represents one way to understand how the system works, including a certain amount of interpretation.

For example, the diagram below depicts an explanation of why "the rich get richer and the poor get poorer"—based on a classic systems thinking model called "Success to the Successful." The idea is that those who are favored by the system (like "A") are able to acquire more and more, while those who are disadvantaged ("B") continue to spiral downwards. [190]

This diagram is an example of a "causal loop diagram" which is one way of portraying how the various important elements of a system interact. The factors are presented as text and the relationships of cause and effect are represented by arrows. In the

---

187 Stroh, "The System Dynamics of Identity-Based Conflict," p. 168

188 In addition to Stroh and Ricigliano works already cited, see Donella H. Meadows, Diana Wright (Ed.), *Thinking in Systems: A Primer.* Chelsea Green Publishing, White River Junction, VT, 2008. Peter Senge, *The Fifth Discipline: The art and practice of the learning organization,* Doubleday, New York. 1990 and Peter Senge et al, *The Fifth Discipline Fieldbook,* Random House, 1994.

189 Ricigliano 13; *Making Peace Last.*

190 Senge ref?] RPP Training Manuals and article on use of systems thinking in evaluation.

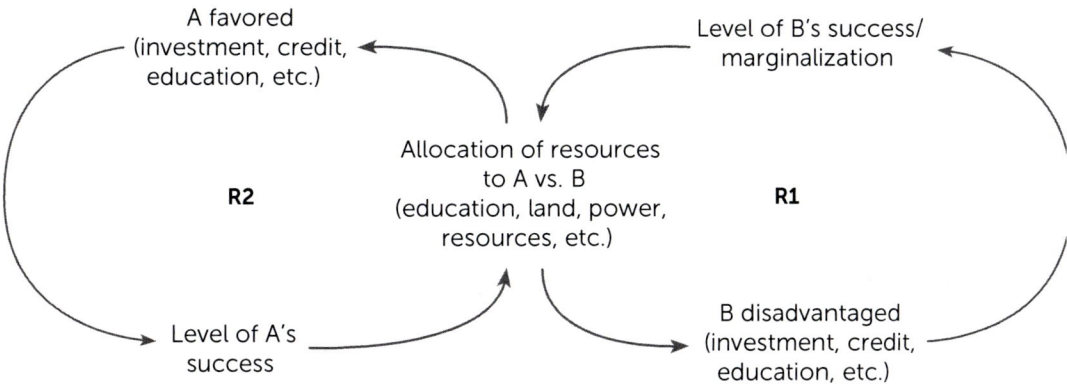

Figure 8.1: Success to the Successful Archetype

Success to the Successful model, there are two interacting "reinforcing loops"—one a vicious circle of poverty and the other a virtuous circle of privilege and prosperity. Over many years, those working on systems thinking have developed a shared set of conventions for depicting systems in diagrams (with some variations), including indications of greater or lesser importance of factors, positive and negative effects, time delays, associated mindsets or mental models, and even ways to indicate numerical values in the system.

We found it possible to use such systems "maps" of conflicts (causal loop diagrams) to identify potential points of leverage for change in the conflict system, as well as to test and revise the theories of change of programs, and to trace potential negative effects or system "pushback" and resistance. In this way, the intervention and actions become included in the analysis.

In order to avoid individual biases or skewed interpretations, we have usually produced such maps through a group process, both for identifying the factors included, and for validating the resulting maps. On occasion, we have produced draft maps, based on a review of multiple conflict analysis narratives—but always present those to knowledgeable groups or a range of well-informed individuals for refinement and corroboration.

The rest of this chapter will discuss how we have used these maps to promote better peacebuilding and conflict resolution programming.[191]

---

191 We will not attempt to provide instructions on how to develop such conflict maps in this volume. The books and articles cited are helpful resources—or the reader may wish to attend a training workshop by CDA or other groups.

An Illustrative Example: Guatemala

On the following page, we have presented a systems map of conflict in Guatemala. This particular conflict map is based on the information provided in the RPP cumulative case study, which was itself based on a series of interviews with a wide range of stakeholders in Guatemala. (Note: a map developed in a face-to-face joint analysis workshop setting in the country among a diverse group would, no doubt, produce a somewhat different map.)

Explanation of the Guatemala conflict map. The conflict map uses many of the mapping "conventions" of causal loop diagramming in systems thinking. The map is organized in a series of causal loops. Those marked with an "R" are reinforcing loops—similar to a vicious or virtuous circle in which the elements support each other in a continuous and increasing process. R1 on the map depicts a central dynamic of social injustice, which is derived from a whole series of other causes, some of them historical (colonialism and racism), and including multiple dimensions as listed. In this central dynamic, social justice leads to protest, instability, and repression, leading back to reinforce injustice. Over time (a delay indicated by the double marks "//" on the arrow) in the R2 loop, oppressed groups shift from protest to revolutionary organization and armed resistance, which again produces instability and a repeated cycle of repression—and, over time, descends into civil war and increased levels of repression. The war (felt differently by different groups in different places) leads to polarization and increased support for authoritarian culture, which again reinforces the core factor of injustice.

The case study notes (R3) that Guatemalan society is split along left/right, urban/rural, and ladino/indigenous lines, based on each group's relationship to social injustice. These splits also reinforce the polarization dynamic, leading back to support for authoritarianism and social injustice. At the same time, the effects of war, violence, and militarization undermine government capacity and political will (R4), leading to weak democratic institutions that are unable to control rising crime, drug and gang violence, reinforcing social support for authoritarianism.

Conflict maps can also show efforts to counteract negative dynamics—depicted as "balancing loops" (B). In the Guatemala case, out of the civil war, and partly in response to international pressure, came various attempts at redress and to address grievances through negotiation of peace accords and other commissions of inquiry. The effect of those accords and truth and reconciliation is, however, undermined by the lack of government capacity and political will to implement them, ultimately leading back to the basic and unresolved injustices that persist.

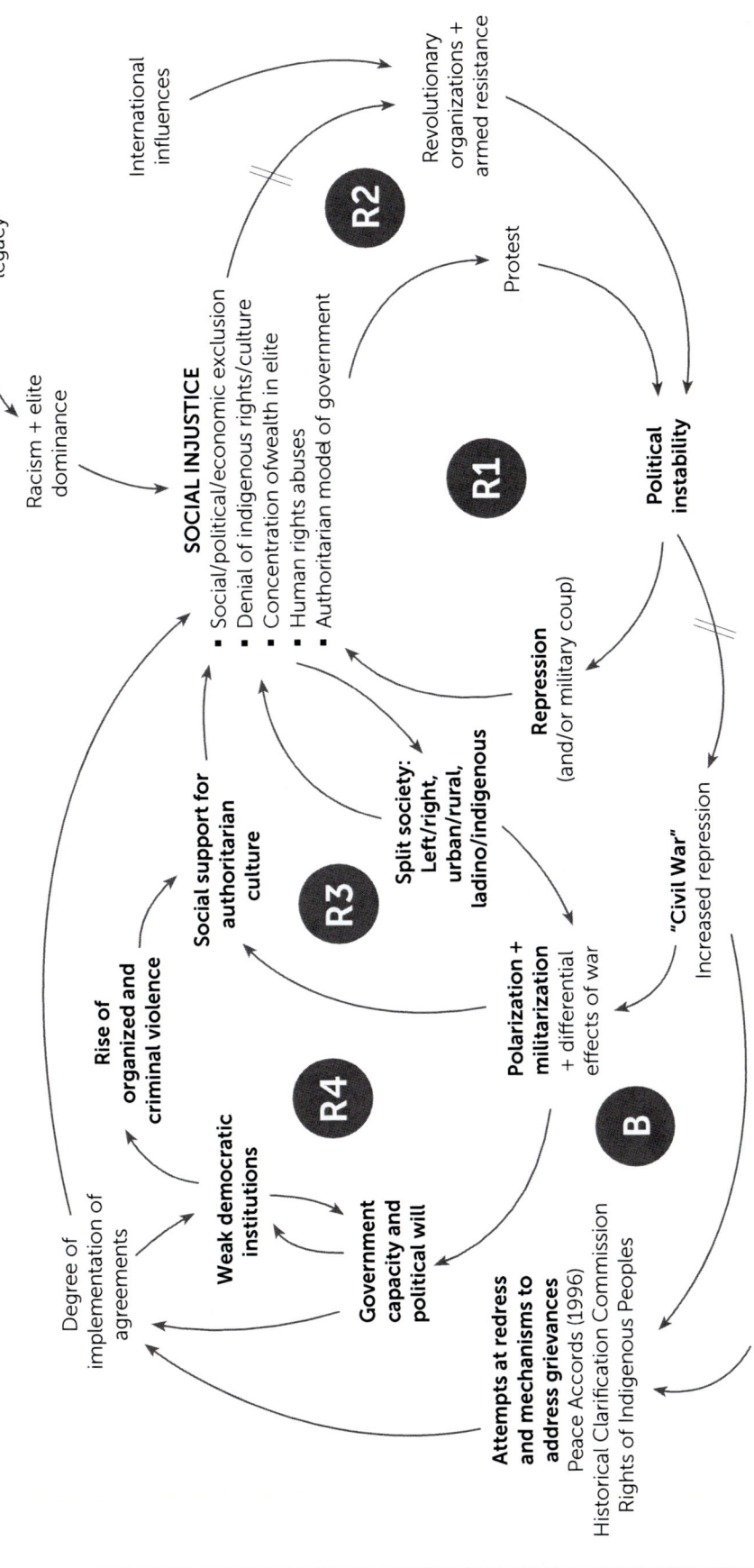

Figure 8.2: Conflict in Guatemala

Using Systems Maps to Develop Strategies

As noted earlier in this chapter, an important critique of "traditional" conflict analysis methods is that they are disconnected from program design processes. That is, even when peace practitioners go to the trouble of performing a conflict analysis, they do not necessarily use the analysis in rigorous ways to develop program strategies. We have produced joint analyses of conflict in multiple locations around the world, and find that the resulting maps are useful tools for generating discussion about how best to intervene to change conflict dynamics.

In using the maps to develop strategy, we found it useful to pose two questions:

1. **What most needs to change in the system?** That is, what leverage points or changes would promote important changes in the *system* dynamics—without considering what is possible or desirable for *us* to do?

2. **Among high-priority issues identified in #1, what are we best able to address in the system,** given the nature of our organization, our mandate, skills, and capacities?

By separating these questions, it is possible to promote awareness of priority peace-building needs, quite apart from organizational biases or programming preferences. We also found that the *process* of mapping conflicts—particularly in a joint process across organizations and among multiple practitioners—draws on the knowledge of all participants, making it more accessible to others and generating a rich basis for discussion of strategies for change.

QUESTIONS FOR IDENTIFYING LEVERAGE POINTS AND STRATEGIES FOR CHANGE USED IN STRATEGY DISCUSSIONS BASED ON SYSTEMS MAPS:[192]

- What changes in the system might affect how the whole system evolves? Are there factors or dynamics that are connected to many loops and dynamics—like centers of gravity?

- Are there factors in the system or in the broader global context that are changing and that will, in turn, affect the system more broadly—either positively or negatively (e.g., global economic downturn and its effects on a patron-client system's capacity to fulfill this functions)?

- How do we think that change CAN happen—and why; what might work? Where is the system changing already? Where can existing momentum for change, positive shifts or bright spots be built on and amplified?

- Which causal connections between key variables/factors in the system are particularly problematic? Can we strengthen productive links or weaken/break problematic causal links? Can we slow down a vicious cycle by breaking links?

- Are there missing feedback loops? Are there parts of the system that should be in communication with other parts? Are there places where additional feedback mechanisms could change parameters for decisions?

---

192 See RPP II Manual; Schirch, op cit. 186-188.

- Are there ways of shortening delays in the system? Or lengthening delays where quick reactions are causing harm?

- Are there ways of changing the factors themselves? Which factors? (Here, a detailed systems analysis related to that specific factor would likely be necessary.)

Generating a sense of the larger picture permits consideration of broader strategies for system-wide change. Using the systems maps to identify key dynamics and points of leverage (where shifts might produce larger changes in the conflict dynamics) helps to bridge the gap between analysis and effective program strategies. Regarding promoting greater collective impact, as discussed in the previous chapter, if there is an effort to create synergies and a useful division of labor across several organizations, the systems map becomes a useful tool for seeing who is working on what, areas of overlap/crowding, and which issues are neglected.

Conflict analysis and program planning in Sri Lanka. RPP was invited to work with the staff and partners of a peacebuilding program in Sri Lanka, as a follow-up to an evaluation. In this case, program staff participated with key partners in developing a systemic analysis—and then used the resulting "map" as the basis for a discussion of programming strategy for the subsequent two years. Visualizing potential (and actual) effects of programs within the map provided a dynamic understanding of how the program might interact with the conflict context it was trying to affect, including how the system itself might "push back" against efforts to promote change.

Using Systems Maps in Combination with Peace Progress Factor Trees

One might ask: how do the causal loop diagrams (conflict systems maps as above) compare with the Peace Progress Factor Tree as presented in Chapter 2? These are both systems thinking tools, but how are they different and how might they be used together to perform somewhat different functions?

We have amassed considerable experience working with partners in the field to perform joint conflict analyses using systems mapping—and, as noted, we have then proceeded to use those maps for setting priorities and program strategies. We have also developed systems maps in the context of evaluation, as a way to identify the key drivers of conflict and to assess the extent to which the program being evaluated had addressed those factors.

Although we have applied the factor tree framework to all of the RPP cumulative cases, we have not yet found opportunities to apply the Peace Progress Factor Tree with partners in the field or to experiment with the application of both causal loop diagrams (maps) along with the factor trees. Therefore, our understanding of how these two systems tools might work in tandem is still in development. Nevertheless, we have some initial ideas about how the two frameworks might complement each other. We will be testing and refining these and will provide further reports of those experiences over time.

Factor trees and causal loop diagrams ask two related but different questions. The factor tree seeks to identify where progress has been made or not made on important factors that support durable peace. They ask: "Where has progress been made and what remains to be done to continue progress towards peace?" Causal loop diagrams or conflict maps identify the dynamics among key conflict factors. They ask: "What are the key drivers of conflict and how do those factors interact with each other and key actors to create the essential dynamics of conflict?" Conflict maps can also incorporate peacebuilding initiatives and positive dynamics, essentially including the peace actions into the system, even if their effects are still small.

Logically, then, one could use a conflict map to determine the most important factors of conflict and then use the Peace Progress Factor Tree to identify whether or not progress has been made on those key drivers. Similarly, groups determining how to focus their efforts could use both tools together. As noted, we have found the conflict maps to be useful for identifying potential points of intervention or points of leverage for change in the conflict system—and then for considering how successful work might prompt successive changes, resistance to change or even unintended negative consequences. Applying the factor tree in context would provide an additional dimension by highlighting areas needing attention—which would align with key drivers of conflict. The color-coded factor tree provides a compelling visual presentation of the remaining peacebuilding work to be done—which should help in priority setting.

Factor Tree for Guatemala

The Peace Progress Factor Tree for Guatemala is presented in Figure 8.3. (This is the same factor tree presented on p. 56, at the end of Chapter 2.) This assessment of where progress has been made and what peace work remains to be done is based on the RPP case study, reflecting how local observers saw the situation when the case was written. Clearly, some progress has been made in acknowledgment of the problems—although the case study emphasizes that many in Guatemala do not understand the causes of the war or the need for concerted efforts to address the fundamental issues of injustice.

The Peace Accords of 1996 brought a formal end to the civil war and laid the groundwork for a transition to civilian government and greater democratization—thus the "durable political arrangement for handling power" is in blue, denoting some progress in this area. However, the governmental structures are under extreme pressure from organized crime and citizens do not have faith in government institutions, many of which have been undermined or taken over by criminal elements. Thus, physical security and governance are in need of urgent attention. The long-term issues of economic fairness and opportunity and social cohesion persist—reflecting the centrality of the justice issues in the conflict map, also echoed in the global variables of horizontal inequalities, sense of grievance and patterns of exclusion. Despite a series of post-war efforts to deal with the past (several commissions, exhumations, legal claims, and commemorations), distrust continues across groups, contributing to the lack of social cohesion. While the RPP case study on Guatemala was written in 2011, the issues identified, especially on the security front, have only gotten worse, triggering a new wave of migration from Guatemala, especially of young people. Note that issues marked with an asterisk (*) are unique to the Guatemala case and are not on the generic factor tree.

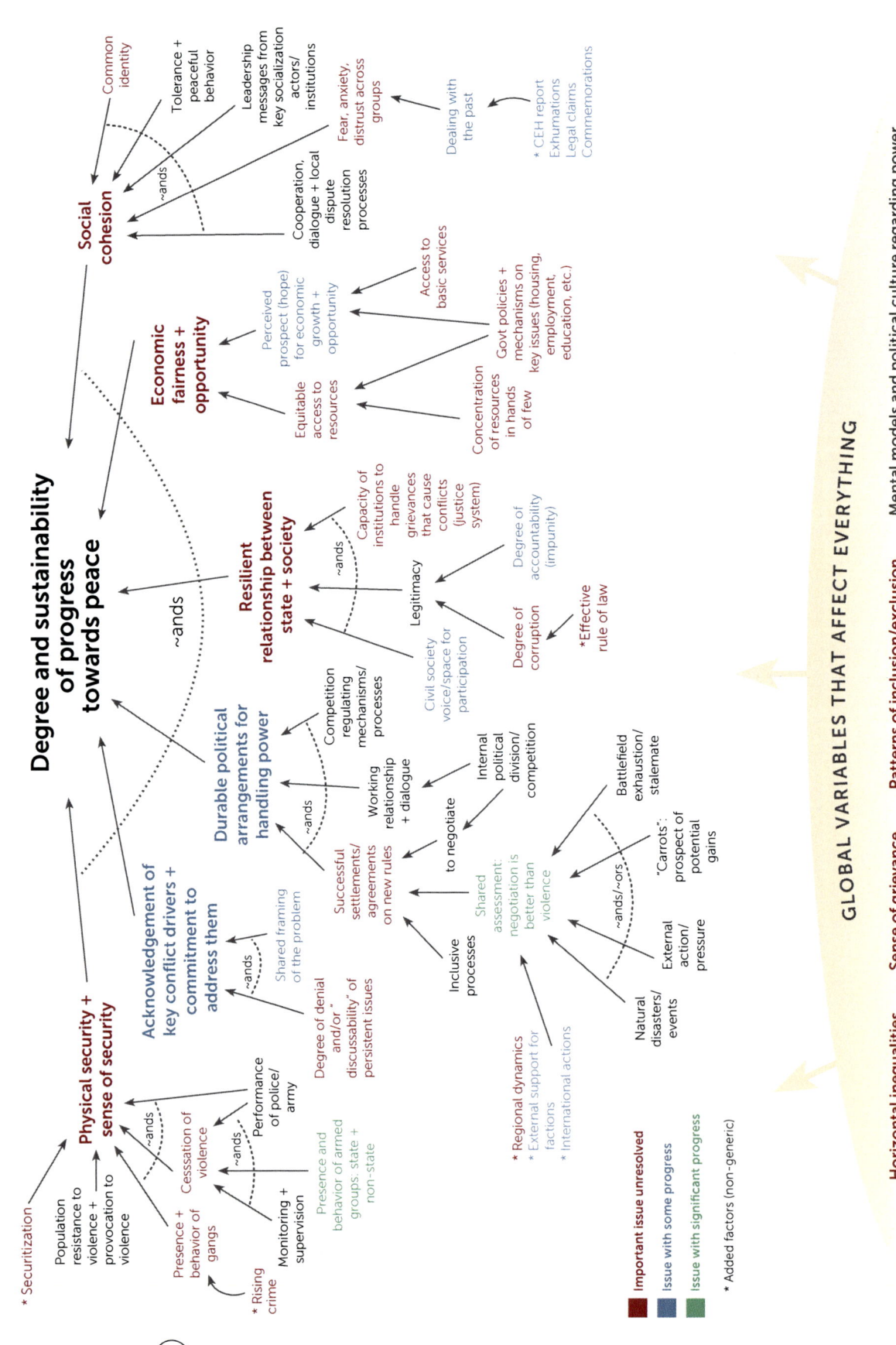

Degree and sustainability of progress towards peace

* Securitization

Population resistance to violence + provocation to violence

Physical security + sense of security

Presence + behavior of gangs

Cessation of violence

~ands

Performance of police/army

~ands

Presence and behavior of armed groups: state + non-state

Monitoring + supervision

* Rising crime

Acknowledgement of key conflict drivers + commitment to address them

Degree of denial and/or "discussability" of persistent issues

~ands

Shared framing of the problem

Durable political arrangements for handling power

Successful settlements/agreements on new rules

~ands

Working relationship + dialogue

Competition regulating mechanisms/ processes

to negotiate

Internal political division/ competition

Inclusive processes

Shared assessment: negotiation is better than violence

Battlefield exhaustion/ stalemate

"Carrots": prospect of potential gains

~ands/~ors

External action/ pressure

Natural disasters/ events

* Regional dynamics
* External support for factions
* International actions

Resilient relationship between state + society

Capacity of institutions to handle grievances that cause conflicts (justice system)

~ands

Legitimacy

Degree of accountability (impunity)

* Effective rule of law

Degree of corruption

Civil society voice/space for participation

Social cohesion

Common identity

Tolerance + peaceful behavior

Leadership messages from key socialization actors/ institutions

Fear, anxiety, distrust across groups

Dealing with the past

* CEH report
Exhumations
Legal claims
Commemorations

~ands

Cooperation, dialogue + local dispute resolution processes

Economic fairness + opportunity

Perceived prospect (hope) for economic growth + opportunity

Access to basic services

Govt policies + mechanisms on key issues (housing, employment, education, etc.)

Equitable access to resources

Concentration of resources in hands of few

~ands

GLOBAL VARIABLES THAT AFFECT EVERYTHING

Mental models and political culture regarding power

Patterns of inclusion/exclusion

Sense of grievance

Horizontal inequalities

Important issue unresolved

Issue with some progress

Issue with significant progress

* Added factors (non-generic)

Figure 8.3: The Peace Progress Factor Tree for Guatemala

9

TAKING ACTION: WHERE DO WE GO FROM HERE?

Waxing Prescriptive

This concluding chapter builds on all of the previous chapters and is unabashedly prescriptive, regarding the peacebuilding field as a whole can move towards greater effectiveness and increased collective impact. We will present a series of recommended actions that summarizes elements discussed in earlier chapters.

These ideas draw on our learnings from the RPP cumulative cases, as presented fully in Part I, and incorporate additional learning from the authors' experiences working with peace practitioners in the field since 2003, as well as our previous years of work in peace and conflict resolution both before 2003 and since. We should also acknowledge that systems thinking has been a critical set of tools, both in the analysis of the cumulative case material and in RPP work on peacebuilding effectiveness more broadly. Our prescriptions for the field are, therefore, shaped by a systems perspective, as clearly reflected in the earlier chapters.

Chapter 6 discussed challenges facing the peacebuilding field and presented a systems map of those issues and dysfunctions. In developing our conclusions and recommendations, those challenges and dysfunctions have remained at the forefront of our thinking. We will not repeat the assessments here, but, instead, will lay out a series of actions that will, in part, address those issues.

Taking Peacebuilding to the Next Level

We have organized our recommended actions in six broad categories—each one, in turn, comprising several related ideas. The six categories are:

1. Applying basic principles consistently

2. Attaining shared understanding

3. Creating effective peacebuilding initiatives

4. Addressing challenges of strategy development

5. Reaching beyond coordination to collective impact

6. Advancing the prevention conundrum

We will address each of these in turn. Each one starts with a key point, framed as a question posed to the peacebuilding community and field.

1. Applying basic principles consistently

How can we ensure that widely-accepted principles in peacebuilding practice are applied consistently, including seeing that efforts contribute to societal level peace (Peace Writ Large), supporting local leaders and initiatives, and guaranteeing conflict sensitivity?

Practitioners are advised to:

• **Ensure that peacebuilding programs contribute to Peace Writ Large**—that is, they develop program logic and theories of change that explain how activities and intermediate objectives will reinforce progress towards larger peace goals.

• **Listen to and support local initiatives and leadership** and identify appropriate external or "outsider" roles that add value and strengthen local partners.

• **Practice conflict sensitivity** (Do No Harm) in all peace programming, as peacebuilding is not exempt from doing harm, just because the programmatic aim is reduced violence.

These principles are widely accepted among peace practitioners. However, they are worth repeating here, because they are still not applied consistently. As noted in *Confronting War*, many peace initiatives operate at a very local level and have not determined how to contribute to the societal level peace (Peace Writ Large), or work entirely on individual change processes without extending them to connect with needed changes in social norms or institutions in the socio-political realm.

Listening to and supporting local leadership and initiatives is appropriate for practical reasons—because it works. For many, this is also a matter of principle that has gained widespread acceptance in recent years. However, donors are still mainly channeling funding through international organizations, and partnerships continue to reflect power imbalances and external control. At the same time, it is important to recognize that in-country politics and relationships are always complex, making it difficult for outsiders to determine which voices to listen to and which local efforts to promote.

Confronting War reiterated the norm of conflict sensitivity, asserting that peace efforts must apply Do No Harm practices, just as humanitarian and development programs do (or should). Because an initiative aims at peace does not automatically exempt it from paying attention to its potential impacts on conflict factors. Yes, peace efforts can and do cause harm! At their most fully developed, conflict sensitive programs can overlap with peacebuilding, as they not only avoid harm but begin to address drivers of conflict, and avoiding inadvertent negative consequences is still an important goal.[193]

2. Attaining shared understanding

Conflict analysis is now an accepted imperative in peacebuilding programming; how can we close the analysis-to-programming gap that prevents a better understanding of conflict dynamics from resulting in more effective programs? How can we combine resources to develop more joint analyses across organizations and stakeholders regarding what is most urgent and important to do?

Practitioners are advised to:

- **Continue to expand the use of systems thinking tools** for exploring conflict dynamics and for identifying progress towards peace goals, as well as priorities for action—through use of causal loop diagrams (conflict maps) and the Peace Progress Factor Tree[194]).

- **Apply stakeholder mapping and identification of who is doing what** as key analytical processes.

- **Promote joint analysis** whenever possible, including listening respectfully to multiple local perspectives, sectors, and stakeholders in diagnosing the nature of conflict.

As we have stated repeatedly, it is important to treat conflict as a *system of interacting parts*, rather than a series of freestanding factors. We have described the function of causal loop diagrams that serve as conflict maps (Chapter 8), and we introduced the Peace Progress Factor Tree in Chapter 2, which suggests six key domains of advancement towards sustainable peace. These two systems tools can be used together to deepen our understanding of conflict dynamics and to determine urgent needs for programming, rather than setting priorities according to favorite methodologies or even what donors are funding.

In our experience, conflict mapping and priority setting must be accompanied by rigorous stakeholder mapping, for which many tools are available.[195] Stakeholder mapping focuses on identifying the key conflict parties, their interests and sources of power (etc.)—which supplements conflict mapping and assessments of progress, which are

---

193 See "A Distinction with a Difference: Conflict Sensitivity and Peacebuilding." Peter Woodrow and Diana Chigas, Reflecting on Peace Practice Project, CDA Collaborative Learning Projects, 2009.

194 See Chapter 2.

195 Among the many resources available, see *Working with Conflict: skills and strategies for action*. Simon Fisher, Dekha Ibrahim Abdi, Jawed Ludin, Richard Smith, Sue Williams, & Steve Williams, Responding to conflict. London, Zed Books, 2000. Also, *Conflict Analysis Framework: Field Guidelines and Procedures. Global Partnership for the Prevention of Armed Conflict*, The Hague, 2015.

both oriented more towards issues and conflict factors. In addition, conflict mapping, assessments of progress and stakeholder mapping can be accompanied by a process for determining which groups and individuals are undertaking specific peace-oriented initiatives, to avoid overlapping efforts or neglect of critical issues.

As noted in Chapter 6, one of the current challenges for the peacebuilding field is the lack of *shared analyses* as the basis for developing shared goals across practitioners and organizations. Many peacebuilding organizations do various kinds of analysis, but few of these are available to others. More importantly, such analyses are more often than not performed with only a small group of participants, based on a single organization and its partners, rather than seeking a broad set of perspectives from many stakeholders and across multiple organizations. While facilitation of such joint analysis processes can be challenging (and, in some circumstances, can cause harm), it is possible. There is now sufficient experience of successfully performing joint analyses in conflict zones all over the world to say this with confidence.[196] A shared analysis is also a fundamental requirement for collective impact, as discussed in Chapter 7 and discussed in point #5 below. Without a shared understanding of the problem at hand, it is difficult to move on to consideration of shared goals and measures of success.

3. Creating effective peace initiatives

> *How can practitioners assure that their initiatives reflect a clear understanding of conflict dynamics and address key driving factors of conflict? Can we treat program design as an ongoing process that is never fully "done," but continues, based on regular feedback, repeated analysis, and M&E systems?*

Practitioners are advised to:

- **Focus on priority areas** (determined, as noted above through joint analysis and priority setting)—which may not always fit individual/organizational preferred topics, approaches or expertise.

- **Avoid two errors in setting goals and objectives**: a) "overclaiming" beyond the realistic ability to deliver in a reasonable time period, (usually framed in broad, general terms, such as "peace" or "reconciliation") or b) describing a series of activities that, in themselves, do not constitute sustained and significant change.

- **Apply the RPP Matrix** as a tool for exploring overall strategies and articulate Theories of Change (why we think that change will result from our approaches).[197]

- **Create linkages** that serve to build momentum for change, gain allies working in other realms, and connect disparate efforts for greater impact (see collective impact under Program Strategy below). Explore multiple dimensions of linkage: vertically

---

196 We noted the systems mapping exercises performed by RPP in Chapter 8. See also, *Making Sense of Turbulent Contexts: Local Perspectives on Large-Scale Conflict*. Garred, M. with O'Reilly-Calthrop, S., Midgley, T., and Scott, M. 2015. World Vision International.

197 See information on the RPP Matrix at www.cdacollaborative.org

from the local community to subnational, national, regional and international levels—and horizontally across sectors and constituencies.

- **Pursue adaptive management** that requires ongoing analysis, gathering and acting on feedback, and shifting tactics and strategies based on learning, while maintaining focus on achievable goals.

- **Address the learning and accountability challenges of adaptive management,** since classic M&E approaches will not work. Ensure accountability to affected populations, to donors, to partners, and to the peacebuilding field.

We have already noted an analysis-to-programming gap in peacebuilding. We have found that organizations often perform some form of conflict analysis, but program designs often fail to address the most important issues. Among the many reasons for this are attachment to favorite methods or approaches, and donor priorities that may not match the most urgent needs or reflect priorities determined in capital cities far from the conflict zone. The previous point discussed the array of analytical processes that can be applied; the challenge is actually paying attention to the results of those processes in designing initiatives with maximum potential for impact.

In working with peace practitioners in conflict zones around the world, RPP staff have frequently encountered an issue regarding the setting of goals and objectives, essentially aiming too high (a lofty, unattainable or vague goal) or too low (a series of activities that are not expressed as a desired change). At times, organizations claim they will achieve an oversized goal (for example) "reconciliation" or "social cohesion," because they assume this is what donors want to hear. In essence, the aid system inadvertently encourages "inflation" and "overclaiming" of promised delivery.

At other times, practitioners have not thought through the *program logic*: how activities lead to intermediate changes, and how intermediate changes contribute to larger goals. We have found that use of the RPP Matrix helps to explore the program logic and underlying Theories of Change—which then aids in setting appropriate goals/objectives, expressed as observable changes that can be measured.

As noted in Chapter 3, the design of initiatives and programs needs to incorporate *linkages*, including vertical linkages from local community work to national and even international dynamics, as well as horizontal connections among different constituencies (women, youth, religious leaders, ex-combatants, etc.) and sectors (development, humanitarian relief, human rights, and others). Such linkages are also an aspect of pursuing collective impact among multiple stakeholders, as discussed in Chapter 7.

There is growing recognition, among peace practitioners and some donors, that peacebuilding programming needs to embrace an *adaptive management* approach, characterized by flexible methods, ongoing analysis, continuous gathering of feedback and regular program adjustments. Usually, it is possible to maintain the overall goal(s), while making more modest modifications in activities or taking an altered route to the same longer-term results. At times, however, it is necessary to reassess the fundamental goals, based on significant changes in the context (outbreak of violence, fall of a government…) or clear evidence that the approach taken is not working. At the same time, if programming efforts are constantly shifting activities, methods/approaches, and even goals, how can they be held accountable? This remains an ongoing area for further learning and experimentation with innovative forms of monitoring and evaluation, including how to assess, in real time, how multiple efforts are adding up or not.

4. Addressing challenges of strategy development

Stepping back from the details of the design of individual initiatives and programs and the challenges of implementation, how will peace efforts achieve timely and sustained change at a sufficient scale to make a real difference? What forms of leadership are required? Who is typically left out?

Practitioners are advised to:

- Consider macro-level theories of change;

- Figure out how to bring peacebuilding efforts to a big enough scale to achieve significant changes;

- Identify the forms of leadership needed at multiple levels, supporting them to acknowledge key driving factors of conflict and to commit to dealing with them; and

- Engage the "hard to reach," other marginalized groups, and women.

As noted in Chapter 6, one of the dysfunctions of the peacebuilding field continues to be fragmentation, competition, and dispersed programming. Peace practitioners and their organizations tend to focus only on their own programs, with scant attention to how their efforts might contribute to a broader, coherent strategy for durable peace. Micro-level theories of change within limited participants or geography fail to take into account larger conflict dynamics that can overwhelm the good, yet inadequate programs that emphasize personal change and/or community-level results.

Applying the RPP Matrix[198] at the strategic level—essentially outlining a realistic overall pathway to peace—would be a useful exercise showing how multiple peace efforts add up to more than the sum of the individual parts, even if they are not closely coordinated within a joint strategy. On the other hand, if multiple

stakeholders can agree on joint strategies and goals, they are more likely to achieve collective impact (see point #5 below).

The RPP cumulative cases revealed only a few cases where peace efforts—beyond completion of a peace agreement—achieved significant scale. Those examples include the Culture of Peace training of thousands of people in Mindanao, which appears to

198 See the CDA website at www.cdacollaborative.org for an introduction to the RPP Matrix.

have changed behavior in response to shocks, the White Lotus campaign in Sri Lanka, which was only short-lived in its effects, a series of smaller actions that added up in Northern Ireland, and the huge structural changes achieved in South Africa. Also, expansion of civil society and concerted media work shifted conflict dynamics in Burundi—at least for a time.

Other than those examples, while at least temporary gains were made in most cases, efforts that were specifically labeled as peace work were often limited in scope, constrained by authorities or donors, and short-lived. We are often reminded of the massive efforts to achieve reconciliation among whole populations in Europe after World War II, especially between France and Germany. These included large-scale structural changes (the Common Market and later the European Union), as well as programs of student and arts exchanges for many decades. Oddly, we have not learned from those successful experiences to undertake more ambitious and sustained efforts to consolidate peace and to address the underlying causes of violence in other settings.

Leadership is an important ingredient. As noted in Chapter 2, it is a key domain for progress towards peace. And Chapter 5 addressed leadership issues more broadly, drawing on the case evidence. As repeated throughout this book, a basic function of leadership is to acknowledge conflict drivers and make a commitment to address them. Such leadership must almost always come from within the conflict zone itself (whether country or subregion), while outsiders can support such leadership and provide resources to enable progress.

Finally, as a matter of strategy, peace efforts must engage several key constituencies, including the "hard-to-reach," other marginalized groups and women. The "hard-to-reach" is a broad category that includes people who are sometimes termed "spoilers" of peace processes, groups that are dispersed, such as ex-combatants, groups that are geographically isolated, or groups that are ideologically extreme in some way. Some such groups may deliberately exclude themselves from negotiations or other efforts at reconciliation; others would like a seat at the table but are excluded for a variety of reasons. This latter category includes groups that experience political, social and economic exclusion, often a fundamental driver of conflict. While it requires time, effort—and sometimes courage—peace processes are strengthened by greater inclusion.

As noted earlier, considerable programming has been undertaken to include women in peace processes, as promoted by UN Resolution 1325. While the RPP cumulative cases did not show much impact from the participation of women, this lack of evidence in our particular study does not disprove the notion that women should be included—and a considerable body of scholarship and programming is building the case for this important principle.

5. Reaching beyond coordination to collective impact

How can we achieve significant progress towards sustainable peace through more effective alliances (consortia, networks, platforms...) among multiple stakeholders, including local civil society organizations, NGOs, INGOs, governments, multilateral organizations, and private sector entities?

Practitioners are advised to:

- **Apply the Framework for Collective Impact in Peacebuilding** (see Chapter 7);

- **Experiment with broker and backbone functions;**

- **Create more linkages:** connecting with development, human rights, justice—and nonviolent action modalities; and

- **Advocate for donor policies and practices that encourage collaboration** rather than competition.

Some the key dysfunctions of the peacebuilding field, as noted in Chapter 6, include ongoing competition and fragmentation (at times exacerbated by donor policies/practices), as well as the lack of shared understanding and shared goals. Chapter 7 then presents a framework for achieving greater collective impact in peacebuilding, borrowing a model developed in other fields and adapting it to the requirements and conditions of peace efforts.

The analysis in Chapter 6 also identifies a challenge regarding the lack of credible and trusted entities (individuals or organizations) that can bring peacebuilding practitioners and other stakeholders together to forge alliances, consortia, or platforms dedicated to achieving common peace goals. One aspect of this missing role is simple convening: bringing disparate groups together to perform joint analysis and explore the possibilities of shared goals, etc. Beyond convening, we see the need for a "broker" role that can facilitate the process of analysis, goal setting, establishing a division of labor, and setting up ongoing communication, feedback, and mutual learning. At times, it may be possible to find people from within the conflict context who can perform these functions, with support from both insiders and outsiders. In other circumstances, outsiders may need to play a catalytic role, while shifting responsibility to local leaders as soon as possible.

The framework for collective impact in Chapter 7 also discusses the need for a "backbone" organization. While this is related to the "broker" role described above, the broker would, presumably, perform a limited set of functions—either for a relatively short time or using a light touch. A backbone organization would be more integral to the ongoing functioning of a network, consortium or platform, providing an organizing role, such as calling meetings and compiling agendas, facilitating communications, ensuring data collection, and so forth. This role and function will necessarily be customized to fit the needs and desires of the organizations involved in a collective impact effort.

The collective impact idea includes the principle of engaging multiple stakeholders in peace efforts; peacebuilders cannot do it alone. We need to create greater linkages—among peacebuilders, but more importantly with other sectors involved with long-term development, humanitarian relief, human rights and nonviolent social change mobilization. Which brings us to the next point.

6. Advancing the prevention conundrum

How can we move beyond a fascination with the constantly changing dynamics of conflict to focus on the persistent, slow-moving and deep structures of injustice, inequality, marginalization, and exclusion that underlie most violent conflict? What linkages are needed among peacebuilding, human rights, development, humanitarian, human rights and nonviolent action practitioners to attain sufficient scale and reach to generate sustained change in those factors?

Practitioners are advised to:

- Recognize that the **deeper structures of conflict resist change,** persist, and shift only slowly, in contrast, the often-cited constant change of conflict;

- **Apply the "precautionary principle"** to conflict, rather than focusing on prediction and warning of violence and attempting to avert crises; and

- Partner with development organizations to undertake **development with a conflict lens** (as opposed to conflict-sensitive development);

Practitioners are often heard stating that conflict dynamics are in constant flux, conditions change rapidly, and so forth. Among other things, the reality of constant change lies behind the call for adaptive management—which we support fully. Nevertheless, we also consider that the constantly shifting dynamics can be seen as relatively superficial "noise in the system" rather than fundamental change.

In places where we have performed repeated conflict analyses over a number of years, we have found very little change in the underlying drivers of conflict. The Global Variables depicted at the bottom of the Peace Progress Factor Tree (Chapter 2) are usually involved in one way or another: horizontal inequalities, sense of grievance, mental models regarding how power is held, and patterns of inclusion/exclusion—usually based on attempts to hold political power, and issues of race, religion, ethnicity, or geography, among other things.

The "precautionary principle"[199] would suggest that, while we cannot reliably predict that violence will occur in the future due to identifiable key drivers of conflict, we know that such factors have resulted in violence, either previously in the conflict area in

---

199 The precautionary principle suggests taking action on issues considered to be uncertain, where there is insufficient scientific knowledge to prove future harm or risk. Despite the lack of confident proof of likely harm, policymakers can justify discretionary actions to protect the public (or, for instance, an endangered species) from exposure to risk. Summarized from http://www.precautionaryprinciple.eu/

question (sometimes repeatedly), or in similar circumstances. The fundamental conflict drivers have shifted in Northern Ireland and South Africa—to the point that further cycles of violence are less likely (though not eliminated). On the other hand, in Sri Lanka, Burundi, Liberia and most of the other RPP case study locations, the underlying conflict conditions have not changed. While we cannot predict when a new round of violence will occur—or what the trigger will be—we can be reasonably confident that an outbreak of violence will take place. *The precautionary principle should provoke us to address those key drivers of conflict, even though we are not able to make firm predictions.*

As we have seen in the Peace Progress Factor Tree, the principal conflict drivers are involved with deep structural problems, associated with security, leadership, governance, social cohesion and economic equity—and the global variables cited above. These are, essentially, long-term development issues. Yet most development programming is "conflict blind"—that is, those designing most development programs do not take the drivers of conflict into account. And, the amounts of Overseas Development Assistance (ODA) devoted to classic development efforts dwarf the amounts dedicated to anything recognizable as peacebuilding or conflict prevention.[200] Peace practitioners would be well advised to create active linkages with development organizations and programs, promoting approaches to "*doing development with a conflict lens.*" Note: this would be different from conflict-sensitive development that avoids inadvertent negative consequences; it would address conflict drivers directly.

Concluding Comments: Ongoing Challenges and Outstanding Questions

Inevitably, CDA's collaborative learning projects generate interesting and practical findings. They also raise questions that are not yet answered or for which there is insufficient evidence. We mention a few of those as grist for further discussion or research, some of which have already been mentioned in passing.

Shared measures

While the Framework for collective impact in peacebuilding (Chapter 7) includes a call for developing shared measures, in addition to shared understanding and shared goals, this is an area that deserves focused attention. Information in fragile and conflict-affected areas is often difficult to obtain, and can even be politically sensitive. Asking the wrong questions can cause harm, and information can be interpreted or manipulated to meet the needs of conflict parties. If peace-oriented consortia or networks are able to agree to shared goals, they will also need to identify how they will measure progress, through both monitoring and evaluation mechanisms. To date, we have seen few experiences of establishing common measures across multiple organizations in conflict contexts. Experimentation and learning are needed.

---

200 Discussions with colleagues at the OECD reveal that it is difficult to calculate the precise ratio of total ODA to anything that might be labeled as "peacebuilding"—largely due to incomplete information and vague categories for reporting contributions to ODA.

Broker and backbone functions

We have already noted the need for further understanding and experimentation with both broker and backbone functions in relation to peacebuilding consortia, platforms or networks. It is too soon to tell how the convening/facilitating/supporting role of a broker might evolve. While there is considerable evidence—and variation—in how the backbone tasks have been carried out in other contexts, we also need to examine how this has worked in past or current peacebuilding groups, and to encourage testing a variety of models.

M&E under adaptive management and consistent with systems approaches

Adaptive management implies the possibility of constantly shifting activities and even goalposts. While systems tools are useful for supporting adaptive management, and the whole approach is oriented towards continuous learning, it is more difficult to imagine how to maintain accountability—to affected populations and donors. Some evaluation approaches, such as goal-free evaluation, most significant change, outcome mapping and outcome harvesting[201] may serve well for adaptive management programming. However, additional experimentation is needed, likely focused on the nodes of change and the documented rationale for program adjustments and significant shifts in direction.[202]

Looking towards the future

In addition to the ongoing questions and challenges cited above, we look forward to observing—and participating in—the further development of the peacebuilding field. We are intrigued by the possibilities of greater synergies and impacts through more collaborative action and will be interested to see how new forms of collective action are able to manage some of the issues identified in Chapter 7, including shared analysis, measures, evaluation and the backbone role.

In closing, we would simply underline the need for peace practitioner of all kinds to form greater connections (linkages) with colleagues from allied fields—to the benefit of all. Peacebuilders should see themselves less as narrow specialists and more as generalists who build bridges across related fields, integrate a conflict lens into development, human rights, and humanitarian assistance efforts, and link creatively with nonviolent movements for social justice.

---

201 Descriptions of these approaches to evaluation can be found on the DM&E for Peace website: http://www.dmeforpeace.org/

202 An article exploring the topic of monitoring and evaluation under adaptive management will appear in the *International Journal on Conflict Engagement and Resolution* in 2018. See Isabella Jean and Peter Woodrow, "Scrambling after Moving Targets: Monitoring & Evaluation Applied to Adaptive Management Approaches in Peacebuilding."

ANNEX A:
LIST OF CUMULATIVE CASE STUDIES

Aceh, Indonesia: "The Impacts of Peacebuilding Work on the Aceh Conflict." Rachel Schiller, 2008.

Burundi: "The Cumulative Impacts of Peacebuilding in Burundi: Strengths and Weaknesses of a Process." Christophe Sebudandi and Juliette Kavabuha Icoyitungye, with Willy Nindorera and Etionette Nahimirimana, 2008.

Cambodia: "Cambodia's Post-War Struggle for Peace." Soth Plai Ngarm and Tania Miletic, 2009

Cyprus: "The Impacts of Peacebuilding Work on the Cyprus Conflict." Dr. Maria Hadjipavlou and Dr. Bulent Kanol, 2008.

Guatemala: "Consumed by Violence: Advances and Obstacles to Building Peace in Guatemala Fifteen Years after the Peace Accords." Tani Marilena Adams, 2011.

Haiti: "Haiti's Fragile Peace: A Case Study of the Cumulative Impacts of Peace Practice." Marie Pace with Ketty Luzincourt, 2009.

Israel-Palestine: "Much Process but No Peace: Israel-Palestine, 1993-2008." Isabella Jean and Everett Mendelsohn, 2008.

Kosovo: "Has Peacebuilding Made a Difference in Kosovo: A Study of the Effectiveness of Peacebuilding in Preventing Violence: Lessons Learned from the March 2004 Riots in Kosovo. Diana Chigas, 2006. [Note: this study was not originally undertaken as an RPP cumulative case, but the focus and lessons were found to be quite relevant, so included in the overall analysis.]

Liberia: "The Cumulative Impacts of Peacebuilding in Liberia." Christof P. Kurz, 2010.

Mindanao, Philippines: "The Diverse Terrain of Peacebuilding in Mindanao: Gains and Challenges in the Peace Process between the Government of the Philippines and the Moro Islamic Liberation Front." Jonathan Rudy and Myla Leguro, 2010.

Mozambique: "The Cumulative Impacts of Peacebuilding in Mozambique." Janet Murdock and Alfiado Zunguza, 2010.

Northern Ireland: "How Did Northern Ireland Move Towards Peace?" Niall Fitzduff and Sue Williams, 2007.

Solomon Islands: "Attempts at Building Peace in the Solomon Islands: Disconnected Layers." Jack Maebuta and Rebecca Spence with Iris Wielders and Michael O'Loughlin, 2009.

South Africa: "Reflecting on Peace Practice: A South African Case Study." Jonathan Mulcahy and Michael Mulcahy, 2009.

Sri Lanka: "The Cumulative Impact of Peace Work in Sri Lanka: Conceptualizing Peace beyond Parties to the War." Farzanna Haniffa and Kanaka Abeygunawardana, 2008.

Tajikistan: "Conflict and Peacebuilding in Tajikistan." Isabella Jean and Parviz Mullojanov, 2008.

Future Generations Cases (Used in case analysis and for a consultation: Available at https://www.future.edu/research/peacebuilding-research.html)

Nepal: "People's Participation in Conflict Transformation: A Case Study of Jana Andolan II in Nepal." Occasional Paper: Peacebuilding Series No.1, Future Generations Graduate School, Bandita Sijapati (Social Science Baha), February 2009. (Note: This is a somewhat longer version of the case than the one used by RPP.)

Guyana: "Towards Ethnic Conflict Transformation? A Case Study of the Cumulative Impact of Citizen Peacebuilding Initiatives on the 2006 Guyana Elections." Roxanne Myers and Jason Calder, Future Generations Graduate School, Occasional Paper: Peacebuilding Series No. 4, 2011. (Note: this is a greatly expanded version of the draft paper used by RPP.)

ANNEX B:
TERMS OF REFERENCE FOR CASE WRITERS

Background on RPP and Cumulative Case Studies

From 1999 though early 2003, the Reflecting on Peace Project (RPP) engaged over two hundred agencies and many individuals who work on conflict around the world in a collaborative effort to learn how to improve the effectiveness of peace practice. The agencies included international peace and conflict resolution NGOs, as well as local organizations and groups working for peace in their countries. RPP conducted 26 case studies, and consulted with over 200 agencies and over 1,000 people to analyze peacebuilding experience. The findings of three years of analysis and consultation are presented in *Confronting War: Critical Lessons for Peace Practitioners*,[203] which reviews recent peace practice, assesses elements that have been successful (or not) and why, and points to learning on how to improve effectiveness.

Since September 2003, CDA has been working with active peace programs in three regions of the world to test how the lessons of *Confronting War* might be applied in practice. The goals of the Utilization Phase are a) to improve the effectiveness of existing peace programs through application of the RPP learnings; and b) to gather the experiences gained through using the RPP lessons, in order to improve the impacts of subsequent peace practice. We have been working with agencies in the Balkans (Serbia and Kosovo), Central Africa (Rwanda, Burundi, Congo) and West Africa (Liberia) since 2004 to help them apply the findings in their work and to learn from their experience. In the Balkans and Central Africa, RPP is working with groups of fifteen to thirty NGOs in each country, on an ongoing basis, to reflect on whether and how their programs have an impact on the broader peace, individually and collectively.

RPP has focused on the effectiveness of programs vis-à-vis Peace Writ Large – the overall conflict situation. Assessing contribution to Peace Writ Large is difficult as most peacebuilding programs are discrete efforts aimed at affecting one (often small) piece of the puzzle, and no one project can do everything. Outcomes are also difficult to assess. As one practitioner noted: "Peace requires that many people work at many

---

203 Available at http://cdacollaborative.org/publication/confronting-war-critical-lessons-for-peace-practitioners

levels in different ways, and, with all this work, you cannot tell who is responsible for what." Moreover, when the goal of "just and sustainable peace" is so grand, and progress toward it immeasurable in its multitude of small steps, then anything can qualify as peace practice. In the face of this complexity, practitioners often say, "I have to assume that, over time, all of our different activities will add up."

The evidence gathered by RPP suggests that although many people do, indeed, work at many levels, conducting good programs at each level, these programs do not automatically "add up" to peace! RPP found that peace programs that were effective in contributing to Peace Writ Large addressed key factors driving the conflict; many programs, however, did not relate their objectives to the driving forces of conflict, and consequently had little impact on the overall situation. Often, programs that had powerful impacts on participants' attitudes and relationships did not lead to activity or changes that to affect a broader constituency of people, and programs working at the elite or grassroots levels were often not linked. Good programs had impact on the local situation, only to see this undermined by national regional developments. In addition, experience showed that peace programs were not linked to each other in ways that improved joint effectiveness and efforts at coordination did not necessarily result in synergies and increased effectiveness.

RPP's findings to date have pointed to many factors that have *prevented* programs from "adding up" to have an impact on the overall conflict situation, but yielded less evidence on what contributes to the "adding up" process. Key questions remaining include:

- How do multiple different peace efforts have cumulative impacts on a situation? What elements and/or processes determine whether there is a positive cumulative impact of multiple programs, reinforcing what others are doing as well as responding to changes in circumstances?

- How can we link micro ("peace writ little") and macro ("peace writ large") levels in programming decisions in order to improve the impacts of all programs on the broader peace? Many practitioners are uneasy with the emphasis on Peace Writ Large as the standard of effectiveness. They question whether it is possible or fair to hold small, often grassroots initiatives to this standard. Further, they do not want to undervalue the success of "peace writ little"—positive impacts at the community level. But here we are challenged to reconcile the findings of the first phase of RPP about "adding up" with the concerns raised by our field colleagues. It is important to figure out how to link these small, community-level, geographically limited programs to impacts at the macro level.

RPP is addressing these questions in new case studies reflecting on situations that changed in the direction of peace (even if "peace" was not achieved, and in some cases later was reversed). The cases completed or underway include: Northern Ireland,

Cyprus, Sri Lanka, South Africa, Guatemala, Burundi, Israel/Palestine, Kosovo, Haiti, Aceh (Indonesia), Liberia, Cambodia, Tajikistan and Guiana. In these cases, there has been a great deal of peacebuilding activity at multiple levels in all, and there has been a shift in the situation, even if settlements were only achieved in a few. By reflecting retrospectively on situations that have changed, it may be possible to identify what and how the various efforts contributed to that change. After commissioning case studies on several situations, RPP will convene a consultation of many of those involved, in order to reflect together and share insights.

Cumulative Case Studies: Approach and Process

Purposes.

The purposes are:

- To develop new insights about how cumulative impacts come about and what constitutes effective linkages.

- To facilitate reflection and strategy development among peacebuilding actors (agencies, donors) to improve the collective impact of their activities.

Key questions:

- What efforts and processes had cumulative impacts on peace? How did multiple efforts have positive cumulative impacts?

- What linkages contribute to cumulative impacts: between levels, within levels, between and within different constituencies, between and within peacebuilders, between and within different sectors, etc.?

Whom to talk to:

A range of people should be interviewed to get a complete picture of the story. People from relevant sectors at different levels (elite/decision makers, middle-level leaders, and local leaders, grassroots) of society should be interviewed, including also people representative of the agencies/groups doing peacebuilding work, donors/agencies supporting peacebuilding, governmental and intergovernmental agency representatives and participants in peacebuilding work. The interviews should not be limited to people who have been directly involved in peacebuilding or peacemaking as practitioners or as participants/beneficiaries. People (at different levels) who have not been directly involved in peacebuilding or the peace process but who are good observers of the process over time should also be consulted for their perspectives. To the extent possible, the perspectives of people from the key parties in conflict should be included.

Sectors might include:

Peacebuilding Practitioners	NGOs (internationals and local actors), international organizations, Diplomats, etc. who have organized peacebuilding efforts/ programs in a variety of areas, and at different points in time. A variety of people: representative of the different kinds of programs, working at different levels/with different constituencies/in different sectors, and at different times (i.e., some older, some newer).
Political Leaders	Representatives of multiple perspectives/tendencies, including those who were involved with the negotiation process and the "turning points."
Civil Service	Ministry representatives (e.g., foreign ministry, ministry of economy, police, army, other ministries implicated with issues in conflict)
Business	Business association, chamber of commerce
Media	Radio, TV and print journalists, editors
International Community	UN, bilateral embassies, donors, regional organizations
Academia/ Education	Academics working on issues related to the conflict

Lines of inquiry

The following framework covers the topics and questions that should be covered in the case study. It is not intended as a full outline or structure for the case study, nor is it an exhaustive list of the questions that would be useful to address. You should not force information and analysis into these categories or questions if people's own framing of the issues, factors, or impacts are different from what is asked.

1. **Understanding of causes of conflict and obstacles to settlement.** The case study should contain:

a. A (very) brief overview of the context, such as a description of the economic, political, development situation.

b. A (very) brief historical overview of the conflict.

c. An analysis of the conflict, based on literature review, interviews, and your own experience, highlighting the driving forces of conflict, obstacles to settlement and key parties/people/actors (either those who have a stake in the continuation of conflict/might block progress and those who could have a strong influence on creating peace).

2. What were the main positive turning points in the conflict (especially recent ones)?

a. What do NGO and peace workers, politicians, civil servants, academics and ordinary people think were key events, initiatives, processes, people, etc. that led to positive change? Why did they occur? To what do people attribute those changes?

b. What laid the groundwork for those changes to happen – at different levels of society? In other words, why did the change happen at that point and not another? What needed to be in place for that change to happen?

c. What were significant obstacles to peace, and how were they overcome? How did various people working at different levels react or respond to negative developments and setbacks in the process?

3. What peacebuilding was done? (Mapping of peacebuilding efforts)

We are interested in knowing what kinds of peacebuilding efforts have been undertaken over time. How far back in time each case study should go for this mapping is up to each case writer; it will depend on what turning points have been identified and what previous developments and activities are important to understand why that turning point occurred.

In some places, this is obviously an overwhelming undertaking. The mapping is not intended to catalogue every effort or evaluate the results of every program in the particular conflict zone over time. Rather it should give an overview of the kinds of efforts undertaken, with whom and for what purpose, and the volume or concentration (in different areas of the country, if relevant). If there are particular efforts that stand out (from people's comments) as especially important, these might be addressed in more detail. As this is a study of cumulative efforts over time, it is important also to capture how the "map" has changed over time.

a. What agencies or groups (not necessarily NGOs or IOs) were/are working? In what areas? How has this evolved from the past into the present? In other words, in broad terms, map:

    i   Volume/density and scale of work (#s agencies/$))

    ii   Doing what (what kinds of activities)

    iii   With whom (who were participants/targets) and scale (how many people and where?)

    iv   On what (what issues did they work on and/or what was their theory of change – why were they doing what they were doing?)

    v   Timing (when, in relation to the conflict) and duration or work

vi With what effects (what are people's impressions/perspectives about the contributions of the activities to peace?)

vii What connections amongst activities or work (if any)?

For the write-up of the case study, identifying categories or types of programs/activities and describing them along these dimensions would be sufficient. Please include for each type of program some detail on an illustrative or representative program (what they did, whom they worked with, with what results), so that the reader can get a more concrete picture of the different approaches looked like.

As information is being collected for the mapping of peacebuilding programming and activities, please highlight the work of women's organizations and work with women in relation to peacebuilding and conflict transformation.

a. How do interviewees think the activities/programs contribute(d) (or would contribute) to peace? What were the programs' goals and their theory of peace/change? What understanding or analysis of the conflict did the programs have and what did they think was needed to promote change?

b. How were decisions made about focus of activities? This is relevant in particular to inquiry into funding of activities—how decisions about funding were made, what kinds of planning processes existed (within donors, between them, among peacebuilding actors)? What effect did that have on programs?

4. Analysis of cumulative impacts: where, when and how did they occur?

This section will bring together and analyze the information in the previous two sections. The broad questions to be answered are: What peacebuilding efforts (or combinations thereof) contributed to the progress that was made? How? Why did these (and not others) contribute? What helped these efforts gain cumulative momentum at that time?

There is no set framework for analysis; you should look for patterns and themes as they emerge from your document review and interviews. Following are some issues/ themes that might be explored:

a. To what do people attribute the positive change? What efforts do people identify as important to stimulating or facilitating achievement of change? Why? What did those efforts do and how? (This question is really an extension of the question in the first section concerning turning points.)

b. How do the relationships and dynamics among four sets of actors affect peacebuilding and the cumulative impacts on peace: a) government (executive/ministries, local government, judiciary, military); b) political structures and processes (political parties, parliament, etc.); c) civil society organizations (disaggregated, with indications of sector, purpose, kinds of activities); d) general population (also disaggregated)?

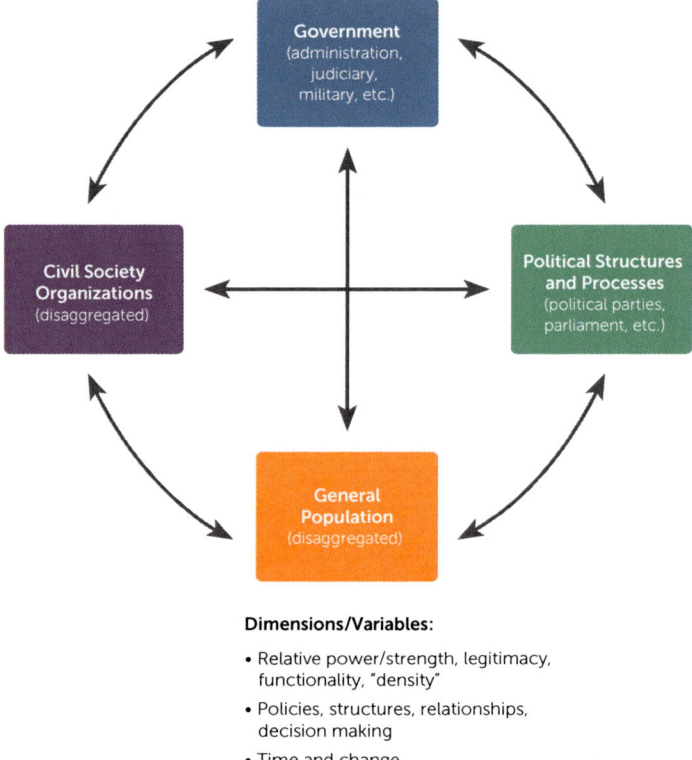

Dimensions/Variables:

- Relative power/strength, legitimacy, functionality, "density"
- Policies, structures, relationships, decision making
- Time and change

Figure B.1: Political Relationships & Dynamics

c. What was the role of women and women's organizations in peacebuilding?

d. How, if at all, did the agencies or activities link with other peacebuilding work being done? Did they know of other efforts? Was there duplication of efforts, and how do agencies and people view the duplication (i.e. why, what was the impact, etc.)? What are people's perceptions of the effectiveness of these linkages?

e. What kinds of linkages existed? Linkages could be direct or indirect, explicit or implicit, and between levels, sectors, activities, and people. For example,

- Horizontal linkages between efforts, both across and within communities. These might include joint planning and/or coordination, coalition-building (across conflict lines and within each community), communication and information sharing, synergies and hand-offs (e.g., working with the same people on different things, building programs on what others did, etc.), across sectors

- Vertical linkages between efforts and processes at different levels, e.g. between official negotiations and unofficial processes and citizen processes, between civil society level activities and political party and processes, between international actors and processes and cross-group processes, between elite and grassroots, etc.

- How did "track 2" and "track 3" (civil society and grassroots) efforts build links to "track 1" or official processes? How did track one build links to unofficial and grassroots efforts and processes? To the broader population?

- Regional linkages—to what extent activities based in the case location were linked explicitly or implicitly with other regional processes or actors

- Between "key people" (people/groups that are key to the continuation or not of conflict, whether or not they are decision makers) and "more people." In other words, linkages between efforts and activities directed at key people and those directed at broadening the constituency for peace.

- Amongst key people themselves, both across divisions and within groups

- Synergies of the focus of activities (i.e. issues addressed, etc.). What were the foci of activities? Was activity focused on a few key factors that seem to be driving the conflict, or more dispersed? What was left relatively unaddressed?

f. What gaps existed? What was NOT being worked on? Who was NOT being worked with? With what effect? How did this change over time?

g. What can you say about leadership in this situation?

5. Analysis of sustainability or reversal of progress

In some places, the positive turning points for peace will have been sustained, while in others (e.g. the Middle East, Cyprus, and Sri Lanka), it was not, and, in some cases, there has been serious backsliding. Questions that might be explored here include:

a. Has the progress achieved been sustained or built upon? Why and how? What allowed progress to be sustained?

- How (if at all) did peacebuilding activities change? What kinds of peacebuilding programs and activities contributed to consolidation or maintenance of progress?

- How did people deal with negative events, setbacks or challenges?

b. In cases where the advances have not been sustained, why was the progress not sustained? Was there really no progress (just the appearance of progress), or was it undermined? By what?

- Were there missed opportunities? What might have been done differently (by various actors, international and national) before and during the positive "turning point" to sustain and continue the progress made?

Data collection and case writing

Each of these case studies could be a PhD dissertation. That is *not* the intent of this process. Each case should take about 20-30 working days from start to completion. It is not expected that each case study will use 20 consecutive days. You may want to spread the days over a longer period of time. Your contract will specify the due date for the case. The case study itself should be around 30-40 pages.

The case studies are intended to tell a story about how and why peacebuilding programming has had (or has not had) cumulative impacts. The case study should reflect the perceptions and analysis of all sides at all levels. You should speak to a variety of people with differing perspectives. The case study should have a story line—decisions on what to include and what to leave out should be based on how important they are to understanding the story. At the same time, we recommend you keep good notes, as it is likely that during the comparative analysis of cases, issues and themes that did not seem relevant at the time the case was being written will become relevant, and you may need to add more information to the discussion.

Literature review

An initial literature review to understand and integrate what has already been researched, compiled and written about peacebuilding efforts should be undertaken. There may already be good maps of peacebuilding programming (or related development, civil society, etc. organizations or programming that might help). There is also likely to be literature on analysis of the conflict and of the various turning points in the conflict that you will want to consult.

ANNEX C:
LIST OF FEEDBACK WORKSHOPS

LOCATION	DATE	NUMBER OF PARTICIPANTS
Bangkok, participants from Cambodia, Thailand, Indonesia, Philippines	December 2012	19
Berlin	December 2012	19
Boston/Cambridge	December 2012	20
Brussels	March 2012	10
Bujumbura, with participants from DRC, Rwanda, CAR, Burundi	March 2012	25
Cyprus, with participants from Egypt, Israel, Lebanon, Iraq, Sudan, Turkey, Palestine, Cyprus	May 2012	28
Geneva	June 2011	20
London	November 2011	
Nairobi, with participants from Somalia, South Sudan, Uganda, Kenya	October 2011	38
Nepal	April 2010	16
Oslo	December 2012	11
Washington, DC	December 2011	33
Panama City, with participants from Guatemala, Colombia, Panama, El Salvador, Argentina	April 2012	18
South Africa, with participants from South Africa, Mozambique, Zimbabwe	November 2012	13
Uppsala	December 2012	13
The Hague	January 2012	16
		299

ANNEX D:
BIBLIOGRAPHY

Adams, Tani M. "Reconstructing Community amid Chronic Social Violence in Post War Guatemala: Four Case Studies." Manuscript. Guatemala: Instituto Internacional de Aprendizaje para la Reconciliación Social, 2010.

Anderson, M., D. Brown and I. Jean. *Time to Listen: Hearing People on the Receiving End of International Aid.* Cambridge, MA: CDA Collaborative Learning Projects, 2012.

Anderson, Mary and Lara Olson, *Confronting War: Critical Lessons for Peace Practitioners,* Cambridge, MA: Collaborative for Development Action, 2003. Available at www.cdacollaborative.org.

Anderson, Mary B. and Wallace, M. *Opting Out of War: Strategies for Preventing Violent Conflict*, Boulder: Lynne Rienner Publishers, 2013.

Autesserre, S. *Peaceland: Conflict Resolution and the Everyday Politics of International Intervention.* Cambridge: Cambridge University Press, 2014.

Autesserre, S. *The Trouble with the Congo: Local Violence and the Failure of International Peacebuilding*, New York: Cambridge University Press, 2010.

Bass, B.M. "From transactional to transformational leadership: Learning to share the vision." Organizational Dynamics, Volume 18, Issue 3, Winter 1990.

Bell, C., & Pospisil, J. Navigating Inclusion in Transitions from Conflict: The Formalised Political Unsettlement. *Journal of International Development 29*: 576–593, 2017.

CDA Collaborative Learning Projects, "Designing Strategic Initiatives to Impact Conflict Systems: Systems Approaches to Peacebuilding. A Resource Manual." Cambridge, MA: CDA Collaborative Learning Projects, 2016.

CDA Listening Project, "Field Visit Report: Kosovo." Cambridge, MA: CDA Collaborative Learning Projects, July 2007

Chandler, D. *Peacebuilding: The Twenty Years' Crisis, 1997-2017* (Rethinking Peace and Conflict Studies). Palgrave Macmillan, 2017.

Chigas, D. "The Harvard Study Group on Cyprus: Contributions to an Unfulfilled Peace Process." In Lund, M. (Ed.) *Across the Lines of Conflict: Facilitating Cooperation to Build Peace*. New York: Woodrow Wilson Center International Center for Scholars and Columbia University Press, 2015.

Chigas, D. and Woodrow, P. "A Distinction with a Difference: Conflict Sensitivity and Peacebuilding." Reflecting on Peace Practice Project, Cambridge, MA: CDA Collaborative Learning Projects, 2009.

Chigas, D. *et al. Has Peacebuilding Made a Difference in Kosovo? A Study of the Effectiveness of Peacebuilding in Preventing Violence: Lessons Learned from the March 2004 Riots in Kosovo*." Cambridge, MA: CDA Collaborative Learning Projects and CARE International, 2006.

Clements, K. "What is legitimacy and why does it matter for peace?" In Wennmann, A. and Ramsbotham, A., Eds. *Legitimacy and peace processes: from coercion to consent*. Accord Series No. 25. London: Conciliation Resources, 2014.

Collier, Paul; Sambanis, Nicholas. 2005. *Understanding Civil War: Evidence and Analysis," Volume 1. Africa*. Washington, DC: World Bank.

Darby, J. "The Effects of Violence on Peace Processes." Washington D.C.: United States Institute of Peace, 2001.

Davis, P. K. (Ed). *Dilemmas of Intervention: Social Science for Stabilization and Reconstruction*. Santa Monica, CA: Rand Corporation, 2011.

Davis, P. K., "Primer for Building Factor Trees to Represent Social-Science Knowledge." *Proceedings of the 2011 Winter Simulation Conference,* S. Jain, R.R. Creasey, J. Himmelspach, K.P. White, and M. Fu, eds.

Department for International Development (UK), "Building Peaceful States and Societies: A DFID Practice Paper." London, 2010.

DM&E for Peace website: http://www.dmeforpeace.org/

Donais, T. and Burt, G. "Vertically Integrated Peacebuilding and Community Violence Reduction in Haiti," CIGI Papers No. 25, Centre for International Governance Innovation, 2014.

Dudouet, V. & S. Lundstrom, "Post-War Political Settlements: From Participatory Transition Processes to Inclusive State-building and Governance." Berghof Foundation Research Report, 2016

Ernstorfer, A., D. Chigas & H. Vaughan-Lee. "From Little to Large: When Does Peacebuilding Add Up?" *Journal of Peacebuilding and Development*, Vol. 10, No. 1: 72-77, 2015.

Evans, W. "A review of the evidence informing DFID's 'Building Peaceful States and Societies' Practice Paper. Paper 1: Political Settlements, Peace Settlements, and Inclusion." London: DFID, 2012.

Fearon, J.D. and Laitin, D. "Ethnicity, Insurgency, and Civil War," American Political Science Review, Vol. 97, February 2003.

Ferrer, M.C., *Framework and Synthesis of Lessons Learned in Civil Society Peacebuilding*. Manila: UP Center for Integrative and Development Studies, 2005.

Fisher, S. and Zimina, L. "Just Wasting our Time? Provocative Thoughts for Peacebuilders," Berghof Research Center for Constructive Conflict Management, 2009.

Fisher, S., Ibrahim Abdi, D., Ludin, J., Smith, R., Williams, Sue & Williams, Steve. *Working with Conflict: skills and strategies for action.*, Responding to conflict. London, Zed Books, 2000.

Future Generations (2009-2012), *Understanding How Communities Create Peace,* at https://www.future.edu/research/peacebuilding-research.html

Galtung, J. editorial in the *Journal of Peace Research*, PRIO), 1964 and Galtung, J. "Violence, Peace and Peace Research." *Journal of Peace Research,* 1969.

Garred, M. et al, *Making Sense of Turbulent Contexts: Local Perspectives on Large-scale Conflicts*, World Vision International, 2015.

Global Partnership for the Prevention of Armed Conflict. "*Conflict Analysis Framework: Field Guidelines and Procedures.*" The Hague, 2015.

Global Partnership for the Prevention of Armed Conflict. "*Multi-Stakeholder Processes for Conflict Prevention and Peacebuilding: A Manual.*" The Hague, 2015.

Gormley-Heenan, C., "From Protagonist to Pragmatist: Political Leadership in Times of Transition," INCORE, Londonderry, 2001.

Haass, R. *Conflicts Unending: The United States and Regional Disputes.* New Haven: Yale University Press, 1990.

Hampson, Fen Osler, Chester Crocker and Pamela Aall, "Negotiating International Conflict," in *Handbook of Peace and Conflict Studies,* Routledge, 2007.

Hanleybrown, F., Kania, J and Kramer, M. "Channeling Change: Making Collective Impact Work." *Stanford Social Innovation Review,* January 2013

Heifetz et al. (2009) *The Practice of Adaptive Leadership: Tools and Tactics for Changing Your Organization and the World.* Cambridge, MA: Harvard Business Review Press, 2009.

Hellmüller, S, & Santschi, M. (Eds.), *Is Local Beautiful? Peacebuilding between International Interventions and Locally Led Initiatives.* Springer International Publishing, 2014.

Institute for Economics and Peace, "Positive Peace Report 2017: Tracking Peace Transitions Through a Systems Thinking Approach." Report # 54. Sydney: 2017. (http://visionofhumanity.org/app/uploads/2017/10/Positive-Peace-Report-2017.pdf)

Institute for Economics and Peace, Global Peace Index (http://visionofhumanity.org/indexes/global-peace-index/),

Institute for Economics and Peace, *Positive Peace Report 2016* (http://visionofhumanity.org/app/uploads/2017/02/Positive-Peace-Report-2016.pdf);

Institute for Economics and Peace, *Positive Peace: The lens to achieve the Sustaining Peace Agenda* IEP Brief, 2017.

Institute for Economics and Peace. "Peace and Corruption: Lowering Corruption—a transformative factor for peace." London, 2015.

John. J. D. & Putzel, J., *"Political Settlements."* Birmingham, UK: GSDRC, University of Birmingham, 2009.

Jones, B., Elgin-Cossart, M. and Esberg, J. "Pathways Out of Fragility: The Case for a Research Agenda on Inclusive Political Settlements in Fragile States." New York: Centre for International Cooperation, 2012.

Kalyvas, S. *The Logic of Violence in Civil War.* Cambridge: Cambridge University Press, 2006.

Kania, J. and Kramer, M. "Embracing Emergence: How Collective Impact Addresses Complexity." *Stanford Innovation Review*, January 2012.

Kania, John and Kramer, M. "Collective Impact." *Stanford Social Innovation Review*: 2011.

Kew, D. and A. Wanis-St. John. "Civil Society and Peace Negotiations: Confronting Exclusion," with Anthony Wanis St. John, *International Negotiation* 13: 11-36, 2008.

Langam, A. & G. Brown, *Building Sustainable Peace: Timing and Sequencing of Post-Conflict Reconstruction and Peacebuilding.* Oxford Scholarship Online, 2016.

Laws, E. "Political Settlements, Elite Pacts and Governments of National Unity: A conceptual study," DLP Background Paper 10, 2012.

Lederach, J.P. *Building Peace: Sustainable Reconciliation in Divided Societies.* Washington, DC: United States Institute of Peace, 1997.

Lemay-Heber, N. "United Nations Stabilisation Mission in Haiti." In Koops, J. T. Tardy, N. MacQueen and P. Williams (Eds.) *The Oxford Handbook of United Nations Peacekeeping Operations.* Chapter 61. Oxford: Oxford University Press, 2015.

Lindemann, S. "Do Inclusive Elite Bargains Matter? A Research Framework for Understanding the Causes of Civil War in Sub-Saharan Africa." Crisis States Discussion

Papers. London: Crisis States Research Centre, London School of Economics Development Studies Institute, 2008.

Mac Ginty, R. and Richmond, O. "Where now for the critique of the liberal peace?" Volume: 50, Issue: 2, page(s): 171-189, Nordic International Studies Association: 2014.

Matveeva, A. "Tajikistan: Peace Secured, But the State of Our Dreams?" in *Across the Lines of Conflict: Facilitating Cooperation to Build Peace*, Michael Lund and Steve McDonald, New York: Columbia University Press, 2015.

McGuiness, K. Ed. *Local First: Development for the twenty-first century*. London: Peace Direct, 2012.

McLoughlin, C., "State Legitimacy." Development Leadership Program, University of Birmingham, Concept Brief 02, December 2014.

Meadows, D. and Wright, D. (Ed.), *Thinking in Systems: A Primer.* White River Junction, VT: Chelsea Green Publishing, 2008.

Meadows, D. et al. *Dynamics of Growth in a Finite World*. Cambridge, MA: Wright-Allen Press, 1975.

Menocal, A. "Inclusive Political Settlements: evidence, gaps and challenges of institutional transformation." Birmingham, UK: International Development Department, University of Birmingham, 2015.

Mercy Corps, "Youth & Consequences: Unemployment, Injustice and Violence." (Case studies of Afghanistan, Colombia, Somalia). Portland, OR: 2015.

Muggah, R. "The Effects of Stabilisation on Humanitarian Action in Haiti," *Disasters* 34, No. S3 (2010)

Nilsson, D. "Civil Society in Peace Accords and the Durability of Peace." *Accord*, Issue 25. London: Conciliation Resources, 2014.

Norwegian Refugee Council. "Searching for Soap Trees: Norwegian Refugee Council's Land Dispute Resolution Process in Liberia," A thematic report, January 2011.

O'Brien Belhoussein, M. "Developing a Model for Collective Impact for Conflict Prevention and Peacebuilding: Summary of Initial Findings," Cambridge, MA: CDA Collaborative Learning Projects, 2016.

Odendaal, A. "South Africa's Infrastructure for Peace." In Mitchell, C. & Hancock, L. Eds. *Local Peacebuilding and National Peace*. London: Continuum Publishing, 2012.

Odendaal, A. *A Crucial Link: Local Peace Committees and National Peacebuilding*, Washington, DC: United States Institute of Peace Press, 2013.

Organization for Economic Cooperation and Development, "From Power Struggles to Political Settlements: Understanding Political Settlements." Paris: International Network on Conflict and Fragility/OECD, 2011.

Organization for Economic Cooperation and Development, "The State's Legitimacy in Fragile Situations unpacking complexity." Conflict and Fragility Series, Paris, 2010.

Paffenholz, T., "Inclusivity in Peace Processes." Briefing paper for the UN High-level review panel, United Nations University Centre for Policy Research, February 2015.

Paffenholz, Thania. *Civil Society & Peacebuilding: A Critical Assessment*. Boulder, CO: Lynne Rienner Publishers, 2010.

Palestinian Counseling Centre, *Evaluation of the WCC Ecumenical Accompaniment Programme in Palestine and Israel (EAPPI)*. Jerusalem: Palestinian Counseling Centre, 2008.

Parks, T., "Political Settlements: Implications for International Development Policy and Practice." Occasional Paper, No. 2, Asia Foundation, July 2010.

Peake, G., C. Gormley-Heenan & M. Fitzduff. *From Warlords to Peacelords: Local Leadership Capacity in Peace Processes*. INCORE Report, 2004.

Reychler, L. & A. Stellamans. "Researching Peacebuilding Leadership." Paper presented at the Conflict Resolution and Peacebuilding Commission at the International Peace Research Association in Sopron, Hungary, July 2004.

Richard Pascale, Pascale, R, Sternin, J and Sternin, M. in *The Power of Positive Deviance: How Unlikely Innovators Solve the World's Toughest Problems*. Cambridge, MA: Harvard Business Review Press, 2010.

Ricigliano, R. *Making Peace Last: A Toolbox for Sustainable Peacebuilding*, London: Routledge, 2012.

Ricigliano, R., and Chigas, D. with AMEX International. *Systems Thinking in Conflict Assessment: Concepts and Applications*. USAID, 2011.

Robert L. Rothstein ed., *After the Peace: Resistance and Reconciliation*. Boulder, CO: Lynne Rienner, 1999.

Schirch, Lisa, *Conflict Assessment and Peacebuilding Planning: Toward a Participatory Approach to Human Security*. Boulder, CO: Kumarian Press, 2013.

Senge, P. et al, *The Fifth Discipline Fieldbook*, New York: Random House, 1994.

Senge, P. *The Fifth Discipline: The Art and Practice of the Learning Organization*. New York: Doubleday, 1990.

Smith, D. "Towards a Strategic Framework for Peacebuilding: Getting Their Act Together: Overview Report of the Joint Utstein Study of Peacebuilding," Royal Norwegian Ministry of Foreign Affairs, 2004.

Stein, J. "Getting to the Table: The Triggers, Stages, Functions and Consequences of Prenegotiation." In Stein, J. Ed. *Getting to the Table: The Processes of International Prenegotiation*. Baltimore: Johns Hopkins University Press, 1989.

Stewart, F. *Horizontal Inequalities and Conflict: Understanding Group Violence in Multi-ethnic Societies*. New York: Palgrave-Macmillan, 2008.

Stroh, D., "The System Dynamics of Identity-Based Conflict." In *The Non-Linearity of Peace Processes: Theory and Practice of Systematic Conflict Transformation*. D. Korppen, N. Ropers, H.J. Giessmann (eds.), Barbara Budrich Publishers: Farmington Hills, MI, 2011.

Stroh, D.P. *Systems Thinking For Social Change: A Practical Guide to Solving Complex Problems, Avoiding Unintended Consequences, and Achieving Lasting Results*, White River Junction, VT: Chelsea Green Publishing, 2015.

United States Institute of Peace and US Army Peacekeeping and Stability Operations Institute. *Guiding Principles for Stabilization and Reconstruction*. Washington, DC: USIP, 2009.

Wachira, G. with Arendshorst. T. and Simon M. Charles, S.M. *Citizens in Action: Making Peace in the Post-Election Crisis in Kenya*, Nairobi: NPI-Africa, 2010.

Wheatley, M. *Finding Our Way: Leadership for an Uncertain Time*. San Francisco: Berrett-Koehler Publishers, 2007.

Wolff, T. "Ten Places Where Collective Impact Gets It Wrong," *Global Journal of Community Psychology Practice*, March 2016.

Woodrow, P. "Framework for Collective Impact in Peacebuilding," CDA Collaborative Learning Projects, Cambridge, 2017.

World Bank, "World Development Report 2011: Conflict, Security and Development." Washington, DC: World Bank, 2011.

Yanguas, Pablo. (2017) "The Role and Responsibility of Foreign Aid in Recipient Political Settlements." *Journal of International Development*, 29: 211–228.

Zartman, I. William. "Timing and Ripeness." In *The Negotiator's Fieldbook*, by Andrea Kupfer Schneider and Christopher Honeyman. Washington, DC: American Bar Association, Section of Dispute Resolution, 2006.

INDEX

Made in the USA
Coppell, TX
04 April 2021

52997110R00117